Fifth Chinese Daughter

Fifth Chinese Daughter

Jade Snow Wong

With a New Introduction by the Author

Illustrations by Kathryn Uhl

UNIVERSITY OF WASHINGTON PRESS

Seattle and London

Copyright © 1945, 1948, 1950 by Jade Snow Wong; copyright renewal 1978
by Jade Snow Wong. "Introduction to the 1989 Edition" copyright © 1989 by
Jade Snow Wong
University of Washington Press paperback edition first published in 1989
Second printing, 1990
Printed in the United States of America

Library of Congress Cataloging-in-Publication Data

Wong, Jade Snow.
    Fifth Chinese daughter/Jade Snow Wong; with a new introduction
by the author; illustrations by Kathryn Uhl.
        p.   cm.
    Reprint. Originally published: New York: Harper, 1950.
    ISBN 0-295-96826-5 (pbk.)
    1. Wong, Jade Snow.   2. Potters—California—Biography.
I. Title.
NK4210.W55A2   1989
738'.092'4—dc19   89-5302
[B]   CIP

The paper used in this publication meets the minimum requirements of the
American National Standard for Information Sciences—Permanence of Paper
for Printed Library Materials, ANSI Z39.48-1984.   ∞

To my mother and father

INTRODUCTION TO THE 1989 EDITION

A T THE AGE OF TWENTY-FOUR, I WAS AWARE THAT MY UPBRING-
ing by the nineteenth-century standards of Imperial China, which
my parents deemed correct, was quite different from that enjoyed by
twentieth-century Americans in San Francisco, where I had to find my
identity and vocation. At a time when nothing had been published
from a female Chinese American perspective, I wrote with the purpose of creating better understanding of the Chinese culture on the
part of Americans. That creed has been my guiding theme through
the many turns of my life work.

Although I felt it was important to record that period of my life,
together with conflicting cultural expectations, I had no inkling of
acceptance for my book. Who would be interested in the story of a
poverty-stricken, undistinguished Chinese girl who had spent half of
her life working and living, without romance, in a Chinatown basement? To my astonishment, readers and literary critics responded with
great interest—and not just in America. *Fifth Chinese Daughter* was
published in both England and Germany. In addition, the U.S. State
Department published translations in the languages and dialects of
Japan, Hong Kong, Malaya, Thailand, Burma, East India, and Paki-
stan. As a result, my book could create more than the hoped-for
understanding of Chinese by Americans. Beyond America (even including Chinese), *Fifth Chinese Daughter* could offer insight into life
in America.

The third-person-singular style in which I told my story was rooted
in Chinese literary form (reflecting cultural disregard for the individual). Since that time, while I have succeeded in establishing my individuality on a local and international basis, I have nonetheless maintained my psychological detachment from my personal importance.

I have been rewarded beyond expectations. I recall a handsome
young paratrooper in full military dress who appeared at my San
Francisco studio on his way to Vietnam. He came to thank me for
writing the book, which he had read in a Texas military base, for he
would better understand the Asians where he was going. I also recall a

long-distance call from a stranger in New York City. She had bought the book in San Francisco and read it aloud as her husband drove their way across the United States. She finished the reading by flashlight while he drove!

In 1953 the State Department sent me on a four-months' grant to speak to a wide variety of audiences, from celebrated artists in Kyoto to restless Indians in Delhi, from students in ceramic classes in Manila to hard-working Chinese immigrants in Rangoon. I was sent because those Asian audiences who had read translations of *Fifth Chinese Daughter* did not believe a female born to poor Chinese immigrants could gain a toehold among prejudiced Americans. I was newly married then; my husband accompanied me at his own expense.

Having discovered kindred Asians halfway around the world, we established a travel agency just at the advent of the jet age. In 1956 my husband and I led a first tour of Americans to Japan. (Japanese freely acknowledge China as mother of their culture.) My early career as potter and enamelist put me on easy terms with those Japanese who were designated "Living Human Treasures." For the next twelve years, we led a number of personally planned tours to Asian countries while, in between, I developed my ceramic arts and mothered two sons and two daughters. Husband and children knew that they held priority over my career. I have spent more time at my kitchen stove than at my kilns. It has been said that food, family, and endurance (in that order) characterize Chinese consciousness. Each of my children did homework in the kitchen while I coached and cooked, and each is now able to create delicious innovations at the wok.

In 1972 my husband and I succeeded in obtaining visas to the People's Republic of China—a month after Richard Nixon's visit. (My book about that experience, *No Chinese Stranger,* was published by Harper & Row in 1974.) Together, we led a number of tours to China; since my husband's death in 1985, I have continued to do so once a year. This has enabled me to witness the remarkable changes there. Thus, I am carrying out my life's creed in another way.

When I first visited China liberated by the Communists, seven years before general travel there, I was apprehensive about relating to those who would represent a way of life much different than that in the United States. Indeed, I found a cult of Mao worship, saw anti-American slogans in public places, and heard daily loudspeaker reminders that Americans were running dogs who must be defeated.

But my husband and I were welcomed as descendants of heroic immigrants who had braved hardship to escape the harshness of an impov-
erished China in waning Imperial days. At formal banquets hosted by
Communist officials, we were completely at home. Table courtesies
were unchanged; our parents' training of half a century ago is as appropriate in Beijing today as it has been in San Francisco's Chinatown.
Everywhere that I have gone, in 1972 and now, I have had the unaccustomed comfort of being in a homogeneous Chinese populace
(though, looking different, I am recognized as being from abroad).

I have learned from my travels that the lot of Chinese immigrants
everywhere has been hard. The injustice of America's past legal exclu-
sion of the Chinese is well documented. My father was prevented
from becoming a naturalized citizen until 1943, a year after I graduated from Mills College. Others of my race in Asia and South America have been denied citizenship, have lost property rights, have
suffered persecution, and have been put on the run—in Japan, the
Philippines, Malaysia, Indonesia, Thailand, Burma, India, and, most
recently, in Vietnam. Less than 150 years ago, Chinese were kidnapped
from Macao for ranch labor in Peru and were physically branded as
slaves. Depending on the period of history and the economic conditions prevailing in various coastal areas of Southern China, different
communities of Chinese have emigrated to specific countries that could
utilize their labor. Cantonese came to the United States, but from
Chaozhou they went to Thailand, and from Fujian they went to the
Philippines. Voluntarily, in ultimate risk-taking by venturing to lands
and languages unknown, or involuntarily, as slaves, they labored to
survive; to survive well, they had to be ingenious. And now, in 1989,
some of their descendants, familiar with their parents' or their own
smarting as targets of prejudice or still finding restrictions in relocated
lands, are returning to invest in China in Special Economic Zones.

In the course of that 1953 mission for the State Department, I met
American Foreign Service personnel abroad, from Nagoya to Calcutta, who belonged to private clubs and who diligently observed
American holidays. Chinese who cling to their customs in America
have followed the same human impulse. My grandmother and parents
established their bit of familiarity in San Francisco. Recreating the
China they knew, enforcing what they thought correct, they gave me a
precious heritage that I have transmitted to my children. As a parent, I
know that it would have been much easier to let our children do as

they wished rather than to shape them patiently in the way I chose.

My father regretted that he had not become rich enough to retire during the depression thirties to his native Chung Shan district, as many of his successful colleagues did. If he had returned with me and my siblings, I could never have had my independent career; instead, I would have endured and perhaps would not have survived the tumultuous times of China in the past five decades.

Having suffered repression, my husband and I gave freedom to our own offspring. Having been cruelly—and sometimes inexplicably—punished, we established the norm of fairness and caring. Having had to conform to restrictions on individual expression, we supported their creativeness. Having been cowed by humiliation, we respected their feelings. Family travel, laughing together—these we also thought important. Thus, our children have developed differently from my generation. From my parents' account, life in China was hard work, grim in its prospects. Rewards were nonexistent. In my own time, life is still primarily hard work, but prospects, though uncertain, have been more promising. Rewards may be brilliant, unexpected. Now my children expect to work hard, but they can also plan to have fun, and they are reasonably certain of rewards. They cherish their ninety-year-old grandmother, with whom they can converse in Cantonese; for their entire lives, they recall her presence at our home or in restaurants during festive occasions.

On the other hand, they and I do not question some positive values which we cherish as our legacy (be they Chinese or particularly our family's). My husband and I chose our home within walking distance of Chinatown so that each child could attend six years of the same Christian Chinese evening school I had. And though they then protested the burden of their studies, which their friends escaped, as adults they are glad to understand the tongue their friends do not. They know well that, in behavior, we emphasize personal modesty, self-reliance, dependability, courtesy, and modulated voices. In values, we esteem love of books and learning, reverence for the natural world, service to fellow man, moderation, living within one's means. Are these values different from those of non-Chinese? Our basic and greatest value is family cohesiveness. From time immemorial, in every culture, for every economic station, the family is the enduring motivation of human activity. Ours is grateful for our Chinese past.

Fifty years ago, as related in *Fifth Chinese Daughter,* I learned in

Chinese school that China was a weak victim of corruption from within and conquest from without; thus, her citizens in the United States did not fare well. In the past twenty years, partly because of the blacks' forging ahead for civil rights, joined by other minorities; partly because of the rising international prominence of China, Korea, and Japan; partly because of Chinese economic success in Singapore, Hong Kong, and Taiwan, a gradual improvement has taken place in American consciousness about Asians. When I graduated from Mills College, I was told to avoid prejudice by looking for work in China-town. I refused to fence myself in; instead, I became the only Chinese face in a series of office positions for which I applied outside of China-town, as well as on numerous San Francisco/California community boards to which I was invited. Yes, being Chinese in America, I have had problems, but they have not stopped me. Now Asian faces are commonplace in the corporate world or in professional offices; some-times Asians are sought for their special attributes. There has been a quiet evolution. Asian Americans, however, know that the battle against race prejudice is not finished.

Despite prejudice, I was never discouraged from carrying out my creed; because of prejudice, the effort is ongoing. My Chinese heri-tage has been my strength and advantage. In Beijing or in Washing-ton, D.C., I can find private doors open to welcome me. To be a mem-ber of the Asian race is to be part of a world majority. As an Asian in Asia, we would not find the freedom of choice which is our particular American birthright. We who did not choose our ancestry can be grateful for opportunities more expansive in this country than in most others, not only for Asians—indeed, for other races as well. To be an Asian American, to be an ethnic American, is a unique combination which is a beginning. With the plus of our rich cultural heritage, to be an Asian in America is our distinction.

AUTHOR'S NOTE
TO THE ORIGINAL EDITION

A CHINESE MAXIM OFTEN REPEATED TO ME BY MY PARENTS IS, "When you drink water, think of its source." The source of this book flows from the continuous encouragement and assistance of Miss Elizabeth Lawrence, who saw the possibilities of such a book, and the patient technical guidance of my friend and teacher, Dr. Alice C. Cooper. Without them, I should not have had the audacity to complete an autobiography at an age when I am, as some amazed persons have pronounced, "not even dry behind the ears."

Included in this story are the significant episodes which, insofar as I can remember, shaped my life. There is no attempt here to judge individuals, only an attempt to evaluate personal experiences, many of which were not "typical." I have not been concerned to discover whether they were good or bad, but rather to what extent they affected one individual's thinking, purpose, and action.

To protect their privacy, people's names have been changed, or disguised. The only exception is Aurelia Henry Reinhardt, for whom a fictitious name seemed inappropriate and unnecessary.

Although a "first person singular" book, this story is written in the third person from Chinese habit. The submergence of the individual is literally practiced. In written Chinese, prose or poetry, the word "I" almost never appears, but is understood. In corresponding with an older person like my father, I would write in words half the size of the regular ideographs, "small daughter Jade Snow" when referring to myself; to one of contemporary age, I would put in small characters, "younger sister"—but never "I." Should my father, who owes me no respect, write to me, he would still refer to himself in the third person, "Father." Even written in English, an "I" book by a Chinese would seem outrageously immodest to anyone raised in the spirit of Chinese propriety.

The drawings are authentic and accurate in detail and represent many hours of careful research on the part of Kathryn Uhl Ball, who co-operated fully to make this book a careful record of an American Chinese girl's first twenty-four years.

CONTENTS

1

THE WORLD WAS NEW

H UGGING THE EASTERN SLOPE OF SAN FRANCISCO'S FAMOUS NOB Hill is one of the unique spots of this continent. A small, compact area overlooking the busy harbor at its feet, it extends only a few blocks in either direction. Above its narrow, congested streets, the chimes of beautiful Grace Cathedral ring out the quarter hours; and tourists and curio-seekers in a bare three minutes can stroll from the city's fashionable shopping district into the heart of Old China.

Chinatown in San Francisco teems with haunting memories, for it is wrapped in the atmosphere, customs, and manners of a land across the sea. The same Pacific Ocean laves the shores of both worlds, a tangible link between old and new, past and present, Orient and Occident.

To this China in the West, there came in the opening decade **of**

1

this century a young Chinese with his wife and family. There they settled among the other Cantonese, and as the years slipped by, the couple established their place in the community.

I tell the story of their fifth daughter, Jade Snow, born to them in San Francisco.

Until she was five years old, Jade Snow's world was almost wholly Chinese, for her world was her family, the Wongs. Life was secure but formal, sober but quietly happy, and the few problems she had were entirely concerned with what was proper or improper in the behavior of a little Chinese girl.

Even at this early age she had learned the meaning of discipline, without understanding the necessity for it. A little girl never questioned the commands of Mother and Father, unless prepared to receive painful consequences. She never addressed an older person by name—it was always Older Brother, Oldest Sister, Second Older Sister, Third Older Sister (she had died at one month without a name, but still she held a place in the family), and Fourth Older Sister. Only her mother and father, or their generation of uncles and aunts, addressed them as Blessing from Heaven, Jade Swallow, Jade Lotus, or Jade Ornament. In short, a little girl was never casual with her elders. Even in handing them something she must use both hands to signify that she paid them undivided attention.

Respect and order—these were the key words of life. It did not matter what were the thoughts of a little girl; she did not voice them. She assumed that her mother must love her, because Mother made her bright silk Chinese dresses for holiday wear, embroidered with gold threads and bright-colored beads, and washed her, and cleaned her white, buckled sandals. Father must love her, because he taught her her first lessons from Chinese books and put her high on his shoulders above the crowds so that she could watch from unobstructed heights the Lion Dances on the streets at Chinese New Year's; and sometimes he took her downtown with him on business errands to that outside foreign American world.

But in spite of her parents' love, she must always be careful to do the proper thing. Failure to do so brought immediate and drastic punishment. Teaching and whipping were almost synonymous. Once, because in fun she had knocked Older Brother's hat off his head when she passed him on the stairs, Father whipped her with a bundle of tied cane; then he withdrew permission for her to go with Oldest Sister to visit the city zoo. Since she had never been to the zoo and had looked forward to this treat for a week, the disappointment and the shame hurt almost worse than the whipping.

Another time, when their neighbor's son spit on her as she was playing, she ran to tell Mother, who was sewing overalls in the factory which was also their home. Mother did not sympathize but reproved her, saying that she must have spit on her playmate first or he wouldn't have spit on her. She was told to bring a clothes hanger, and in front of all the other working women Mother spanked her. Again the shame was almost worse than the pain, and the pain was bad enough, for Mother usually spanked until the wooden hanger broke.

Thus, life was a constant puzzle. No one ever troubled to explain. Only through punishment did she learn that what was proper was right and what was improper was wrong.

At this time, Oldest Sister and Second Older Sister were already married, and Fourth Older Sister was living with Oldest Sister; Jade Snow scarcely knew them. At home, besides Jade Snow there were Father and Mother, Older Brother, who was about twelve, and three-year-old younger sister Jade Precious Stone.

Jade Precious Stone and Jade Snow were closest. They slept in the same room, dressed together, ate, played, cried, and got spanked together. They hardly ever disagreed. Jade Precious Stone was a delicate child, gentle and quiet. Because she was younger, she addressed her sister as Older Sister Snow, and she was taught to respect her Fifth Older Sister's judgment on all things. That meant that Jade Snow was responsible for any trouble they got into together.

The Wongs lived at the back of their father's overall factory on Stockton between Clay and Sacramento streets. The factory-home was huge. To the right on the street floor was a room containing ten or more sewing machines of various kinds. Also on the street floor, to the left, was the office. A forty-inch-wide cutting table ran the length of the room to the kitchen and dining room at the rear. Beyond was a door leading to the bathroom, one of the few in

Chinatown at that time equipped with running water. What fun the children had in that bathtub, which served also for washing the family clothes!

On the second floor were the finishing machines and more long cutting tables where women sat all day examining the finished overalls before folding and tying them into bundles of a dozen each. In front were the family sleeping rooms: one for Mother and Father, one for the two younger daughters, and another for Older Brother.

Home life and work life were therefore mixed together. In the morning, Father opened the factory doors while Mother prepared a breakfast consisting of rice, a green vegetable or soup, a meat or fish, and steamed salted dried fish from China. For the rest of the day Mother was at a machine except when she stopped to get the meals or to do other housework.

The Wong daughters and the children of the workers played hide-and-seek around the high bundles of blue denim, rode on the pushcarts used for loading overalls, climbed onto the cutting tables to talk to the women as they worked. It was the Wong girls' responsibility not to quarrel with the employees' children, who were of guest status.

Instead of playing, Jade Snow often followed her father around as he saw to the placement and repair of the machines or the distribution of work. At first she asked questions, being curious. But her father did not like questions. He said that one was not supposed to talk when one was either eating or thinking, and when one was not eating, one should be thinking. Only when in bed did one neither eat nor think.

However, he seemed to understand a child's need to make noise. To satisfy this need constructively, he started to teach his daughter Chinese history. He would read aloud a sentence, "Wong Ti was the first king of China," and Jade Snow would repeat it after him word for word. So, while her father laid out material, or numbered and labeled the spools of thread, she would trail along near him, reciting the text over and over until she knew it without prompting.

It was not great fun to make a noise in this way, but Father said that all Chinese children in America should learn their ancestral language, and one did not dispute one's father if one were a dutiful little girl taught to act with propriety. From the first Chinese primer lessons of "Ding Dong; Ding Dong; the bell rushes me to attend school," and "Ding Dong; Ding Dong; the bell reminds me to leave school," Jade Snow was gradually advanced to "When Wellington was a boy he would not permit riders on horses to enter his father's fields of grain. . . ."

A primer lesson usually served as a text for a moral lesson too. Wellington, although a foreign Englishman, was an example of a small boy who followed absolutely the instructions of his father. He was told to guard the gate which opened into their grain fields, and he carried out the order to the point of defying a group of soldiers who wanted to take a short cut across these fields. He stood his ground with such determination that the cavalry would have had to trample him before they could trample the grain crop. Of course Wellington won out. Thus, duty to one's father came before duty to one's army.

The children could play out-of-doors if they stayed within their own block and did not cross any streets. They wore dark-blue denim coveralls which Father's seamstresses made, with bright red belt bands and red facings on the sleeves and on the square necklines, and buttoned drop seats—a comfortable garment for climbing around. Sometimes they played in a nearby empty lot where it was interesting to explore all kinds of weeds and bugs. Only one other place in Jade Snow's early experience had any growing plants. That was the Presbyterian Home around the corner on Sacramento Street. She was told that women "in difficulties" sought refuge there, but curious stares yielded only disappointment, for the heavy red-brown brick building always stood in closed silence. Turning to go home she would pause to pick a little spray of yellow broom from its surrounding hedge and hold its delicate fragrance under her nose.

Her father and his bright red wheelbarrow provided Jade Snow with wonderful escapes to the world outside this block. While most Chinese women in San Francisco still had to conform to the Old-World custom of staying at home, her father believed that according to New-World Christian ideals women had a right to work to improve the economic status of their family. Because they couldn't come to the factory, Mr. Wong took their work to them, installed and maintained their sewing machines, taught them how to sew, and collected the finished overalls. On these trips, Jade

Snow was his companion, for Younger Sister was still too small. When the wheelbarrow was loaded with materials, she had to run in quick little steps to keep up with her father's long strides, but after the wheelbarrow had delivered its burden she was privileged to sit inside while he pushed it easily up and down, clickety-clack, over the cobblestone hills of San Francisco. Her father was so strong! Looking around at the world, Jade Snow felt a burst of pride as she saw other children's envious wonder. At such times, she was very happy to have been born her father's fifth daughter.

There were other times when he had to go downtown to see his jobber boss and took Jade Snow with him. There she saw a completely different world which filled her with shyness and wonder. Pretty, strangely dressed foreign ladies with brightly colored faces and curled hair smiled at her and tried to make her speak to them in their language. They sat behind machines that made a clattering noise as they punched out figures which were repeated several times over by means of sheets of black paper. Jade Snow was always given a piece of this magic paper to take home, and very often the jobber boss gave her a booklet of bright cloth samples and a shining new nickel besides.

The nickel was always spent immediately at the corner candy store, which offered a choice among an ice cream cone, a "popsicle," and chewy Chinese toasted dried beef. For a penny one could buy four little packs of hot red ginger or three salty preserved olives twisted in rice paper, which were imports from China.

Lacking money for treats, Jade Snow would hope that the ice delivery truck might happen to stop and the iceman drop a small piece of ice from the big leather bag on his back. If her eyes were sharp she could dart over, pick it up, run home to wash it under the faucet, and enjoy its cool smoothness, sucking it and rolling it around her mouth. But she must never take pieces from the back of the truck while the iceman was momentarily gone, as she often saw other children do. To do this would be stealing, and her father had taught her a lesson in honesty she would never forget.

There had been an old, wrinkled, spectacled peddler, who was always a welcome visitor at the factory. Slovenly and with a white stubble which always needed shaving, he arrived carrying a big bundle whose contents varied from time to time. It might contain shoestrings, corsets, nightgowns, baby slippers, stockings, dish towels, or any number of miscellaneous things tempting to a woman.

Jade Snow had been aware of his visits ever since she could remember but had never paid much attention to his wares. Then one day the peddler's bundle revealed a riot of beautiful colors, for he was selling drapery samples. Jade Snow, hanging around her mother's skirt, gazed enraptured at the pretty posies on the chintz prints, shyly picked up a little square, and fingered it lovingly. The peddler called out, "Buy your girl a piece of material, ma'am. A penny is all I ask. I am almost giving it to her to play with, you can see. A penny, ma'am, a penny."

"Jade Snow, put that material back. Can't you see I am busy?"

Jade Snow looked wistfully at her mother, echoed her "No" by shaking her own head silently, and put the square of red and green back on the pile. Mother turned away, but the peddler followed, coaxing her to buy. Jade Snow looked at the square she had dropped. She wanted that colorful square for her very own! But she had no penny. Why couldn't she have it? She was going to have it. So she quickly leaned down, picked up the square again, hid it in her pocket, and ran off.

She found a box in a corner of the factory and sat there, looking at her piece of material, counting the number of blossoms on it, studying the colors. She twisted it, turned it around, and rubbed it against her cheek. She didn't know how long she sat there, but suddenly she was jolted out of her enchantment by her father's firm voice:

"So there you are hiding. Where did you get that material?"

"I found it."

"Do not lie to me. Where did you find it? Things like that do not grow around here."

"I found it from the peddler's bag!"

"You mean you stole it from the peddler's bag! For shame, that a small girl of mine should begin to steal. I must teach you a lesson you will never forget. You may begin now with a small square, but the next thing will be a whole bolt of material. Go immediately and sit on the front step of our doorway with the material held prominently in your hand, so that when the peddler returns for it, he will find you and take it back. And whatever he does for punishment, you will deserve it."

Not until then did Jade Snow realize that she had committed a sin. She soberly took the material and sat on the front step. There she sat for minutes and then for hours. She grew hot in the afternoon sun. People coming in and out of the factory would ask, "Jade Snow, what are you doing here?" And she would reply miserably, "I am waiting for a man to come back for this material which I took."

She lost her interest in the material and began to dislike it. As she grew more uncomfortable, she hated it. But still the peddler did not return. She imagined the awful things that might happen to her. Perhaps they would put her in jail! She was terrified. She wished that he would come and get it over with. The sun went down; the evening bay breezes began to chill her. She was getting hungry as well as thirsty and cold. The workers all went home. Then her father came to bolt the front door.

"Do you remember that you are never to steal or be dishonest in any way?"

Jade Snow hugged her knees and looked up at the tall figure standing over her. "Yes."

"Very well, you may give the piece of material to me to put away until the next time the peddler visits our factory, and I shall return it to him."

During these years, the one older person who seemed most understanding of a little girl's failure to do the proper thing was Mother's mother. Grandmother was little and stooped and always wore a loose black Chinese coat and trousers. Her hair was fastened into a knot at the back of her neck by a gold brooch set with pretty jade stones. Sometimes she tucked a narcissus or a tuberose blossom into the edges of this knot. If Grandmother happened to be visiting when Mother spanked Jade Snow, she would always snatch the child away and scold Mother instead. To Jade Snow it was remarkable that she should have such power, especially since Grandmother was frail while Mother was strong. Yet her intervention was only mildly disputed.

Sometimes, Jade Snow and her sister were privileged to visit Grandmother's home. This was one small room in an old, dark, run-down building two blocks from the Wongs. In the corner facing the door a large bed was screened off in Chinese fashion; that is, a bamboo frame had been erected four-poster-wise, and draperies veiled it completely. The bed dominated the room, which also held a gas plate, a few chairs, a sewing machine, and an ancestral worship table. On the table, below the pictures or tablets bearing the names of Grandmother's forebears, were cups filled with wine, bowls of fruit and meat, and burning brown punk and red candles, arranged to feed and light their spirits, for Grandmother was not a Christian.

Whenever the sisters visited Grandmother, they knew that she would offer them a treat. On her window ledge she kept a glass jar filled with thick sweetened condensed milk. For child visitors she spread the sticky cream on thin salty soda crackers, as many as they wanted. Since their Chinese diet seldom included sweets, the children usually ate and ate. Sometimes Grandmother would offer instead dried lichees—that delicate-flavored fruit in its crisp, papery shell, which she kept in the sewing machine drawers. Or if she happened to be out of sweets, she would boil an egg for each visitor. But she always managed something.

There was one service Grandmother requested in return for all her kindnesses. She often asked Jade Snow and Jade Precious Stone to clench their fists and hammer her bent spine up and down. She said that the vibrations improved her circulation, that they were relaxing and felt good. Although the girls thought the exercise great fun, they found it hard to understand how their blows could make Grandmother feel better. They had tried the treatment on each other without experiencing any enjoyment.

A vivid memory Jade Snow was always to associate with Grandmother had to do with a live turkey her father brought home one American holiday week and tied to the leg of the dining table. He told his fifth daughter to go into the room alone and make her acquaintance with her first turkey.

Where was the bird in that dimly lighted room? The oilcloth on the table dropped almost to the floor, and the turkey must be hiding under it. Jade Snow lifted the cloth, and crawled in to see better this strange bird that her father had said was related to chickens. Only it was different, he said. . . . It was indeed different! Face to face with the ferocious creature, she sat petrified, seemingly imprisoned between the legs of the table with a bird which looked anything but friendly. Was it a bird? Those ugly blotches on his jerking head. . . . He was coming closer to her, closer, too close. Suddenly, though she could not seem to move, she found her voice and cried out with all her might. Whether such an uproar was proper or improper could not be helped. For the first time in her life Jade Snow was shaken with fright.

As a result, she became sick and insisted on sleeping with Mother, a thing she had never done before. She sweated; and for days and nights, whether she closed or opened her eyes, that turkey kept coming closer, and closer. . . .

The family conferred. It was Grandmother who reminded them that there was an established ritual which would "out the scare." The following evening, the entire family gathered in Grandmother's room, with Jade Snow the center of attention. Never before had she felt so important. The lights were turned off except for candles. Then Grandmother lit a fire in her bronze brazier and threw in a small lump of "Bok Fon," a white mineral with herbal properties. In the semidark room, she began to chant softly: "Out with the scare which is hiding in our Jade Snow. . . ." As she whispered the lines over and over rhythmically, she picked up the child and passed her back and forth above the glowing brazier. The candles flickered; the shadows of the family loomed like dancing giants on the walls. Jade Snow was frightened all over again. She did not like this silent, solemn, strange atmosphere. What were they doing to her? Still, it would not do to cry. Any outburst would surely have been improper at such a time.

It was confusing—that terrible turkey creature, the people quietly watching in the flickering light, Grandmother acting so unlike herself. Then the flames died down, and it was over. The grownups turned on the lights and gave the bewildered child something bitter and hot to drink. It was an herb tea brewed in a pot from which she saw Grandmother remove her jade pendant, a piece of gold ore, and a pearl brooch. The presence of the jewelry assured a "calming" and "precious" tea, they told her. Though the tea puckered her mouth, she felt relief for the first time since coming face to face with the turkey. That night, she slept alone peacefully for the first time in days.

The next day, Grandmother came, bringing the remains of the white substance that she had burned and left to cool overnight in the brazier. She showed it to Oldest Sister, who happened to be visiting but knew nothing of the turkey incident.

"What does this look like to you, Oldest One?" Grandmother asked.

Oldest Sister said unhesitatingly, "Why, that is a turkey."

Why did the "Bok Fon" which Grandmother bought at the herb store bear any relation to Jade Snow's scare? Why did that piece of white mineral burn to the shape of the object which had frightened her? The family did not seem concerned with questions. But although it was difficult to understand such things, Jade Snow remembered them.

2

THE WORLD GROWS

ONE DAY WHEN THE FAMILY WAS AT DINNER, FATHER BROKE THE habitual silence by announcing a new edict: "I have just learned that the American people commonly address their fathers informally as 'Daddy'! The affectionate tone of this word pleases me. Hereafter, you children shall address me as 'Daddy.'" No comment was required; the children mentally recorded this command.

When she was six, Jade Snow's world expanded beyond her family life. Daddy started her in an American public grade school. Before she left home, Daddy and Mother both took her aside and gave her solemn instructions: "Jade Snow, at school a teacher will be in charge, who is as your mother or your father at home. She is supreme, and her position in all matters pertaining to your education is as indisputable as the decisions of your mother or father at home. Respect her accordingly."

Thus, Jade Snow accepted another authority in her life. The schoolteacher was a little Chinese lady dressed in foreign clothes. She spoke the foreign "English" language, although when necessary she could explain in Chinese to her pupils. However, she discouraged them from speaking their accustomed language.

Although Miss Chew had the authority of one's parents and occasionally scolded some pupil who overlooked this fact, she never spanked anybody! School life was comparatively simple, since for some hours each day Jade Snow became less actively concerned with what was proper or improper. In fact, she sometimes became actively concerned with what was really fun to do!

New games in the foreign language were learned—"Farmer in the Dell," "Go Walking Round the Valley," "London Bridge Is Falling Down." Instead of learning about the virtuous Wellington as a boy, Jade Snow memorized a poem about Jack and Jill who climbed a hill to get water but somehow lost it all.

Instead of opening on the left-hand side and reading from right to left in vertical rolls like Chinese books, the new books with gay, colored pictures opened on the right-hand side and were read horizontally from left to right.

One of the most memorable events occurred one afternoon when Miss Chew brought several cases of whipping cream to class. Each pupil received a jar of cream fitted with a wooden disk on a stick. Miss Chew announced, "We are going to make butter."

Butter? Wasn't that what one bought at a store in a cube, wrapped with paper? Did one ever "make" it? Jade Snow remembered her mother's words, "Never question the actions of your teacher." So she followed instructions without asking any question.

After the cream had been churned for some time, sure enough, yellow flecks appeared, and then joined and thickened into a lump of butter! Jade Snow experienced a wonderful new feeling—the pride of personal creation. And when she smeared her own butter made with her own hands on the crackers Miss Chew provided, she thought that she had never tasted anything more delicious in all her life!

School brought new experiences with other Chinese children. During recess, Jade Snow learned to play hopscotch, and to memorize new Chinese and English rhymes which were chanted to find who should be "It" for games of hide-and-seek or tag.

To these pleasant experiences were added her first major problems with other children. There was the day, for instance, when a bigger girl hit her with her fists. In Jade Snow, pain was mingled with confusion. Girls never hit other girls. They might argue, take things away from another, but only little boys were expected to be rough enough for fist fights! At least, that was what Mother and Daddy had taught her. Nevertheless, Jade Snow's first impulse was to strike back. But she seemed to hear her mother's familiar reminder, "Even if another should strike you, you must not strike him, for then your guilt would be as great as his."

While Jade Snow controlled her fists, she burst into tears for relief and ran home. Mama's explanation as she wiped her daughter's tears was that not all Chinese girls were brought up like herself, and some had little family training.

Attendance at an American school did not mean that Jade Snow's Chinese lessons ceased. Shortly after she had entered Miss Chew's class, Daddy told her:

"From this day until I see fit to place you in the Chinese evening school, I shall continue to give you half an hour of Chinese instruction every morning before you go to the American public classes. Years ago, when your Oldest Sister Swallow was a child like you, the Chinese schools in Chinatown were not open to girls. Your sister rose daily at six in the morning, washed her face, combed her braids, and studied Chinese with me for an hour before breakfast. Now she knows enough Chinese to write a learned letter to China."

"Why were not the Chinese schools open to her?" Jade Snow asked wonderingly, as she laid out on their dining table her tablets, brush, inkpad, and first reader.

Daddy explained, "Many Chinese were very short-sighted. They felt that since their daughters would marry into a family of another name, they would not belong permanently in their own family clan. Therefore, they argued that it was not worth while to invest in their daughters' book education. But my answer was that since sons and their education are of primary importance, we must have intelligent mothers. If nobody educates his daughters, how can we have intelligent mothers for our sons? If we do not have good family training, how can China be a strong nation?"

Daddy had forgotten his daughter and seemed to address a larger audience as he stared off into space.

"Confucius said, 'He who is filial toward elders and fraternal toward brothers and is fond of offending his superiors is rare indeed; he who is not fond of offending his superiors and is fond of making revolutions has never been known.'

"So you see, the peace and stability of a nation depend upon the proper relationships established in the home; and to a great extent, the maintenance of proper relationships within the home depends on intelligent mothers. Now I do not want you ever to question why you should study Chinese," finished Daddy.

So they resumed their lesson. They opened the first reader, entitled *Instruction Book to Preserve the National Grammar for the Use of the First Grade.*

The first lesson taught: "One, Two, Three," but this gradually advanced to:

"Big and Little Sisters return home after school. Big Sister in her room teaches Little Sister to do women's work."

Many subjects were embraced in this primer, from lessons in nature to lessons in ethics. They varied from:

"In the little garden the flowers bloom gloriously. Butterflies come in pairs; they fly in coming and fly in going"; to the last lesson in the book, which was:

"Come, come, come. Come and read books. If you do not study your books, you will not know written words. If you do not know written words, you will have a life of sorrow."

This primer constituted only a portion of Jade Snow's lessons. For Daddy also had a book with illustrated lessons on the principles of correct calligraphy. One did not lay down just any stroke as one pleased. First, one must hold one's brush in exactly the correct position. Next, it was necessary to proceed with each stroke in the proper order. Finally, the completed character should be correctly balanced in a square.

Daddy turned to the first page of the book, now golden brown with age. Its paper was thin, and its corners curled a little from frequent thumbing by Jade Snow's predecessors in learning. The right margin had been punched with holes about a half inch from the edge, and at two-inch intervals; the book was handbound with cord threaded through these holes. It had been printed in China with wood type, and the title was still quite legible, *The Practice of Writing Is in Fact Easy*.

The first page discussed the way to hold a brush correctly. The illustration showed that one's fingers should be curved in a continuous fluid line, with the brush held flexibly between the thumb and third finger, while the index and middle finger rested gently on it. In fact, it was much like holding a chopstick.

"When holding the brush, you must not pull your fingers tightly against your palm. Your fingers should be relaxed, curved outward with a hollow space between their graceful line and your palm," Daddy admonished.

Jade Snow corrected herself, but after a few strokes—there were her fingers, with brush clutched hard and tight against her palm again!

She swept a sidelong glance at Daddy. Without a word, he tore off a corner of the newspaper they had spread on the table under their work. He rolled up the paper into the size and shape of a walnut, stuffed the ball between his daughter's curved fingers and palm.

"Now begin again."

The newspaper ball really helped. Her fingers just rested on it, and were blocked into the correct, curved position. Soon she was able to train her fingers to work freely, eliminating altogether the paper-ball crutch.

Daddy now introduced her to the second page, which concerned the correct procedure in forming a character. Each stroke of the one word which filled the entire page was labeled numerically to show which stroke should be brushed in first. The principle in brushing a character was that one always proceeded from top to bottom and worked from left to right.

Daddy emphasized, "Once you learn how to brush a character correctly and beautifully, it will always be yours, no matter how old you grow to be. You may not remember the pronunciation of a word, or the lines of a poem memorized, but you can never brush a character off-balance once you have learned to brush it right."

Thus, Jade Snow, with her brush held correctly, dipped its tip upon her inkpad and began the stroke to her first word, pronounced "wing," which means "forever" and looks like this:

A long time was spent on this word. It embodied the elementary stroke technique of starting her brush in a point at the tip, applying pressure for strength and stroke expansion, and then gradually decreasing the pressure toward the end of the stroke in order to end with the tip of the brush in a point again. The criteria for skilled calligraphy included not only proper placement of the strokes, but also "power," which was the soul of the character.

Jade Snow learned not only how to use her brush; she was also taught how to care for it properly. She learned that in "opening" a stiff new brush, she should get a dish of cold water and slowly roll the point back and forth until the bird bristles fanned out freely. A brush should always be opened up to its base to get maximum action. After using ink, a brush must be rinsed gently again in water, and carefully recapped. Daddy always discarded the hollow bamboo casing, because it permitted a brush to dry hard and stiff. Instead, he used a brass casing, which would keep a brush flexible and damp until another day's brushing.

"Mama, how long do I still have to go to school?" seven-year-old Jade Snow asked one morning after summer vacation was over and she was preparing to return to the public grade school for the fall semester.

Mama was busy putting breakfast on the table. "You have just begun. After your sixth year at this school you are attending, there will be another six years at some other school farther away, where you will have to go by streetcar. After six years there, you will graduate from 'middle school.' Then some people are fortunate enough to have the opportunity to go to college, which continues for another four years."

Jade Snow started on her hot breakfast of fresh-cooked rice, boiled salt fish sprinkled with peanut oil and shredded ginger root, soup with mustard greens, and steamed preserved duck eggs with chopped pork. While she ate, she tried to digest the fact that she would have to spend practically all her life in school. Six and six and four more—a total schooling of sixteen years! She could not imagine what fourteen more years would be like.

Daddy, who concentrated on his Chinese newspapers at all meals, had the remarkable ability of knowing at the same time and in detail all that was said or done at the table. Now he looked up to add his comment:

"Some people who take up a profession study at college six or more years. But you are a girl, so you need not worry about that. It will not be necessary for you to go to college."

Jade Snow was relieved that she would only have to complete middle school.

The third grade offered her two new fields of exploration: painting and the "times tables." While Jade Snow had learned to handle the Chinese brush securely, Daddy had severely nipped her early efforts to draw pictures instead of square characters. "You can learn nothing from your own pictures," he had reprimanded. Now in the low-third grade she was encouraged to draw. She decided that the American school was going to be continuously different in more and more ways from Chinese studies and that there would be little point in wondering why. Even American brushes were different, with very long wooden handles, and short, stiff bristles. Painting was great fun, because no one told Jade Snow what to do or how to do it!

Their arithmetic lessons were on little cards neatly printed with various "times tables." Jade Snow found the figures of these cards interesting to learn and mastered all of them up to 12×12.

At the end of the semester the teacher showed Jade Snow that her report card bore the notation "Promoted from grade 3A to grade 4A." She had skipped a grade! She marched over to the new building with the 3B's and left her 3A friends behind. The teacher and her friends all seemed very much excited, and Jade Snow caught their excitement. Evidently, skipping a grade was not an ordinary accomplishment.

That afternoon, when Jade Snow returned home from school, she ran to Daddy happily and asked him to sign her report card. Daddy made his usual careful study of her grades and signed his usual painstaking signature in English.

"Daddy, did you notice that I have skipped a grade? I am going to a new building! I have been promoted two grades. Isn't it—"

Daddy quietly stopped the child's rush of excited words, "That is as it should be." That was all he said, with finality.

"Yes, Daddy," and Jade Snow suddenly lost her afternoon's excitement. She wandered off in search of Mother. Mother was putting buttons on some coveralls. She tried a new approach, "Mamma, I learned my lessons so well that I am promoted two grades, and now it will be only thirteen more years of school instead of thirteen and a half more years."

"What did your father say?" was Mother's only spoken reaction.

"He said, 'That is as it should be,' " Jade Snow replied, crushed.

"Your father was right," was all Mamma said, also with finality.

In 4A almost all the children were nearly nine years of age, while Jade Snow was barely eight. A year's difference meant that they talked about different things and acted differently. The main difference was that 4A was organized into two crowds, Mabel's and Jeanie's. Jade Snow went with Mabel's crowd. During recess they would cluster about Mabel, whispering, whispering about nothing in particular. The important thing, however, was to continue these whispers, because Jeanie's crowd always whispered around her. The very worst fate was to have your own crowd "mad" at you. Unswerving loyalty was demanded by both leaders, but one day Lily Lum in Mabel's crowd was seen on cordial terms with Jeanie herself! That would never do. Mabel singled Jade Snow out to give Lily the push which meant that they were "mad" at her. Jade Snow did not want to do this; after all, maybe their mothers were friends, or they might be neighbors, Lily and Jeanie.

Mabel demanded the reason for Jade Snow's hesitation: "Are you afraid?"

"Oh, no . . ." How did Mama's instructions apply to this situation? "Oh, no . . . I am not afraid, but wouldn't it mean more if we all went together?"

This appealed to Mabel's imagination, and thus it was that during recess they twined their arms around each other and sailed up in a body to Lily to give her the push of defiance that would banish her from their crowd.

The introduction of a group standard which differed from her home teaching was perplexing to Jade Snow, but she concluded that it would be easier to conform to group action than to enter a one-voice argument against it.

Miss Mullohand, her new teacher, was quite the loveliest person that Jade Snow had ever known. She had wavy, blonde hair, fair skin, and blue eyes, and her manner was gentle. Jade Snow always remembered one experience with her.

Sometimes after school a group of girls would play baseball in the schoolyard, while Miss Mullohand acted as umpire. Jade Snow did not do well in such games because Mama always discouraged physically active games as unbecoming for girls. When Jade Snow had wanted to climb upon signposts as other children did, Mama had made her sit down to embroider bureau scarves. However, one day when she was watching the game from the sidelines, an enthusiastic batter carelessly flung her bat, straight against Jade Snow's hand. As Jade Snow cried out, the teacher was there. She leaned down and held Jade Snow closely, rubbing her fingers, wiping the tears which fell involuntarily as the pain gradually flowed into her numb hand.

It was a very strange feeling to be held to a grown-up foreign lady's bosom. She could not remember when Mama had held her to give comfort. Daddy occasionally picked her up as a matter of necessity, but he never embraced her impulsively when she required consolation. In fact, when she was hurt either inside or outside, it was much better not to let Mama or Daddy know at all, because they might criticize her for getting into such a situation in the first place.

There in Miss Mullohand's arms, with undefined confusion in her mind, she suddenly remembered the time when she and Jade Precious Stone had awakened from Sunday afternoon naps to find the whole store dark and deserted, and the front door locked. They must have been just three or four years old then, and in terror they had climbed down the back stairs, and had helped each other to the only source of light: the front factory window. They had clung to each other weeping. After what seemed like an unbearably long time, Mother and Father had returned home and told them, "Here we are, and stop crying." For comfort, Daddy took a bag of fried soybean curds he had just bought to cook with deep-sea bass and green onions, split them and sprinkled them with white sugar, and gave the two children as many as they wanted as an unusual treat to "mend the hurt." The children were never again left alone.

But Mama and Daddy had not caught them up in their arms in comfort, Jade Snow remembered at first, finding it wonderful comfort to be embraced by Miss Mullohand. But suddenly the comfort changed to embarrassment. What was one supposed to do now in response? The embarrassment turned to panic.

"Does it hurt badly?" Miss Mullohand asked. Jade Snow felt herself stiffen as her panic increased, wordlessly shook her head to say "No." She pulled herself from Miss Mullohand and fled from the schoolyard.

Jade Snow did not tell Mama about the incident. Mama would not understand. Mama would say that she should not have been interested in ballplaying in the first place. But more than that, she was now conscious that "foreign" American ways were not only generally and vaguely different from their Chinese ways, but that they were specifically different, and the specific differences would involve a choice of action. Jade Snow had begun to compare American ways with those of her mother and father, and the comparison made her uncomfortable.

3

FORGIVENESS FROM HEAVEN

FOR THE FIRST TIME IN JADE SNOW'S MEMORY MAMA WAS CONFINED to bed. Jade Snow thought she must be very ill indeed, for all her food had to be brought to her, while Grandmother took over the household duties and meal preparations. Female relatives, including aunts, cousins, and older sisters, came to visit Mama in her close and dimly lit bedroom. But no one seemed particularly worried over her condition; for some reason, her illness appeared quite acceptable.

During the hours when Jade Snow was not at school, she had to remain with Mama, and whenever Mama wanted anything, she went to tell Daddy or Grandmother. But she did not seem to want much; even her meals were quite simple, since she desired only rice and a special steamed dried vegetable from China, which was chopped fine and mixed with peanut oil. Staying quietly with

Mama became so tedious that company was very welcome, for Jade Snow would then seize upon the temporary distraction to edge slowly out through the door.

This enforced vigil continued for days, until one night Jade Snow and Jade Precious Stone were awakened from sleep by a great deal of confused noise, a mixture of clattering pans and excited chatter. This unusual activity came from Mama's bedroom, which was separated from the girls' by a folding partition. Through the cracks in the partition, Jade Snow could see a bright light sifting into their bedroom.

The two sisters consulted with each other in whispers—somehow the situation called for whispers. Jade Precious Stone asked from the depths of her bed: "Shall we get up and see what is going on?"

Jade Snow listened a moment longer—it really was strange—some woman was talking to Daddy, and it was not Mama! She seemed to speak with authority; moreover, she was decisively giving orders!

Jade Snow cautioned her younger sister: "You had better stay in bed because you catch cold easily, and I'll find out what is happening. Perhaps Mama is getting worse."

Jade Snow was not able to see anything through the cracks, but she called to Daddy for reassurance.

Daddy answered, "We do not need you; go back to sleep."

Jade Precious Stone called out, "I heard him too; come back to bed."

For a little while the two sisters continued to whisper their perplexity, but soon fell asleep despite their troubled wondering.

The next morning, Jade Snow went in to see Mama to ask what she would like for breakfast. First she started to ask, "What was all the noise last night . . . ," but she was arrested in her questioning by astonishment, for Mama had in bed with her a very small baby. It did not look like any other baby that Jade Snow remembered, for this one had a red, red face, no hair, tightly shut eyes, and tightly clenched fists.

"Mama! Who left this? While you are sick, must you care for a baby too?"

But she saw that Mama did not look so sick as yesterday, at least not sick the same way. She was very tired-looking, it was true. At the same time, though, the tenseness of the last few days was now gone. It was replaced by an expression of serene happiness.

Mama explained, "The lady doctor whom you may have heard last night brought this baby. I feel much better now and I can take care of him. He is your brother and his name will be 'Forgiveness from Heaven.'"

"But where did the lady doctor get 'Forgiveness from Heaven'?"

"I guess I have not yet told you where babies come from. They are roasted at the hospital ovens. There are three kinds of babies. When they are nearly done, they are white foreign babies. When they bake a little longer, they become golden Chinese babies. Sometimes they are left in too long, and they become black babies!"

Jade Snow turned over this information in her mind, and concluded that it was quite reasonable. Then she looked at her little brother critically. He appeared more red than golden, but seemed basically Chinese. "Good thing he was done just right," she thought.

On her way to school that morning, she met one of Daddy's seamstresses coming to work. She stopped Jade Snow with "Did the baby come last night and is it a girl or a boy?"

Imagine that! How did she know? She could not have heard the noise last night; she had not seen the baby in Mama's room this morning. It was very odd that she should ask such a question.

"Yes, we have a baby done just right, and his name is Forgiveness from Heaven. He is my baby brother, so he must be a boy."

After school, Jade Snow returned home to find all the women of their family gathered. Everybody was talking at once, sitting around in the dining room, and of course the talk was centered around Forgiveness from Heaven. For once, Daddy was sitting idle during working hours, but he never looked happier.

Oldest Sister Jade Swallow said, "Baby has the largest ears in the family, and they are close to his head too."

Then, catching Jade Snow's puzzled expression, she explained, "You know, the larger the ears, the longer one will live; and the closer to one's head, the more they indicate success in life. A person whose ears stick out has genuine cause for worry; he has 'wind-catchers'! A person whose ears are undersized is not supposed to live long. If you don't believe me, look at the ears of old people, and study the lives of those with 'wind-catcher' ears."

They continued to discuss the baby.

"He has Grandmother's beautiful mouth."

"He has a well-rounded nose, which means material prosperity."

"His face finishes nicely at the chin; that means he will have good fortune in later life."

"A nice high brow means great intelligence."

Daddy added his opinion, "At last we have the happiness of another son to carry on the Wong name. We must have a fine celebration when his age reaches a full month. In the meantime, to announce the good news we shall send out red eggs to our friends and invite them to come here to taste pickled pigs' feet."

For days afterward, there was great bustle in the household to prepare the announcements. With Grandmother and older sisters, Jade Snow helped to dye eggs red. They took case after case of clean white hens' eggs, and boiled them in giant kettles. Into the boiling water they dropped red printed rice paper imported from China. The dissolving red dye turned the eggs pale pink, then a deeper pink, and at last they were ready to be lifted out and drained.

Big baskets of fresh-killed chickens were delivered to the house, and these were gently simmered in water until they were just done. Then hot boiled peanut oil was brushed on their plump bodies as they hung to cool. This was the favorite Chinese way of cooking chicken.

Paper bags were filled with the delicious announcements, to be distributed to relatives and friends. Each bag contained some red eggs, a section of chicken, and some slices of pickled white ginger root.

Cooking in the kitchen at the same time were big kettles containing at least fifty pounds of pigs' feet, simmering until tender in black Chinese vinegar and ginger root. Every visitor who arrived to call on Mama tasted some of this "Pigs'-Feet Vinegar." Even the lady doctor liked it. She said that the calcium dissolved in the vinegar was very nutritious. Afterward, whenever Jade Snow smelled this particular brew in Chinatown, she knew that someone was celebrating the coming of a new baby.

In a week Mama was up and about again. A new baby meant much work. There were many diapers to wash. Mama took care of these in big buckets in the bathtub. She said they were fortunate in having an automatic hot-water heater, since most other families in Chinatown had to boil their water. Baby brother cried to be fed all the time, it seemed to Jade Snow, even in the middle of the night.

As the end of a full month approached, Forgiveness from Heaven lost his redness, and became more interesting. Great preparations were now begun for the important celebration. A baby was not supposed to be taken out before this month had passed.

Daddy wanted the feast held at his factory and home, on the second floor. The older sisters bought many bundles of crepe paper in red, white, and blue, and cut it into two-inch widths, unraveling long streamers which were fastened along the ceiling from one end of the store to the other. Long tables were constructed by placing planks over sawhorses. Extra dozens of bowls, chopsticks, and glasses for the occasion were also delivered to the house.

Daddy had an additional stove installed, and not a burner remained idle, as ducks, chickens, squabs, pork and beef were all cooked each in its own best way with appropriate spices, seasonings and vegetables. Aunts and female cousins helped with the cooking. It was the happiest work they had ever done; even Jade Snow had fun trying to help. Laughter, excitement, and anticipation made light work of the activities.

Then came the party! On Daddy's side, his first cousin, who was like a brother to him, came with his wife, son and daughter-in-law, daughter and son-in-law, and all his numerous grandchildren. Other cousins and nephews of Daddy's were also there. On Mother's side, her brothers and Grandmother were there. Many friends, some of Daddy's employees, as well as others that Jade Snow did not know, also came, until she lost count of their numbers.

Those who drank were offered Chinese spirits, and those who did not, like the women, had sparkling apple cider, which was an imitation champagne always served at Chinatown's celebrations or feast occasions.

The arriving guests first greeted Mama and Forgiveness from Heaven, making a great deal of fuss over the baby, and each gave him a present of money, wrapped in red paper for good luck. At the age of one month, Forgiveness from Heaven had a good start toward his bank account.

The dramatic high light of the evening was unexpectedly provided by Third Uncle on Mother's side, who drank too much rice wine and became violent. He started to become quarrelsome, broke some dishes, and finally let fly a few wild punches. At that point, Daddy and one of his cousins took some rope and tied his hands behind him, led him downstairs, and left him on the floor to sober up. Then they returned and the fun went on. No one seemed to be bothered by Third Uncle's behavior. They commented that he often became violent after drinking.

The Wong family had never before seen such merrymaking, and Jade Snow enjoyed all the excitement. Just one remark she had heard, however, marred the perfect celebration, and remained in her mind as she lay in bed after the guests had departed. It was something she had overheard one of her older sisters say to the other while she was helping them twist the crepe-paper hangings.

"This joyfulness springs only from the fact that the child is at last a son, after three daughters born in the fifteen years between Blessing from Heaven and him. When Jade Precious Stone was born before him, the house was quiet. There was no such display."

Under the comfortable warmth of her covers, Jade Snow turned over restlessly, trying to grasp the full meaning of that remark. Forgiveness from Heaven, because he was a brother, was more important to Mama and Daddy than dear baby sister Precious Stone, who was only a girl. But even more uncomfortable was the realization that she herself was a girl and, like her younger sister, unalterably less significant than the new son in their family.

4

GRANDMOTHER AND HER WORLD BACK HOME

EVERYONE IN THE WONG FAMILY MADE MUCH OVER THE FIRST male child born into their family in fifteen years, but Grandmother, Daddy, and Mother especially doted on Forgiveness from Heaven. Over ten pounds at birth, the baby was fed so continuously that he developed remarkably. When Daddy's jobber-boss came to visit their family, he tucked a dime into the child's tightly clenched fist, and accused Mama of feeding her son on elephant's milk!

Jade Snow felt that Forgiveness was a great improvement over her one doll, but much less tractable. He seemed to do little more than cry, drink milk, and wet his diapers, but Mama presided lovingly over all his antics, keeping him spotless. Forgiveness' baby skin was smoother than Jade Snow's nicest white silk Chinese dress, and his smell seemed to her sweeter than the fragrance of any blossom.

Grandmother and Jade Snow helped Mama to care for the new

baby. Every day after school, Jade Snow's first responsibility was to take in from the line his clean clothes which Mama had washed the night before, and fold them neatly in a pile. If Forgiveness was not already asleep, she would roll his baby buggy back and forth to lull him into his nap. She had a favorite song, learned in the American school, which she sang to him:

> Bye lo, baby bunting, Daddy's gone a-hunting,
> Gone to get a rabbit skin,
> To wrap his baby bunting in.
> Bye lo, baby bunting, bye.

She didn't know exactly what the song meant, but she liked the tune immensely and Forgiveness seemed to like it too. During the day, while Mother was usually busy at her sewing machine, Grandmother was with them regularly, helping to feed and take care of Forgiveness. Their shared responsibility for Forgiveness' well-being meant that Grandmother's and Jade Snow's activities coincided. For this period, therefore, Jade Snow spent more of her after-school time with Grandmother than with anyone else. Sometimes, of course, Jade Precious Stone was with them, but most of the time she was playing with the other children in the factory or on the street.

Grandmother was full of wonderful surprises and delightful stories from another world—the world she called "back home in China." After the diapers were folded, Forgiveness was asleep, and his bottled milk prepared, Grandmother and Jade Snow would start one of their favorite pastimes, either folding squares of white paper into miniature pagodas, mandarin hats, airplanes, long-legged cranes, dragon boats, or playing a wonderful string game called "making baskets" (cat's cradle), in which one of them would start a basket on both hands with a circular piece of string, then her partner would transfer the string pattern to her own hands while she changed its form or design. As they played back and forth, the pattern often became quite intricate, and Grandmother invariably developed an arrangement that baffled Jade Snow completely. During these games, Grandmother heightened the entertainment with her stories, and after a while Jade Snow pieced together a picture of Grandmother's former world.

Grandmother had adopted Mama and two older boys, for she had no children of her own. Life in their village was simple, as a result of stringent economy. The food of the family was mostly polished white rice, steamed and flavored with a little oil and salt, and occasionally included a small quantity of dried salted root vegetables. A farmer cousin supplied them with fresh vegetables; in this they were much more fortunate than some of their neighbors. But meat and fish were rare items on their menu. Chicken and eggs were also dear; and they never heard of or used dairy products in their cooking.

It was not that they were poor, exactly. Grandfather had gone to America to seek his fortune as a partner in a poultry business in San Francisco's Chinatown. He was a conscientious and good provider for his family in China. But Grandmother was a woman of courage and ambition, and instead of living well on the money sent home to her, she aspired to make more money with it.

"I saved and saved our money from your grandfather—the average woman cannot work to make any money in China," Grandmother explained. "With some capital, I decided to raise pigs. Pork was everyone's favorite meat, and it could be salted and cured. I thought it would be a simple matter to raise hogs on the low hills behind the house. Buying a few pigs at a time, I finally accumulated a drove of forty-five. And then disaster struck. An epidemic swept them, killing them one by one until I had only eight left."

Jade Snow asked, "Where was your doctor, Grandma?"

"Do you think we would have doctors for animals when even people suffered for lack of proper medical care?" was her reply.

"Well, what about the eight which were left?"

"I became discouraged and left them in your mother's care. In fact, I was so annoyed at those pigs that I decided to forget my disgust over the failure of my first venture by leaving home altogether for a while. So I went to visit my country cousins, leaving both the pigs and the house with your mother, who was eleven at the time."

But Grandmother still had not accounted for the last eight pigs. Jade Snow had to know what had happened to them. So she approached Mama. Watching Mama expertly running a pair of trouser legs through a seaming machine, Jade Snow burst out: "Mama,

what happened to those eight pigs that didn't die when they were
left by Grandma after she went away?"

Mama was caught by surprise, and did not respond readily. Then,
slowly, she finished the story.

"I fed them and drove them near the house. Not one died after
I took over. I wasn't much older than you then, but every night I
had to bring them heavy pails of hot mash. I remember still how
their sudden grunts in the darkness would frighten me, and I would
throw out their food hastily. I could not flee fast enough back to
the house, to climb shivering into the comfort of my bed, while
their grunts seemed to pursue me in the darkness."

"Mama, what happened to those eight pigs?" Jade Snow persisted.

Mama replied quietly, "Your grandmother sold them after I
raised them." She paused, then added bitterly, "But I didn't see any
of the money."

Jade Snow felt very close to that frightened little girl who like
herself had to do what her mama wanted, not for reward, but because it was proper.

According to Grandmother, living in China was based on an
economy of conservation. Having little fuel, they steamed whole
dinners in one pot by stacking bowl upon bowl, resting them on
bamboo sticks. They slept on a teak or marble slab to keep cool in
the perpetually warm nights of the southern provinces. Food was
sold in earthenware containers, because cans and glass bottles were
too costly. If Grandmother needed oil, salt, or sauces, she would
send Mama to the store with a porcelain bowl, and Mama would
return, climbing the hills and walking most carefully, guarding the
filled bowl so as not to spill anything. Of course, paper bags and
newspapers were nonexistent.

Not only did Grandmother indulge Jade Snow with tidbits, play
with her, and fascinate her with stories, but she also aroused in her
an appreciation for growing things.

"I am going to show you how plant life develops," she said one
day as she took a glass from the kitchen cabinet. Then she rolled
a piece of white blotting paper around the inside of the glass and
poured in a half inch of water. Jade Snow could see the moisture
slowly traveling up the piece of blotter.

After that Grandmother showed Jade Snow a handful of black

and white striped seeds, which she called "polly seeds." Choosing some nice plump ones, she slipped them in between the blotter and the glass, with their sharp ends pointed up.

"Now we shall have to wait," she said, putting the glass up on the kitchen window sill.

For days Jade Snow watched the glass without discovering any change. According to Grandmother's instructions, she kept the blotter wet. Then one day she saw that a little white point was piercing its way through the blunt end of one of the seeds, heading for the water supply in the bottom of the glass. In a few days all had sent out roots, which lengthened to the water line. About this time the pointed ends of the seeds opened to release little green shoots which pushed their way up into the free space above their glass home and then changed to brilliant wings of leaves, while the fine white roots grew into a tangled mass in the bottom of the glass.

"Grandmother, those seeds all looked alike when you planted them, but now one has hardly grown at all, and some are much taller than the others," Jade Snow observed.

"That is the way with growing things and even with people," was Grandmother's reply. "We have provided all of them with the same care, but some just cannot avail themselves of this opportunity, while others have made the most of what they have and are bursting forth with their best for us to admire."

Grandmother peered at Jade Snow over her dainty gold-rimmed eyeglasses, and announced, "Now we are going to continue this lesson by transplanting the best of these plants. We will discard the weak ones, just as in life those who do not try are left behind."

Miraculously, Grandmother produced from the back-porch sink a pot of earth. Skillfully she worked the soil loose with a pair of sturdy bamboo chopsticks; then gently holding a "polly seed" plant, she dropped the root and covered it, tamping down the earth with care. When she had completed her work, four of the healthiest seedlings were planted with their leaves proudly raised.

"I am going to take this home and care for it, as you do not have enough sunshine here. Later I shall bring the pot to you again so that you can see what has happened," Grandmother promised.

Jade Snow periodically asked about the welfare of the little plants, until one day Grandmother did bring the flowerpot back to her.

The plants were several inches tall now, and one was just bursting into a bright yellow bloom; but one showed no promise of bloom at all.

Grandmother continued her lesson, "Now you can see that, when conditions change some will adjust readily and come out first, while others may still be left behind."

Jade Snow nodded. She could see again that handful of all-alike seeds lying in Grandmother's open palm, and she reflected on the wonders which water and soil could accomplish for those which would try.

Grandmother added an afterthought. "However, the Chinese also believe that there is heaven's blessing in a person's ability to make things grow. If an established plant blooms one year with unusual beauty, it is a sign that heaven has chosen to bless its home with special good fortune for that year. The same seed and the same care oddly produce different plants for two different people. Sometimes, you will even find that for a crooked person, a plant will grow crookedly. Some people have not been blessed with the ability to nurse life—plants, animals, fishes, even children may not grow for them. You remember, your mother could raise pigs, but I couldn't. These are your plants; be happy that they will grow for you."

At the age of eight, when Jade Snow had been promoted to the fourth grade at the American school, one night at dinner Daddy looked over his newspaper and announced, "I think it is about time Jade Snow was enrolled in Chinese evening school. She needs more diversified Chinese subjects than I have time to teach her. She should learn now about China's great rivers, T'ang poetry, and provincial differences, and she should compete in class essays."

There was no discussion—the plan was simply announced.

Accordingly, Jade Snow set out at four-thirty the next afternoon with her hand in Daddy's; a few blocks away they reached the Hip Wo Chinese evening school, which was operated and subsidized jointly by the American boards and Chinese branches of three churches: Presbyterian, Congregational, and Methodist. The principal knew Daddy, who was on their board of directors. Mr. Lee was a scholarly-looking man with an animated expression and greying hair. To determine Jade Snow's grade level he asked her to read from some books on his desk. Daddy told him modestly that his daughter had had some preparatory lessons.

The principal was surprised to find Jade Snow maneuvering successfully through the third-grade lessons. After due conference the two men decided that she could be placed in the third grade because she had not studied a balanced program of subjects, although she had an advanced vocabulary.

Mrs. Ling, the third-grade teacher, was a pale, small woman with brilliant, straight black hair drawn into a tight bun at the nape of her neck. She always dressed in a conservative, dark Chinese dress.

Studying Chinese at school was quite like studying at home with Daddy, except that it was easier. Instead of individual response to a watchful father, it was group response to a teacher, who, no matter how watchful, could not possibly detect the careless response of a particular individual. Mrs. Ling read a line which the class of twenty-five students supposedly repeated after her. However, even if tempted, Jade Snow could not daydream comfortably over her lessons, because upon her return home Daddy always had her review them aloud with him.

The worst part of the Chinese school was that it left Jade Snow without any time to play with Jade Precious Stone after day school, or to chat with Grandmother, or to observe the daily changing antics of brother Forgiveness. After day school, there was scarcely an hour left for folding diapers and getting something to eat before starting for the Chinese school. School was not dismissed until 8:00 P.M., after which there were more lessons at home.

And soon another duty was added to eat even further into Jade Snow's rare free hours, for Daddy now decided that her Chinese and American education should be balanced by some training in Western music. Second Older Sister Jade Lotus had already worked her way through and graduated from a San Francisco music conservatory. She played Beethoven, Chopin, and Mozart to perfection at important Chinatown socials and taught piano lessons. To her judgment Daddy entrusted the selection of an upright piano, which he purchased second-hand for the awesome sum of forty dollars and had installed in the girls' bedroom.

The Chinese Y.W.C.A. office where Second Older Sister worked as executive secretary was a half block from where the Wongs lived. Here, elderly Mrs. Schumann, who specialized in music lessons for young beginners, was engaged to give Jade Snow an hour's lesson each Saturday afternoon. Mrs. Schumann had an energetic love of the piano, and tremendous patience in teaching a Chinese girl who found English difficult and had not the faintest idea what Western music was.

Before her music lesson, Jade Snow was sometimes privileged to have her lunch with Second Older Sister in the Y kitchen. Since the Wongs never ate at the home of friends or at restaurants except at rare banquets, a change in cooking seemed the most wonderful treat in all the world. The Wong meals were confined to those foods found in the grocery stores of Chinatown, which carried either things imported from China or domestic crops of Chinese origin. But Second Older Sister cooked American dishes of strange and deliciously different flavors.

Her visit to the Y.W.C.A. was a bright spot in the week for Jade Snow. Even though its real purpose was a difficult piano lesson, to see other faces than those of her friends at school and at the factory, and to play without care for an hour or two were real joys.

Like Chinese studies, piano lessons were not wholly bad nor wholly good. They were a duty to be gotten through by trying one's best. Jade Snow wouldn't have minded them if she could have been rewarded with immediate results, but a year of effort found her still concentrating on finger exercises, despite an hour's practice every day with an extra hour on Saturday morning.

One evening as Jade Snow was absorbed in practicing her calligraphy lesson at Chinese school, she was startled to discover her third uncle on Mother's side, the one who had had too much to drink at Forgiveness' birth celebration, in conversation with Mrs. Ling. Mrs. Ling announced that Jade Snow was to go with him at once. In great wonder, she packed her books. On their way home, he explained: "Your Grandmother has become very ill, and your Mother had her taken to the hospital today. We did not want to tell you, but now Grandmother is asking for you. Be quiet and be careful not to upset her when I bring you to her."

Jade Snow had never before visited the Chinese hospital. Its atmosphere was strange to her and somehow oppressive. In a self-operated elevator they went up to find Grandmother's room.

Grandmother looked so tiny and colorless! Alone in a white room, she was enveloped in white covers and pillows on a high bed. A strange pallor had spread over her face and hands. For the first and last time in her life, Jade Snow saw her customarily neatly-dressed long, straight hair falling carelessly over her pillow.

She opened her eyes when Jade Snow stole quietly up to her bedside, and she took the child's hands in her cold ones, clasping them weakly.

Jade Snow could not bear the silence. "Grandma, why are you here? What is the matter? Come home with me and I will help take care of you!"

Grandmother managed an attempt at a smile, but her eyes were clouded with pain and sadness. As she stroked Jade Snow's brow and swept back the child's bangs in a habitual gesture, she said, "I don't think, Jade Snow, that I shall be coming home with you. But will you remember your grandmother always with this precept? Be a good girl, and in your years of schooling, study your books very hard with your heart's full interest. Remember, the ones who do not try are left behind."

That was all—Jade Snow gently squeezed Grandmother's hand in response, and bade her a quiet and last farewell.

5

LUCKY TO BE BORN A CHINESE

THE MONTHS FILLED WITH SCHOOLWORK, MUSIC LESSONS, AND home chores were broken in routine by a few days which glowed. These were the seven days of the Chinese New Year. According to the Chinese lunar calendar, New Year's fell in the American February, unless it was a Chinese "leap year," which gave the year an extra seventh month. These holidays climaxed the year and the American-Chinese children at public school were excused for their festivities.

Mama made preparations by cleaning house completely until everything was gleamingly neat; starched white curtains, polished floors, new oilcloth on the dining table were the first signs of the pleasant days to come. The Wong children, all scrubbed and with their hair washed, were dressed in new clothes, for New Year's literally meant that everything should be new, renewed, or clean.

The children also tried to be very good, for a scolding on New Year's day foretokened frequent scoldings during the year. It was also poor taste to talk about unpleasant subjects, such as death, for that would also bring bad luck; therefore visitors uttered the most flattering remarks and offered exaggerated good wishes, such as, "May you be blessed with a hundred sons and a thousand grandsons!" or "May you enjoy the best of health and longevity!" or "May you find your great material fortune this year!"

The sidewalks on both sides of Grant Avenue were lined with colorful exhibits when "The Year's Thirtieth Night" or New Year's Eve approached. Huge branches from blossoming trees, such as the peach, pear, or apricot, were placed beside open-tiered shelves laden with pots of flowering azaleas, camellias, gardenias, cyclamen, and early-budding bulbs of narcissus and daffodils. Because of its delicacy and heavenly fragrance the traditional narcissus bulb with double blossoms, which grew in water, was always the favorite.

Beside the plant displays were huge wicker baskets piled high with fresh greens or root vegetables, or big pans with dried vegetables or sea foods from China soaking in water. At this time of the year the Chinese grocery stores did their best business. The merchants cleaned their shops, placed fresh plants and oranges in their windows, and displayed new stock imported for the occasion from China.

Mama took Jade Snow and Jade Precious Stone and Forgiveness from Heaven through the streets to see all the sights, for although Mama would not leave the house the year 'round, on "The Year's Thirtieth Night" it was her privilege and desire to go out and enjoy the community gaiety for one evening.

The streets, narrow to begin with, were now made even narrower by the displays; they were also jammed by shoppers looking for choice purchases. The busy hum of the crowd and the merchants' cries created an undercurrent of excitement. A festive spirit flowed from the well-dressed children and their dressed-up mothers, all seemingly relaxed and carefree in their holiday mood and costumes.

Mama did not buy anything; she had her hands occupied with Forgiveness and Jade Precious Stone. Besides, Daddy had already bought all their groceries for their wonderful New Year's meals—

one feast tonight for "Rounding Out the Year" and one day after tomorrow to "Open the Year."

On New Year's Eve, when they got home, they discovered that Daddy had gone out too by himself and had brought back a huge branch of pink blossoms, which now graced their one and only antique vase, a handsome black porcelain piece with a colorful dragon decoration. The faint perfume of almond blossoms pervaded their dining room.

Mama said, "Daddy, such a luxury to buy a branch which will shed its blossoms in a few days. I heard the prices they were asking for these!"

But Daddy smiled happily. "Once a year is reasonable enough for a luxury," and Mama really looked pleased.

The Wongs expected callers every day of the New Year week, and they were prepared not only with a spotless home but also with decorations of bright oranges and tangerines neatly stacked on plates, new potted plants, and red hangings and pillow covers.

Jade Snow helped Mama pass sweetmeats and red melon seeds to their guests. The sweetmeats were candied melon, coconut, or kumquats, and lichee nuts from China. The red melon seeds were consumed by the visitors with remarkable skill. They cracked the tiny kernel's outer shell with their teeth, and extracted the thin white seed expertly without breaking it, continuing this tirelessly all afternoon without interrupting their conversation. (In a Chinese gathering melon seeds took the place of cigarettes; and during visits, at the theater, and at banquets, the click, click, click of cracking shells always told of a sociable occasion.) The red and green colors, the fruit, the green plants, the flowering branches, the seeds, the sweets—all were propitious: they meant life, new life, a fruitful life, and a sweet life.

During New Year's, Chinese women worked at jobs irregularly or not at all; the most important thing was to celebrate properly. The women who were regularly employees of Daddy's visited his home as guests. There were many exchanges of sweets, and Jade Snow was never hungry during that week. In addition, callers tucked into the children's hands at least a quarter and sometimes fifty cents or a silver dollar, wrapped in red paper for a good-luck token of material wealth during the year. Mama reciprocated by giving the callers' children similar good-luck packets. Some of Jade Snow's schoolmates returned to class with tales of the amount of gift money they had kept for themselves, but she always had to give hers back to Mama.

The delicious tidbits exchanged at New Year's varied according to the pride and custom of individual households. Some prided themselves on steamed sweet puddings, made of brown sugar and special flours, and decorated with red dates or sesame seeds. Others specialized in salty puddings, made with ground-root flour (something like potato flour), fat pork, chopped baby shrimps, mushrooms, red ginger, and green-topped with parsley (baby coriander leaves). Some families brought a special deep-fried dumpling filled with ground soybeans and rolled in sesame seeds, to be eaten piping hot. Still other women spent considerable time in making tiny turnovers which consisted of a delectable filling of chopped roast pork, bamboo shoots, and spices, rolled in a thin, chewy, translucent paste, and steamed on bamboo racks.

In China, Jade Snow was told, one of the New Year rituals centered around a live carp. The carp, favorite motif for decoration on dishes, was a long-lived fish. It could be kept out of water for an hour or so and yet live when returned to it again. It was also a common superstition that the carp could, after long meditation and practice, develop into that king of creatures, the fiery dragon. At New Year's, therefore, it was the custom in some parts of China for a family to obtain a live carp, tie some red paper around its middle, and lay it (often with difficulty to keep it laid) on a bed of fresh green lettuce leaves. This literally formed a lively dish. After it had served its purpose, the fish was quickly released to swim out again into its river or pond home.

At the Wongs', the New Year week got a good start at the "Opening of the Year" with an extra-bountiful dinner which featured Daddy's special chicken dish and a huge roast duck. The celebration also had a good wind-up on its seventh and last day called "The Day Man Was Made," with another feast. Of course, the dinner did not end with chicken or duck; there were special dried-vegetable-and-oyster stews and other time-consuming dishes which were not usually served.

To "Open the Year," Daddy—who cooked only when he was

enormously pleased with the occasion—
chicken. First, he simmered two young cl
just done. Then he cut green peppers into
them. Opening two cans of lichee fruit from
the syrup with cornstarch. Then he boned
chicken. A layer of chicken, a layer of lichees, a
pepper, a trail of lichee sauce, and then he repea,
The dish was served cold, and the unusual comb,
always drew forth compliments from the Older S
husbands.

During the week that followed, there were Lion Da
the streets. Daddy took them to watch the dancing,
Forgiveness high on his shoulder, to watch the perforn
unobstructed heights. It was the custom in San Francisco
Chinese hospital to raise its yearly funds by engaging a
dance for his money. A group of acrobats trained in the te,
relieved one another in these dances. They used a large and
cious-looking but very colorful "lion's head," fitted with bright
on springs, and a jaw on hinges. From this head there hung a fa
satin "body" and "tail" piece, sewn together with different-color
scalloped strips of coral, turquoise, red, green, and blue silk. On
man who set the tempo for the dance manipulated the head, holding it up in both hands, with only his brightly trousered and
slippered legs showing below. As the huge Chinese drums beat in
quickening tempo, he danced hard, raised the head high, and jerked
it from side to side in an inquiring and delighted manner. His
partner, holding up the tail, danced in accompaniment. Their lively
movements simulated the stalking, attack, and retreat of a lion.

Citizens of Chinatown co-operated by hanging red paper tied
with currency and lettuce leaves in front of their doorways. The
lion approached and danced up to the prize. Sometimes, he had to
dance onto a stool to reach it. As he stretched his hand out through
the mouth to grab the money, his feet keeping time on the stool all
the while, the occupant of the house or store threw out strings of
bursting firecrackers, both to welcome him and to scare away the
evil spirits. Daddy, with Jade Snow, Jade Precious Stone, and Forgiveness from Heaven, followed the lion's trail, treading the red

nts of burnt firecracker wrappings which carpeted the gray
lks.

e Snow was always fascinated by the Lion Dance—the insist-
trong beat of the drums was exhilarating, and the colors and
hm were unforgettable. But sometimes she felt sorry for the
, especially when it was hot, or when the bursting firecrackers
re thrown right at the "fearless" animal.

The firecrackers were set off to frighten away any lingering evil
irits, and to make the New Year fresh and clean. They came
om China and were of various sizes. The tiny ones were hardly
vorth burning, and were useful to pack with stored clothing to keep
away moths. The next size was most popular. In a continuous string
they made a great deal of noise, and singly they were still effective.
In fact, when Jade Snow was once careless enough to allow one of
these to pop off in her hand, it felt numb for a long time. There
were still bigger ones which Jade Snow was not allowed to burn.
These were called "big lights" and could blow up a bottle or lift
a tin can. Only big boys played with those.

Another festival which was traditional with the Chinese and
therefore with the Wong family was the Moon Festival.

As long as Jade Snow could remember, their family had un-
failingly and appropriately observed the holiday, which was said to
have originated in ancient China. According to the Chinese lunar
calendar, on the fifteenth day of the eighth month the moon would
rise rounder, larger, and more brightly golden than at any other
month of the year. Then, specially baked cakes filled with a thick,
sweet filling were eaten by the Chinese in recognition of the beautiful, full harvest moon. The round Chinatown moon cakes which
Jade Snow knew were about four inches in diameter and an inch
and a half thick. Thin, short, sweet golden pastry was wrapped
around rich fillings of ground lotus pods, or candied coconut and
melon, or ground sweetened soybean paste. Jade Snow's favorite
filling was "five seeds." This was a crunchy, sweet, nutty mixture
of lotus pods, almonds, melon seeds, olive seeds, and sesame seeds.
Each cake was cut into small wedges, to be enjoyed slowly with
tea. Daddy always said that his father in China used to be able
to cut his cake into sixteen to thirty-two wedges; one cake would

last him all afternoon as he sat on his front porch to eat and drink and leisurely watch the rest of the village go by his door.

At Moon Festival time, Grandfather also called for a special rice-soup dinner for a large crowd of friends and employees. A thick soup was prepared with rice cooked long hours in chicken stock. Pork chopped fine was seasoned and formed into little balls which were dropped in toward the last part of the cooking. The basic soup was ladled boiling hot into individual bowls. The table was already set with attractive dishes of thinly sliced meats and condiments: red tender beef, fresh raw bass fillet, minced green onions, red ginger, pungent parsley, shredded sweet baby cucumbers, chopped peanuts, crisply fried fine noodles. Each person busily helped himself to these additions according to his taste. A rice-soup dinner was informal and a social occasion for fun.

Yes, it was sometimes very lucky to be born a Chinese daughter. The Americans, Jade Snow heard, did not have a Moon Festival nor a seven-day New Year celebration with delicious accompaniments. Besides, they burned their Chinese firecrackers five months later on one day only—the Fourth of July!

6

UNCLE KWOK

A MONG THE WORKERS IN DADDY'S FACTORY, UNCLE KWOK WAS ONE of the strangest—a large-framed, awkward, unshaven man whose worn clothes hung on him as if they did not belong to him. Each afternoon around three-thirty, as some of the workers were about to go home to prepare their early dinners, Uncle Kwok slowly and deliberately ambled in through the Wong front door, dragging his feet heavily, and gripping in one hand the small black satchel from which he was never separated.

Going to his own place at the sewing machine, he took off his battered hat and ragged coat, hung both up carefully, and then sat down. At first Jade Snow was rather afraid of this extraordinary person, and unseen, watched his actions from a safe distance. After Uncle Kwok was settled in his chair, he took off his black, slipper-like shoes. Then, taking a piece of stout cardboard from a miscel-

44

laneous pile which he kept in a box near his sewing machine, he traced the outline of his shoes on the cardboard. Having closely examined the blades of his scissors and tested their sharpness, he would cut out a pair of cardboard soles, squinting critically through his inaccurate glasses. Next he removed from both shoes the cardboard soles he had made the day before and inserted the new pair. Satisfied with his inspection of his renewed footwear, he got up, went to the waste can some seventy-five feet away, disposed of the old soles, and returned to his machine. He had not yet said a word to anyone.

Daily this process was repeated without deviation.

The next thing Uncle Kwok always did was to put on his own special apron, homemade from double thicknesses of heavy burlap and fastened at the waist by strong denim ties. This long apron covered his thin, patched trousers and protected him from dirt and draft. After a half hour had been consumed by these chores, Uncle Kwok was ready to wash his hands. He sauntered into the Wong kitchen, stationed himself at the one sink which served both family and factory, and with characteristic meticulousness, now proceeded to clean his hands and fingernails.

It was Mama's custom to begin cooking the evening meal at this hour so that the children could have their dinner before they went to the Chinese school, but every day she had to delay her preparations at the sink until slow-moving Uncle Kwok's last clean fingernail passed his fastidious inspection. One day, however, the inconvenience tried her patience to its final limit.

Trying to sound pleasantly persuasive, she said, "Uncle Kwok, please don't be so slow and awkward. Why don't you wash your hands at a different time, or else wash them faster?"

Uncle Kwok loudly protested the injustice of her comment. "Mama, I am not awkward. The only awkward thing about my life is that it has not yet prospered!" And he strode off, too hurt even to dry his hands finger by finger, as was his custom.

Jade Snow, peering around the corner, came into the kitchen after he left, and began to help her mother with the dinner preparations. Seeing that her mother appeared amused over the incident, Jade Snow asked, "Mama, why is Uncle Kwok so queer?"

"I don't know why he is so queer, but I can tell you something about him," her mother replied. "He is no blood relation to you, but he used to work with your father at a match factory before your father started this business. In making the match tips the factory used sulphur, which was supposed to be harmful to the teeth unless the worker washed it from his hands most carefully. Well, one of the workers scoffed at this precaution, but soon suffered from a serious tooth decay. Uncle Kwok took no chances; he washed and rewashed his nails almost every hour. He was ridiculed by everybody, but he still has his natural teeth today. Now he is a habitual handwasher.

"Uncle Kwok is a converted and devout Christian, who has spent almost a lifetime studying the Confucian classics. He likes to think of himself as a scholar. All his life, his one ambition and fondest dream has been to become a private tutor. He did manage to save some money, but a swindler assured him that he could invest his savings to bring in big dividends, and with these Uncle Kwok hoped to be able to establish the little school where he could teach the Chinese classics. The 'investment' dividends have never materialized."

"Mama, why doesn't he come to work earlier and make a little more money?"

"He is a janitor at a Chinese church across the Bay in Oakland, which gives him a room in return for his services. Each morning after he has cleaned the church building, he sits and waits until the last possible moment of the afternoon, hoping to be notified that this is his 'day of opportunity.' Then he picks up his satchel, just in time to come over on the last afternoon ferryboat for his work here," Mama explained.

"Mama, have you ever seen what is in Uncle Kwok's satchel? I have always wondered why he never goes without it," Jade Snow asked.

"You will be surprised to learn that his satchel does not contain a miser's fortune, as some gossipers suppose. It contains only Chinese classics. Since we have known him, he has worn out three satchels carrying these books. If you ask him about the meaning of one Chinese ideograph, he begins looking through all his books for different versions, but in his great excitement at being consulted, he is never able to find even one intelligent answer."

"But, Mama, he only works here a little while, even after he finally arrives."

Mama enlightened her further. "He goes to another janitor's job at a neighboring apartment house, which pays him fifteen dollars a month. After he pays for his commutation ticket there is hardly enough left to buy him food and clothing. That is why you might have noticed that whenever I have a pot of noodles or soup, I always give him a big tureenful. He has never yet left a speck of food in his dish."

Jade Snow mourned aloud, "My, I feel so sorry for Uncle Kwok!"

"Oh, but he wouldn't want you to feel sorry for him," replied Mama. "He has more pride and dignity than you or I. He is older than either your father or I, but it pleases him to call me 'Mama' and your father 'Papa.' Sometimes, when I haven't enough extra food and I know he is hungry, I offer him a quarter for a meal, but he always refuses angrily. Your father tried to buy him new shoes, but he would not accept them on any condition."

Jade Snow tried to understand how a grownup could become so queer, but though she continued to watch Uncle Kwok from a distance, she never found an answer that satisfied her.

7

LEARNING TO BE A CHINESE HOUSEWIFE

IN THE EARLY 1930'S THE LIFE OF THE WONG FAMILY CHANGED radically: they moved from the factory home where they had lived and worked for almost ten years. For some time Jade Snow had been conscious that her parents were discussing the matter of rent, concluding that they could no longer pay for a street-level store-front location. In this period of economic depression, the factory which had always kept Daddy and Mama busy was now idle for six months of the year.

One night Jade Snow came home from Chinese school to find the whole family prepared to go out. Jade Precious Stone and Forgiveness were wrapped up snugly in caps and coats.

"Jade Snow, drink this milk and come along with us. Your daddy has found a possible new store location where we may move. We have borrowed the keys from the landlord and want to inspect it tonight," explained Mama.

The Wongs moved along the street in a body, Daddy first with Younger Brother in hand, and Mama arm-in-arm with her daughters, one on either side according to established habit. They had not gone many steps before they met one of Daddy's acquaintances, who addressed him familiarly by his first name.

"Brother Hong, seldom do I see your family and you together on a little expedition," said Daddy's friend.

"Yes, Uncle Bing; have you met my inferior woman?"

Mama nodded, smiling ever so slightly, and remained absolutely silent.

Daddy continued, with beaming pride, "And this is my baby son!" He flourished his arms at the little figure by his side.

Uncle Bing complimented Daddy: "What a fine boy; what intelligent features! Here is a piece of money to buy some candy." He tucked a coin in Forgiveness' hand in accordance with customary practice. To be the baby of the family, and a boy at that, qualified one for the sole honor of receiving special gifts from one's parents or friends or relatives.

Daddy turned to the girls. "And these are my small daughters, Jade Precious Stone and Jade Snow. Address Uncle Bing!" Daddy commanded.

Jade Precious Stone and Jade Snow obediently complied with the expected courtesy: "Uncle Bing, have you had your dinner?"

"Thank you, I have. Brother Hong, your Thousand Gold [daughters] are certainly growing fast," replied Uncle Bing.

They made their farewells and continued on their way. As they passed an herb store a block farther, Daddy suddenly said, "Oh, I remember that I must see Brother Sing about a school matter. Take Forgiveness a minute and wait for me here. I shall be back right away." And he left Mama with the three children standing in the darkened street.

Mama exploded, "Your father always does that when we go out. That is why I dislike to accompany him. Once he left me, and in his absent-mindedness forgot to come back. So I walked on and on alone, and finally went to a foreign movie in the American section of town. When I returned home, I found he was consumed with anxiety, and had called upon our relatives to look for me. But still that hasn't improved him! As long as he assists in so many community affairs besides running his business, he is likely to be absent-minded!"

This evening, however, Daddy did not forget his family, and in due course they went on together to the vacant store, which was only five blocks from their present home, and on the same street.

Daddy opened a door, and his family descended a steep flight of wooden stairs into a two-story basement, which was cold, damp, pitch-dark, and smelled unpleasant. Daddy picked out their way with the beam from a solitary flashlight.

In the eerie, lonely light, Jade Snow clutched Daddy's rough, hardened hand, and saw that they were in a room which ran the length of the narrow building. The dusty foundation walls were of rough brick, and the unpainted rafters were hung with spider webs. Jade Snow shivered, wondering how Daddy had found such a place and why on earth he would want to look at it twice! She looked at him. His face held no horror. In fact, as he talked now his expression was one of imagination and controlled excitement. He was selling the place to them, but he was already sold himself.

"We can cut some windows here and here. This basement is below street level, it is true, but it adjoins an empty lot which is level with the floor down below. Therefore, we can get air and light and some little sunshine by cutting small windows through this wall which opens on the lot. Of course, we will always run the risk of someone building next door, but we must trust the future to God.

"Now on this upper floor," Daddy swept on, "we can erect partitions for our rooms, and downstairs we can install our sewing machines for factory work. I have measured the place and have drawn a tentative plan."

With his family clustered around, he directed the beam of his flashlight onto a piece of cardboard on which he had drawn to scale a plan of their future quarters, all neatly labeled with measurements and names.

After studying the plan, Daddy began pacing off imaginary rooms to show Mama how the measurements would work out. As they talked about the kitchen, Jade Snow began to catch a little of Daddy's enthusiasm, and to think of the cold expanse in terms of working and living.

Daddy and Mama finished making some readjustments in Daddy's plan. Mama kept saying that the rooms must follow a "central unity."

As they made their way home, Daddy figured for Mama. "The rent there will be about fifty dollars less than what we have been paying. It will cost us about a thousand dollars to move from the old place and to reinstall and rewire all our machinery. It will cost us at least another thousand to partition and paint the place and to install proper plumbing. Thus we will have to live there for some years to recover our investment, but we shall be ahead after that."

In the following months, Daddy directed the renovation of the basement. He hired some Negroes to chisel out part of the brick walls for windows, and supervised the work of carpenters, plumbers, electricians, and painters. Finally the Wongs moved into their new quarters.

Daddy had asked Mama to choose the colors, which she did without hesitation. The dirty cobwebs on the rafters and brick walls had been replaced by fresh whitewash. The partitioned-off kitchen was a warm red-brown with battleship linoleum on the floor. It was fitted with a new sink and a beautiful, large, overhauled second-hand stove—complete with oven, warming oven, and broiler, as well as four burners—which Daddy had bought on McAllister Street for six dollars. Never before had the Wongs had an oven!

The bedroom shared by Mama, Daddy, and Forgiveness, and the dining-living room next to it were painted a bright watermelon pink, with blue-green woodwork. Jade Snow and Jade Precious Stone shared built-in bunk beds in a room with cream-colored walls and brown linoleum floors. Older Brother had a study and adjoining bedroom to himself, which he painted apple-green accented with metallic silver. On his walls were tacked numerous bright-colored banners with college names. Each bedroom had a window, and the living-dining room had two.

Really the new home was not so bad as it had at first appeared. But Jade Snow wondered how Daddy could foresee so clearly the possibilities of a basement which had been unrented for years because it was rumored that someone had hanged himself there. The rent was low because people said that the building was haunted. But Daddy, who believed in none of the usual superstitions of the

Chinese, always said that anyone who believed in Jesus Christ could defy any ghost; and in accordance with his conviction he had once spent the night in a room where someone had hanged herself. He said that it was one of the nights he had slept best.

The part of the upper floor that was not taken up by living rooms was given over to a fenced-in office area, finishing machines and packing tables. The main production and bulk of the work, however, was done on the floor below, to which the bales of denim material were slid down a portable wooden chute through the sidewalk opening.

The manufacturing process now became, even more than it had been before, an inseparable part of Jade Snow's life. As much a part of home as her bedroom were the sewing machines she passed before she came to her bedroom door. She talked above the din of a factory full of motors and machines in operation, and practically breathed in rhythm to the running stitches. Daddy's garment manufacturing operations were so much a part of her that she never gave them conscious thought.

When a cutting order was received, Daddy laid his material smoothly down the length of the cutting table, layer on layer, usually, piling up a stack of five dozen. Then he rolled out on top a heavy, brown paper stencil which was perforated in the outlines of the pattern. In his careful way he had managed to include in the stencil all the pockets, belt-loops, flies, trouser legs, and other necessary parts for the exact number of each size in the lot, as specified in the jobber's order. To Jade Snow this achievement seemed miraculous. Not only did Daddy end up with the correct number and faultless fit; he also saved as much material as possible. In cutting as in other activities, Daddy wasted nothing. Daddy always tried to save *something*. Daddy was one of a very few men who knew how to mark stencils so expertly; sometimes other cutters brought their patterns to consult with him.

After the stencil was laid, white talc was dusted over the holes of the outline. When the stencil was lifted, it was time to cut! The cutting machine was a roaring menace, its vertical blade vibrating, its gleaming edge sharpened even more keenly than Daddy's old-fashioned razor-blade. With his hand on the steering handle, Daddy guided the machine steadily and skillfully through the piled depths of the material. One wrong move would be multiplied by sixty pieces, and Daddy could neither economically nor morally afford that loss. After cutting, bundles of trouser parts with their trimmings were assembled by size and distributed to the seamstresses.

After preassembling by the seamstresses, it was Mama's job to pick up the semifinished overalls and run their main seam through her double-seaming machine, which joined two pieces of material by rolling in the raw edges completely and locking them with twin needles. The various bundles were then returned to the seamstresses for final hemming. Since all overalls had to pass through Mama's hands before completion, she was constantly lifting heavy bundles, but she never complained.

When the hemming was finished, the overalls were taken to the upper level for final finishing with buttonholes and bar-tack reinforcements. These expensive special machines were as necessary to complete one pair of pants as a thousand pairs, and for many years Daddy was burdened with the payments on them; somehow these had to be squeezed out of his earnings before he could feed and clothe his family.

Completed overalls were picked up by the "folders," who cut loose threads, examined the work for damage or incompletion, folded the overalls neatly, and tied them in bundles of a dozen each, preparatory for final pickup.

Pickup was a dramatic event during these basement factory days. The sidewalk entrance was flung open, and the various Wongs stationed themselves along the steep stairs. The overalls were ready, stacked according to their lots. Daddy would pick up a bundle from the stack, pass it to Mama, who would throw it to Jade Snow perched somewhere on the stairs, who would throw it up to Older Brother on the sidewalk. Older Brother, who could throw the farthest with unerring aim, would land the bundle in the truck.

From this family factory Daddy's overalls were sent to the jobber, who distributed them all over the United States to department stores and mail-order houses. Jade Snow often wondered where they all went, and sometimes she thought she recognized the overalls or jeans she saw on strangers or friends.

After the Wongs moved, Daddy's factory continued to be idle most of the year, even as he was faced with meeting the expenses of moving. He threw together all his funds for rent, utilities, payments on machinery. He went into debt. He borrowed from his jobber. And he stopped buying groceries.

Jade Snow was barely eleven in this depression year of 1933.

Some of their relatives who had relied wholly on wages for income became unemployed and had to apply for government relief.

Daddy faced the grim times with Mama. They were exploring ways for more severe economy, and in their discussion, Mama said, "Jade Snow is old enough to take over my housework so that I can do as much sewing as possible. Perhaps you can go out and solicit odd work which I can do at home. It is time for our daughter to learn the meaning of money, the necessity for thrift, and how to keep house. I shall provide her with the money for groceries.

"But it is my desire not to apply for relief, even though we may need it. I do not want my children to experience getting anything without first working for it, for they may become selfish, and a selfish person can wander the world over and still starve for lack of food. Selfishness often starts with a spirit of dependency; therefore I want my children to learn to cope with the world, and to understand that they get what they want only after working for it."

Mama had spoken, and had spoken beyond her customary habit in both length and determination. When she gave her verdict on these rare occasions, Daddy silently accepted her judgment.

Almost overnight, the life of Jade Snow, heretofore characterized by gravity keyed to propriety, became weighted with the gravity which only anxiety over money can cause.

Now, every day after school she reported immediately to Mama, who gave her the usual fifty cents to purchase groceries for that evening's dinner and tomorrow's breakfast. Lunch was composed of leftovers. With prudent management, it was possible to get a small chicken for twenty cents, three bunches of Chinese greens for ten cents, three whole Rex soles or sand dabs for ten cents, and about a half pound of pork for the remaining ten cents. The household staples, such as rice, oil, salt, soy sauce, and soap were bought by Daddy.

The small chicken would be cut up, bone and all, into pieces which could be handled by chopsticks, marinated like beef or pork with a standard seasoning of a tablespoon each of flour, soy sauce, sugar, and oil and then placed in a bowl for steaming. This dish would be saved for breakfast. The sole to be served at night would be fried with a little chopped fresh ginger root, which was used more frequently than garlic in the Chinese kitchen. Ginger root in this instance neutralized any fishy odor—no fish was ever cooked without it—but it was also indispensable as an herb for the relief of certain types of colds and stomach or intestinal upsets.

The pork was sliced thin and used to make soup stock in which the greens were cooked. The three bunches of greens made sufficient soup and vegetable for both dinner and breakfast. Together with generous bowls of rice this menu fed three adults and three children.

In shopping for groceries, Jade Snow soon learned which stores carried the best of a particular thing; and after scathing criticism from Mama, she learned how shiny a fresh fish should look and how firm it should feel; how solid a head of cabbage should be before it could be considered solid, how an old turnip looked as distinguished from a young one, how pink good pork was, how crisp a bean sprout should be, and how green a young onion. Jade Snow never tried to bargain, as Mama often did from Chinese habit, or to get more than her money's worth by begging or flattery, as she heard fellow shoppers do, but under Mama's watchful checking at home, she certainly had to get her money's worth.

Most of the Chinese vegetables and condiments were purchased at the small general grocery stores, which were a clutter of canned goods on shelves, huge open baskets of vegetables along the wall, cured sausages, dried sea foods, and pressed ducks hanging overhead, jars of preserves and sauces here and there, sawdust on the floor, and always a fat cat watchful for mice. Mama said that they were much like the grocery stores in China.

The meat market was more American-looking with its long, refrigerated counters and white uniformed butchers. For fish, Jade Snow shopped at the stores which usually sold fish at counters in front and live poultry in the back. At the end of Chinatown, however, was one store which sold poultry without selling fish; it was Uncle Jan's store.

Uncle Jan was called "Uncle" because he was Daddy's good friend; also Mama had gone to school with his wife in China. He was Jade Snow's friend too, and she never had to watch him to be sure she got a good chicken.

Uncle Jan never bothered to make an inviting window display; he had paper sacks piled there. But he had more business than any other poultry store—he supplied restaurants, and many Caucasians came to get their chickens from him. Uncle Jan sometimes sat at his counter taking telephone orders, or making entries in his books, but whenever a customer came in, he jumped to wait on him personally. He was a good salesman without apparent effort, for he loved people. He would ask you how you were cooking your chicken, how many you were feeding, and would give you exactly what you wanted at the most reasonable price in Chinatown. He would put his hand into one of the many cages which filled his store to the ceiling and pull out a loudly protesting chicken. By the feel of its breastbone he could tell you when it had been hatched.

When Jade Snow went to Uncle Jan's, he always smiled happily, showing a flash of gold-crowned teeth. A cigar hung perpetually from a corner of his mouth, a cigar which he chewed but didn't smoke. Here and there on the white tile floor, Jade Snow could see little black wads of chewed tobacco. Uncle Jan inevitably asked, "How is your father? He is always working so hard. But so do we all nowadays, with many mouths to feed. And your mother? I still think of her as 'the little one' from habit, for that is what I used to call her in China." After Jade Snow had murmured replies, he might continue, "Why don't you get some squabs instead of chicken today? They are fat and tender."

Jade Snow would be doubtful, "Mama said chicken."

Uncle Jan would grin and wave his hand, "You tell your mother that I want you to have squabs for dinner."

Jade Snow would ask cautiously, "But the price?"

"Don't even think about the price; I will figure it correctly for you."

While live white squabs were killed and dressed by his wife or employees, Uncle Jan would continue his conversation. He never left Jade Snow waiting alone in his store.

"And what about the oldest sister and your other sisters and brothers? Is the little one growing fast? And what about you? Are you being a good scholar? I always have admired the way your father has taken his stand on educating his daughters. He is a scholar while we are just businessmen."

As she left, Uncle Jan would call out with the usual courtesy, "Tell your mother that she is welcome to visit us at our home any time she is free."

And Jade Snow would reply, "Thank you, and you feel free to visit us too." She always felt a warm glow after talking to Uncle Jan. At American Thanksgiving, for some years now, they had served turkeys given to them by him, for he had a standing agreement with Daddy that if Daddy would help him sell turkeys on the rush day before Thanksgiving, he would receive as a gift as large a fowl as he desired.

By four in the afternoon Jade Snow had usually completed her shopping and rushed home, where Mama would have started dinner preparations. The rice always received first attention. "Get your rice on the stove first," Mama said, "and if it is cooked well, the other accompaniments are secondary. But if the rice is underdone or improperly cooked, the most delicious meat or vegetables cannot make up for it. The reputation of a good cook begins with good rice."

They had only half an hour to prepare dinner, then only twenty minutes for the meal, before it was time for Jade Snow to grab her Chinese books and be off to the Chinese school with Jade Precious Stone. Returning home at eight o'clock, Jade Snow first washed the dinner dishes and then washed the rice for the next morning's breakfast. To wash rice correctly is the first step in cooking rice correctly, and it is considered one of the principal accomplishments or requirements of any Chinese female. When Jade Snow was six, Daddy had stood her on a stool at the kitchen sink in order to teach her himself this most important step, so that he could be personally satisfied that she had a sure foundation.

First, she dipped out the required amount of raw polished white rice from the rice barrel. In their household, the barrel held a hundred pounds of rice, and an abalone shell was the measure. This shell had been used in the family for years; Mama said it was older than Jade Snow. Its luster was dulled, but infallibly, one-and-one-half measurefuls would insure enough rice for one meal (a little more for dinner; a little less for breakfast; and two measures when there was company). The rice was scooped into a heavy aluminum pot with a tight cover, and was washed in the pot.

It was first dampened with a little water, then rubbed for a while with both hands (if you were a child like Jade Snow) or with one hand (if you were a grownup). White starch would come off the rice and bleed into the water. You rinsed after the thorough first rubbing of about a hundred strokes. Then rub, scrub, and rinse again. Rub, scrub, and rinse again. Then rinse, rinse, rinse. Three scrubbings; six rinsings; these were the minimum treatments. When the water came out clear, the rice had been thoroughly cleaned.

Now it was ready for cooking water. Cold water was added until it reached one of Daddy's first knuckle joints above the level of the rice. Jade Snow usually allowed on her fingers a knuckle and a half. Then she checked the quantity of water by tilting the pot gently so that the rice remained undisturbed on the bottom. In this position, the knuckle-or-so of water, if allowed to flow to the edge of the tilted pot, would reach to the diameter of the rice on the bottom of the pot.

The cooking of rice was not less important than the washing. The pot, with its lid tightly in place, was set over a burner with the flame turned high until the water began to bubble and boil over. Then the burner was turned very low, and the steaming rice water was gradually absorbed. Daddy said that this was a most delicate stage in the cooking and that one should never lift the cover of the pot to peer at its contents. Instead, one should give the rice the full benefit of its steam and only by observation of the escaping steam should one conclude how nearly done the rice was. At the first bubbling stage, the steam rose straight up, strongly. At the completion of cooking, the steam curled ever so gently around the edges of the lid.

If by carelessness one forgot to turn down the flame when the water boiled, the rice would scorch. At times, this could happen in the best of families, but Daddy had a remedy. He would place a little saucer or Chinese teacup full of cold water in the pot on top of the rice to absorb the scorched taste.

Ideally, however, the rice would be cooked just right in about a half hour, into tender, smooth, snowy, fluffy, separate morsels. Under no circumstances did one stir or drain or rinse. Of course, this formula for faultless rice which would be beyond reproach of the most critical future mother-in-law depended entirely on the kind of rice which was chosen. During the prolonged waterfront strike in San Francisco, when it was not possible to obtain imported Chinese rice, Daddy bought the only available substitute—blunt-grained California rice. Despite the most careful efforts of Daddy and Mama by turn to coax, treat, and nurse this rice through washing and cooking, the result was a sticky, yellowish mass. The Wongs ate bread for the period of this strike.

Clearly Jade Snow's shopping list never included a few pounds of rice. Choosing a season's supply (about five hundred pounds) required the combined wits of both Daddy and Mama. Where rice was concerned, Daddy was perhaps more opinionated than many other Chinese, because his father used to own a rice store among his other businesses in China, and he had grown up among rice-husking activities.

When the Wongs were dipping into their last fifty pounds of rice in the rice barrel, it was a signal for Daddy to go to his favorite rice dealer, who imported his merchandise from China.

"Fellow Villager, we wish to choose our new supply of rice. May we have some samples of your current stock?" Daddy would ask.

"Good morning, Mr. Wong," the proprietor would reply. "I know you like the firmer type. I have a shipment of such rice, which is whole and smooth, and absorbs very little water. It is also comparatively free of foreign matter."

"That is very important," Daddy would answer, "for our last supply contained an abnormal amount of husks and gravel particles. It would be best if you would let me take home some samples to discuss them with my woman before I order."

The half dozen or more sample packets which the rice dealer supplied were wrapped in squares of cotton material, blue lined with bright pink. Each was labeled with type and price. Once home, Daddy and Mama sat down at their round dining table and carefully opened the little parcels, spreading them out in orderly rows.

Daddy put on his glasses and pointed out to Mama the sample recommended by the rice dealer. "This new import is supposed to take little water and be quite free from grit and husks."

Mama studied it a minute and then pointed to another sample.

"However, the grains of this type are formed more perfectly and have a nice shiny fat look on the surface, which shows it is from fresher stock. Rice cooked from these grains will have the firmer texture which we like."

Then she added, "But it costs fifty cents more for each fifty-pound sack. Perhaps we should get the type the rice dealer recommended."

Daddy, who had previously decided on the kind the rice dealer recommended, was suddenly aroused, "What is more important than the rice which we eat twice a day and which is our main food? It is what we are, or we are what it is. Better to have what we want at whatever price, and economize on something else. It is decided—we shall have this most expensive type."

And so Daddy returned the samples and ordered the kind selected. Soon several hundred pounds of rice in its fifty-pound sacks was delivered and stacked in a corner of the store.

Now to the Wong children, this delivery by no means ended the story of buying rice. For the rice came from China packed in double thickness straw-mat sacks, the open ends hand-sewn with strong hemp twine; as reinforcement, double strips of flexible cane about three-eighths of an inch wide, were wound around the sacks. From each sack of rice Daddy opened to fill the rice barrel, he, who wasted nothing, carefully untied the cane, straightened it out, and saved it to make switches for whipping disobedient or improper children, because Daddy firmly believed that severe whipping was the most effective means of bringing up creditable daughters and illustrious sons.

So it was no wonder that the Wong children always watched a delivery of new rice with sad eyes and heavy hearts. It was also no wonder that Little Brother Forgiveness, who as a son dared to be more articulate than his older sisters, would plead unhappily with Daddy when he saw him come home with new rice samples, "Daddy, please don't buy any more rice!"

8

THE TASTE OF INDEPENDENCE

IN CHINESE SCHOOL, JADE SNOW HAD NOW PASSED BEYOND THE vocabulary stage to the study of essays, which she was required to memorize both by oral recitation and writing. The correct spelling of a word could not be hazarded from the sound, but depended on one's remembering the exact look of a character, including the location of the tiniest dot.

The only subject which permitted students to exercise their imaginations and to demonstrate their knowledge of the language was composition. Once a week they were given a subject title, such as "The Value of Learning," or "The Necessity of Good Habits," and the class hummed with anticipation as the words were written on the blackboard. They worked first on a rough draft, and afterward copied the draft with fine brushes onto the squares of a tablet page, which they submitted for correction.

On Saturday mornings, an assembly was held in the chapel of the Chinese Presbyterian Church, where members of the advanced classes took turns in practicing public speaking before the student body. Their talks were usually moral clichés, many patterned after sermons heard from their minister. Patiently, the students suffered with the speakers through such subjects as "It Is Time for China to Unite," "The Little Boy Who Cried Wolf-Wolf and Betrayed Only Himself," or "You Can Trust Some Animals More Than You Can Trust Some People."

Sometimes at these assemblies, they heard sermons or guest speakers. But always the meeting began with prayer and hymns; Jade Snow and Jade Precious Stone learned to sing in Chinese the words to such melodies as "Bringing in the Sheaves," "Day Is Dying in the West," "He Arose," and the stirring "Onward, Christian Soldiers."

Order, in the most uncompromising Chinese sense, was enforced strictly. Not a sound was tolerated from the rows of black-topped heads in the audience. A dean or disciplinarian preserved order and punished offenders for a multitude of infringements—from assembly misconduct to cheating in class. During assembly, this unpopular man paced up and down the aisles with a long rod held menacingly in his hand. At the slightest noise he was instantly there, and the guilty one was told to stand in the aisle to be shamed publicly for misbehavior. The boys were seated on the right side of the hall, with the girls on the left, arranged by grade. Several boys were notorious for disrupting the peace at almost any assembly. They seemed to enjoy their brief sojourn in the limelight as they stood in disgrace. Rarely was a girl stood out for punishment, but when she was, all heads turned toward her as if by signal.

One Saturday morning, Jade Snow's most humiliating Chinese school experience occurred in this setting. Simply for the pleasure of outwitting the disciplinarian, Mr. Dong, some of the girls had agreed upon the idea of passing notes surreptitiously from one aisle to the other. One assembly passed off successfully; another assembly found the girls still triumphant. The third week, Mr. Dong, who was conscious of a disturbance, decided that he must find a culprit or suffer a serious loss of face. Unfortunately he decided to pull out a culprit exactly at the moment when the note slid into Jade Snow's hand.

The next move was swift—the long rod tapped Jade Snow's shoulder. Shrinking, she looked up to find Mr. Dong, his face wreathed in triumph, motioning unmistakably for her to come out and stand in the aisle.

Jade Snow had never before been mortified so completely, sud-denly, and publicly. Slowly she made her way from her seat to the aisle. She stood, perspiring and blushing, keeping her eyes down to screen her agony. She wished that her straight bangs were long enough to conceal her whole face from the curious eyes that she knew were turned to stare in surprise, disapproval, and sympathy. Her tears gathered, hung, and finally dropped unchecked. The green Victorian design on the faded red aisle carpet stamped itself indelibly on her memory during the interminable wait until the end of the assembly.

As usual, her first thought was "What would Daddy and Mama say?" Mostly it was "What would Daddy say?" Daddy probably would never have been party to passing notes. He would not mind refusing to co-operate in a project to which all others had agreed, if he thought it was not exactly right. But as just another little girl in a whole row of classmates with whom one had to get along every evening of the week, Jade Snow had not felt equal to resistance. It was her own fault, as usual.

Finally, the last hymn was sung, the students received the bene-diction, and as the assembly was dismissed, Mr. Dong announced, "All those who have been stood out at assembly will go to the principal's office immediately to receive their punishment."

"To receive punishment"—wasn't standing out enough? This aftermath had not occurred to Jade Snow. She picked up her books from her seat and trailed out after the dwindling crowd, turning off to enter the principal's office instead of going downstairs to the street as usual.

Guilty boys were waiting inside the office, which held two old-fashioned desks and a couple of old wooden chairs. Into this color-less, cluttered-looking place, Mr. Dong hustled with brisk anticipa-tion. He went to his desk and found a long cane switch, heavier and tied more securely than Daddy's salvages from the bindings of the rice bundles. Evidently the boys were seasoned to this routine, for they quickly stepped up to Mr. Dong and held out their right palms. The switch cut the air and cracked down loudly three times on the open palms. The boys did not cry out, but stuck out their chests manfully before their lone female audience, and nonchalantly scampered off.

Mr. Dong began his treatment of Jade Snow more ceremoniously. "Wong Jade Snow, I am surprised at such misbehavior in a young lady, and you must be punished to teach you a lesson."

Jade Snow was terrified. Then indignation routed terror as it suddenly occurred to her that she need not necessarily submit. Nobody except her parents had ever whipped her. It was one thing to be stood out as a martyr for her friends, but nobody should whip her for it. According to Mama's and Daddy's instructions, she had never before argued with a teacher, but she needed no practice for the scornful words which she flung recklessly because she knew that they were righteous.

"Yes, I did pass a note, and for that perhaps I deserve to be stood out. But I am no more guilty than the girl who passed it to me, or the girl who had passed it to her, and even less at fault are we than the girl who started it. If you whip me, you should also have here all the girls from my row, with their palms outstretched. And I won't hold out my hand until I see theirs held out also!"

There was a stunned silence. Mr. Dong could not have been any more surprised than Jade Snow herself. From where had all those words tumbled, so suddenly and so forcefully?

Mr. Dong recovered somewhat and clutched his vanishing dignity. "So you dare to question me!"

The new Jade Snow spoke again, "I speak only for what is right, and I will always question wrong in the way my Daddy has taught me. I am willing to bring him here to submit this matter to his judgment. Until then, I hold out no hand."

There Mr. Dong was held. Obviously he did not wish to have a director of the school board brought in to arbitrate between the disciplinarian and his own daughter, Jade Snow. He generously waved his hand. "Very well, I shall let you off gently this time, but don't take advantage of my good nature to let this happen again!"

As Jade Snow went home that Saturday afternoon, her thoughts were not concerned with her victory, unprecedented as it was. She was struck with this new idea of speaking for what she knew was right. All the vague remarks which Mama and her older sisters had dropped from time to time, and the stories they had told about Daddy's well-known habit of speaking out forthrightly and fearlessly for what he believed was right, no matter what everyone else thought, had borne their first fruit in Jade Snow.

At the American day school, Jade Snow was now ready for junior high school. Most of her classmates went on to a local junior high school where the student body was a mixture of Italian-American and Chinese-American youngsters. Daddy, however, made some investigations first, having heard rumors that this was a "tough" school, not in the sense of academic requirements, which would have been pleasing to him, but in the behavior of the boy students.

Although the accuracy of this report could not be ascertained, Daddy judiciously was not taking any chances on undermining the delicate sensibilities and disciplined character which he and Mama had so carefully and strictly forged in Jade Snow. At eleven, this daughter could hardly find a moment of her life which was not accounted for, and accounted for properly, by Mama or Daddy. She had not yet been allowed to visit any friend, of any age or sex, unaccompanied. She had never even gone to the playground, a block away from home, without a grown-up relative or friend in attendance. When she was old enough to go alone to school, to the barber shop, or to the grocery, she either took Younger Sister, or was allowed exactly enough time to accomplish her purpose and return without any margin for loitering on the streets.

About this time, Jade Snow and Jade Precious Stone together suffered their last whipping at Daddy's hands, to teach them unforgettably the importance of keeping a promise and the necessity of accounting to their parents for their time and their activities.

Oldest Sister Jade Swallow was organizing the citizens of Chinatown to roll bandages for shipment to the Chinese front in the Sino-Japanese war. One Saturday evening she asked her two younger sisters to come over to the Y.W.C.A. to help her. Jade Snow asked Mama for permission to go.

"It is all right with me as long as you get all your household duties done before you leave. But you must also obtain your father's permission," said Mama.

Jade Snow went to Daddy.

Daddy debated, "I do not like to have you begin the habit of going out at night. However, it is a worthy cause. Be back not later than nine."

The Y.W.C.A. was about four blocks away. There the sisters had a fine time rolling bandages. It was fun to chat with Oldest Sister again, for they did not see one another often. Before they knew it, it was nine o'clock, but Jade Snow and Jade Precious Stone were loath to depart. Tomorrow would be Sunday, and only a few more bandages were needed before their quota would be filled.

"We are supposed to be home by now, Big Sister," Jade Snow anxiously reminded.

"If you stay a little longer to finish this job, I will telephone Daddy and tell him that you are still working here and will be home a half hour later."

This Oldest Sister did. She reported that he had consented. In happy confidence that all was well, the two sisters finished their bandages and went home at 9:30.

They raced down the flight of entrance stairs, walked through the store, and just as they were entering the hallway to their room, they saw Daddy rise from his desk in his office cubicle. He came out to meet them, and they saw that he held in his hand the bundle of whipping cane.

"Look at the clock and observe the time!" was all he said.

They looked. The big old-fashioned Seth Thomas wall-piece gave the date of the month, the day of the week, and its time hands leered down at them. Nine-thirty-seven, they read.

Daddy loomed large and menacing; there was no kindness in his face. Swiftly the switch cut the air and whistled sharply just before it landed across the back of Jade Snow's bare calves.

"You are older and you must be punished first," thundered Daddy angrily. "You are responsible for leading your younger sister, and I shall teach you not to disregard the time and your word to me again."

Down whistled the switch again on little nine-year-old Jade Precious Stone's bare legs. "And you are to learn not to follow your Older Sister in her sins."

Across Jade Snow's thighs, then against Jade Precious Stone's.

again and again both children were roundly whipped; but Mama had put one limitation on her own and on Daddy's whippings—the children were never to be struck near or on their heads, because such blows might affect their brain and injure their intelligence!

"Are you not ashamed that big girls like you must be taught by physical punishment! Now off to bed quickly before I become more angered," said Daddy in a roar.

The girls jumped and winced under the strokes but knew that it was best to submit silently. Jade Snow knew that Daddy's generation in China were whipped even more severely—they were suspended from their wrists while receiving punishment. The girls limped off and climbed into one bed for mutual comfort, and under the covers they rubbed each other's sore, red welts. With heavy hearts, they quietly sobbed themselves to sleep.

The daughters of the Wong family were born to requirements exacting beyond their understanding. These requirements were not always made clear, until a step out of bounds brought the parents' swift and drastic correction.

Now after eleven years of continuous vigilance, Daddy was not going to let Jade Snow go to any school that "tough" boys might be attending. He called upon Oldest Sister for assistance. Oldest Sister suggested a junior high school eight blocks from home which she thought superior to the other school. As it had no Chinese students, Jade Snow would be forced to learn more English, Oldest Sister convinced Daddy.

Complying with their decision, Jade Snow found herself the only Chinese student in a small neighborhood school. Here she did not make new friends. She missed her grammar school companions, but she hesitated to take the initiative in making friends with the first "foreign" classmates of her own age. She was not invited to any of their homes or parties. Being shy anyway, she quietly adjusted to this new state of affairs; it did not occur to her to be bothered by it.

Since the new school was a little farther than comfortable walking distance over the steepest part of Nob Hill, Jade Snow received fifty cents from Mama twice a month to buy a car ticket. On nice days, however, Jade Snow usually walked home from school to save two-and-a-half cents.

It was on one of these solitary walks home soon after she had transferred to the new school that Jade Snow was introduced for the first time to racial discrimination.

She had been delayed after school. Everyone had gone except herself and a little boy to whom she had never paid much attention —a very pale, round-faced boy with puffy cheeks, an uncombed thatch of sandy hair, freckles, and eyes which strangely matched the color of his hair.

"I've been waiting for a chance like this," Richard said excitedly to Jade Snow. With malicious intent in his eyes, he burst forth, "Chinky, Chinky, Chinaman."

Jade Snow was astonished. She considered the situation and decided to say nothing.

This placidity provoked Richard. He picked up an eraser and threw it at her. It missed and left a white chalk mark upon the floor. A little puff of white dust sifted up through the beam of the afternoon sun streaming through the window.

Jade Snow decided that it was time to leave. As she went out of the doorway, a second eraser landed squarely on her back. She looked neither to the right nor left, but proceeded sedately down the stairs and out the front door. In a few minutes, her tormentor had caught up with her. Dancing around her in glee, he chortled, "Look at the eraser mark on the yellow Chinaman. Chinky, Chinky, no tickee, no washee, no shirtee!"

Jade Snow thought that he was tiresome and ignorant. Everybody knew that the Chinese people had a superior culture. Her ancestors had created a great art heritage and had made inventions important to world civilization—the compass, gunpowder, paper, and a host of other essentials. She knew, too, that Richard's grades couldn't compare with her own, and his home training was obviously amiss.

After following her for a few blocks, Richard reluctantly turned off to go home, puzzled and annoyed by not having provoked a fight. Jade Snow walked on, thinking about the incident. She had often heard Chinese people discuss the foreigners and their strange ways, but she would never have thought of running after one of them and screaming with pointed finger, for instance, "Hair on your chest!" After all, people were just born with certain characteristics, and it behooved no one to point a finger at anyone else, for everybody was or had something which he could not help.

She concluded that perhaps the foreigners were simply unwise in the ways of human nature, and unaware of the importance of giving the other person "face," no matter what one's personal opinion might be. They probably could not help their own insensibility. Mama said they hadn't even learned how to peel a clove of garlic the way the Chinese did.

When she arrived home, she took off her coat and brushed off the chalk mark. Remembering the earlier incident of the neighborhood boy who spit on her and its outcome, she said nothing about that afternoon to anyone.

During the next two years, Jade Snow found in eager reading her greatest source of joy and escape. As she now understood a fair amount of English, she stopped at the public library every few days after school to return four books and choose four new ones, the number allowed on one library card. Every day she read one book from cover to cover while with one ear she listened to her teachers. Temporarily she forgot who she was, or the constant requirements of Chinese life, while she delighted in the adventures of the Oz books, the Little Colonel, Yankee Girl, and Western cowboys, for in these books there was absolutely nothing resembling her own life.

About this time, to help her in her studies, Daddy bought Jade Snow her own desk. It was exactly like his, of yellow oak, with a kneehole, a set of three drawers on the right side, pigeonholes facing on the back, and a cover of flexible slats which could be rolled down to lock the desk. Daddy believed firmly in providing each of his children with a personal desk, light, and pair of scissors. He hated to have anyone disturb his belongings, and to teach his children the importance of leaving other people's personal property alone, he saw to it that each had his own essential tools for orderly living and studying.

Thus well equipped, Jade Snow had no excuse for not doing her homework to perfection. Because of this and because her last name began with "W," which seated her at the back of the classroom, she was able to manage those two fancy-full happy, daydreaming years in her storybooks while she obliviously sailed through junior high, received a blue-and-white block sweater emblem for outstanding citizenship, and woke up to find that her teachers had skipped her half a grade. At twelve she was qualified to enter high school.

9

SATURDAY'S REWARD AND SUNDAY'S HOLIDAY

T HE BRIGHTEST SPOT IN JADE SNOW'S WEEK WAS SATURDAY NIGHT.
But first there was Saturday afternoon. Then she did the
family washing in big galvanized buckets in the bathtub. Bed linens
and Daddy's shirts were sent out, as well as Big Brother's laundry,
but Jade Snow washed all the underwear, night clothes, sweaters,
blouses, dresses, and towels for herself, Younger Sister, Daddy,
Mama, and Forgiveness. She also dusted the rooms and swept them
thoroughly, and about once a month did extras like cleaning the
woodwork, polishing the aluminum kettles, and giving the big
stove a good scouring. Mopping and other housework beyond Jade
Snow's physical capacity, Mama did herself, though it meant that
she had to stay up one night a week until two in the morning.

For the chores which Jade Snow did, Mama paid her fifty cents a week. On Saturday afternoon, for another fifteen cents a week, Jade Snow also cleaned Big Brother's room and changed his bed. If she had time for it, she persuaded him to let her do some of his light laundry, for which she was paid at the rate of a penny a piece. In this way she sometimes earned as much as twenty-five or thirty extra cents a week. These activities, together with the twelve-and-a-half cents she saved from carfare almost every week, gave her an income of about three dollars every month.

Those three dollars gave Jade Snow a wonderful feeling of freedom. Since Daddy provided her with shelter, Chinese school tuition and books, and Mama with her major clothes requirements, American school supplies and expenses, and food, her own three dollars could buy an extra sweater, a pair of new shoes, or an occasional ice cream.

Yes, it was worth the household chores to be able to claim independent earnings. Besides, Saturday afternoon was rewarded by Saturday night. That was the one night of the week on which Mama usually stopped working to indulge in their one luxury. She took her children to the "foreign" movies.

At the neighborhood theater a few blocks from their home, the attractions of Western life or jungle thrillers were supplemented by the serial, which was one of Mama's greatest passions. For a few hours, she and her children forgot who they were, how hard they worked, or how pressing were their personal problems, as they shared the excitement of six-shooters, posses, runaway stagecoaches, striking cobras, the unconquerable Tarzan, and organized apes.

Home after the movies, Saturday night was not yet ended; Big Brother would have bought the Sunday paper, so there were the funnies to pore over. Jade Snow, Jade Precious Stone, and even little Forgiveness, looking over each other's shoulders, would eagerly devour "Bringing Up Father," "Dick Tracy," and "The Katzenjammer Kids."

"As long as I have been in America," Mama often said, "those little mischief-makers (the Katzenjammer Kids) have never grown an inch!"

On this night, Mama had to chase them to bed. She said invariably, "You don't want to go to bed now; when you are older, you will wish for more sleep and you won't be able to get it."

By contrast, Sunday was sober and peaceful. On this day the machines were inactive. The Wongs arose as usual, but after breakfast it was time to study the Bible, pray, sing hymns, and review the Sunday-school lesson under Daddy's supervision. Jade Snow translated the English lesson into Chinese, while Younger Brother and Younger Sister listened with a minimum of squirming under Daddy's watchful direction. Daddy read the Scriptures from his Chinese Bible, well-thumbed from a lifetime of usage.

Daddy's unshakable, profound faith in Christianity had been established when he came alone to a tough and growing San Francisco after the turn of the century, a young Chinese unacquainted with the American language and customs. He had been sent by a firm in China to audit the books of their San Francisco branch. The frauds he found which discredited the management of this branch created no popularity for him among his own people in Chinatown.

Eager by nature and habit for knowledge and self-improvement, Daddy discovered one source of organized friendly assistance. The Cumberland Presbyterian Chinese Mission, operated with enthusiasm by a Chinese pastor who became his lifelong friend, welcomed him. The mission not only taught him English at night school, it introduced him to hymns and sermons, and educated him in a new doctrine of individual dignity and eternal personal salvation which revolutionized his traditional Chinese thinking, centered around reverence for his ancestors. In a few years, he left his business and was ordained a minister.

Daddy's wife and two oldest daughters were waiting for him to return to China after he reached his goal of a few thousand dollars. Under the influence of his newly found philosophy, he wrote his wife, who had little, two-and-a-half-inch, bound feet.

"Do not bind our daughters' feet. Here in America is an entirely different set of standards, which does not require that women sway helplessly on little feet to qualify them for good matches as well-born women who do not have to work. Here in Golden Mountains [America], the people, and even women, have individual dignity and rights of their own."

Then later, when he could afford to arrange for his women to share in America's new life, he joyfully wrote, "I am forwarding you and our little girls your passage fares and passports to come over and join me here in the Great City of Golden Mountains [San Francisco]."

Daddy became as serious about Christian precepts as he was intent on Confucian propriety. It was a blend which was infused into all his children, by example as well as by instruction, from the time they were old enough to distinguish "Yes" from "No." His stern edict to Jade Snow, "Respect your older sister in all matters," was somewhat softened by his addition of "Love your brother and sister, according to Christ's teaching."

The daily indoctrination of Jade Snow and her brothers and sisters in the requirements of correct personal conduct which would bear Daddy's closest scrutiny was augmented by Sunday training in the Christian ideals of a serviceable life which would bear God's closest scrutiny. They attended the Methodist Chinese Mission, which confirmed Daddy's standing as a "local preacher" when he transferred there. After finding it necessary to establish a business for support of his family, he had left his full-time minister's duties at the Cumberland Presbyterian Mission.

The Wongs' Sunday morning hour of home devotion ended when Sunday-school time approached. At Sunday school, Daddy taught a class of boys. Jade Snow and Younger Sister were in a class taught by a Caucasian lady.

Sunday school was followed by the regular church service. Mama came to this service, at which, with other church members who did not know English, she sang hymns in Chinese. The service was conducted by a Chinese minister, whose sermon was delivered mainly in Chinese, with which a little English was mixed.

After church service and a late lunch, Mama and her children liked to go for a walk. Daddy did not join them, since he was the church treasurer and had to count the offering every Sunday.

Next to the Saturday movies, these Sunday walks were the best part of the week.

Chinatown was almost in the middle of San Francisco's central area of interest. Only a few blocks away was North Beach, the Italian section; the Embarcadero, or the waterfront section; Nob Hill, a residential section; and the downtown business center.

Mama might decide to go window-shopping. The family would then thread through narrow and colorful Grant Avenue, past the Chinese-style grocery stores. Here crisp Chinese greens were stacked out on racks in the streets in front of the windows to attract passers-by, and at night, wooden boards were fitted over glass windows to protect them.

Above the shops the buildings rose three and four stories, topped by red-tiled eaves and yellow and green pagoda corners. They were usually owned by family associations, the size of the building varying according to the association's numerical and financial strength in its exclusively male membership. The association offices, conference halls, and social rooms were on the top floor, from which French doors opened out onto the surrounding balcony. Within, the high-ceilinged rooms were always orderly, and extremely light and spacious, in contrast to almost all other interiors in Chinatown. Moreover, the walls were covered with scenes of butterflies or birds exquisitely embroidered in delicate hues on silk, or with the brushed characters of poetic phrases, all framed in dark teak and set with mother-of-pearl. Around the room in an unbroken row, square, carved teak armchairs were arranged. During festive occasions like New Year's, red satin embroidered seat covers adorned them. In the center of the conference hall was a long rectangular table used for business discussions. Altogether, the association buildings presented a formal appearance both within and without, and could be identified from the street below by the elaborate gilded signs with black characters mounted over the French doors of the top floor.

On some Sundays they saw impressive funeral processions. These varied according to the importance and wealth of the deceased. Before the procession came into sight, they could hear the band, mournfully playing "Nearer, My God, to Thee." One Sunday they saw one of the most elaborate displays arranged for a funeral. The wealthy, powerful, and prominent Chinatown figure who had died left a family divided between Christian and traditional Chinese beliefs; therefore, both elements had to be satisfied that the spirit of the deceased would rest in peace.

A marshal led the procession. He was followed by a band playing Western funeral music. Their faces were Chinese, but they were dressed in conventional American gray band uniforms. After them, an open convertible held a huge flower-framed portrait of the deceased. A pair of stuffed white doves were mounted at the top of the frame. White-gloved close friends in the back seat of the convertible steadied the props supporting the portrait. Then came the hearse, with white-gloved honorary pallbearers on foot flanking both sides. The bent figures of the immediate family followed. First came the oldest son, with black crepe on his left sleeve and tied around his waist. He was followed by younger brothers, and then by his sisters, also with the oldest one first. The women, however, were covered by waist-long black hoods, under which they wept loudly and continuously. Their heavy mourning was complete, even including thick black stockings. A friend who would be paid a fee for his services was at the side of each family member to guide him or her.

The immediate family was followed by more distant relatives who also wore black crepe on their sleeves (left arm for men; right arm for women). Then came the friends in pairs—men first, then women. There were hundreds attending this funeral. After the friends on foot came another hired band. This Caucasian one did not attempt to harmonize with the first band in the melodies it chose, which created a great din. The second band was an unusual sight, since most families could afford only one. Limousines followed; some fifteen shiny new black ones driven by liveried Caucasian chauffeurs had been hired for this occasion. This was also a conspicuous luxury. The automobiles of friends followed, driven by their owners. Some had passengers; others had not.

And then came a strange sight: Buddhist priests in flowing somber robes trailed along, chanting prayers of their religion for the dead. Two of them held a pole from which a drum was suspended; a third priest kept time with the prayers by soft rhythmical beats. After these priests came huge open trucks, laden with large and small floral offerings, which left a lingering trail of fragrance in the streets. Each wreath was tied with a pair of long white satin ribbons, about three or four inches wide. Although these were waving merrily in the breeze as the truck drove along, the spectators could see black brushed characters on them. The ribbon on the right of a wreath was inscribed "To ———, now of the thousand ages," and the left streamer carried the name of the sender, and his relationship to the dead. Still another truck held the clothes of the deceased. These would be burnt at a special incinerator at the cemetery, in the belief that the rising smoke would return them to the spirit of the dead.

Here and there among the procession, hired help scattered squares of yellow paper, which flew hither and yon along the street. This golden "paper money" would bribe the evil spirits which always lurked unseen, so that they would not detain the spirit of the dead from his destined rest.

The procession wound its way slowly. It had first gone past the deceased's home to lead his spirit past in a last gesture of farewell. After going through the heart of Chinatown, the temporary end of the journey was reached at old St. Mary's Church, which the Chinese called "The Building of the Big Clock" because of this feature. After dispersing, the family would distribute to friends white paper packets each containing a nickel. The recipient must use it immediately to buy a piece of candy to "sweeten the taste"; he was not to spend it for any other purpose. Then the immediate family and close friends would continue in the hired limousines to the cemetery for burial rites. After these rites, the friends who drove out to the cemetery would be given red paper packets containing a dime—also to buy candy.

Mama explained that this was roughly patterned after the funeral processions in China, although mourning there was sometimes in white. And because there were no automobiles, the family must walk on foot to the burial grounds, while the sons and male relatives bore the coffin. The evening before a funeral, at which relatives gathered from great distances, there were private mourning services, when the family knelt on straw mats before the body to mourn aloud their loss. Incense and candles were burnt to give the spirit's journey a fragrant light. In most localities, these services were conducted at home; the "funeral parlor" was unknown. And instead of Chinatown's habitual choice of Sunday for a funeral to facilitate people's attendance on their day off, in China the day was chosen by necromancy to be sure that the spirit would be sent to his home in harmony with all other spiritual forces. Mama added, "This custom is rarely observed here because of its inconvenience. In America, the role of human beings is performed with eyes on the clock."

After the burial rites, a big dinner at a restaurant followed to extend hospitality to those friends who had "given face" in going to the cemetery. It also gave the crowd an opportunity to relax from the tension of the day.

Mama also explained, "Here in America, mourning is not diligently practiced. In China, severe full mourning, the garb of filial piety, for one's father and mother must be maintained for three years; for one's grandparents, one year. This means wearing blue, black, or white; no jewelry, no make-up, no parties, no dressing of one's hair."

Leaving the association buildings and the grocery stores behind, Mama and the children would pass through the fashionable Grant Avenue shopping center of downtown San Francisco, where Mama would linger before the window displays of the latest new merchandise.

Sometimes, however, Mama and her family went to North Beach. Here the wares in the windows told of an entirely different variety of goods within—panettóne and French bread, hanging sausages, herbs, and ravioli. Even the smells were different in "Little Italy." Then a right turn and a climb up steep steps brought them breathless to the top of Telegraph Hill and to a magnificent view of sparkling San Francisco Bay.

Still a third walk which Mama liked included a stop at a playground, where there was a wonderful sloping lawn. Jade Snow and her sister and brother loved to start at the top of the incline and roll over and over as fast as they could until they came to the bottom; with the smell of grass on their clothes and in their disordered black hair, they would lie there breathless and laughing, blinking in the bright sun.

On their way once more, they entered another world, a world permeated with the aroma of bubbling caldrons of shellfish, with the fiesta spirit of the tourists who crowded the streets under gay awnings, with the persistent tang of the sea, the creak of swaying fishing boats, the cries of sea gulls, and the persuasive cries of noisy Italian barkers inveigling customers into the sea-food restaurants. The parked automobiles with little trays of sea-food cocktails hooked onto the open windows, the rows of white-tiled counters neatly stacked with clean, red, cooked crabs, lobsters, and prawns— where else would you find all these sights and sounds and smells but at Fisherman's Wharf in San Francisco? And what other city offered so many happy explorations?

10

"ONE WHO OR THAT WHICH SLIPS"

IN THE WINTER OF 1934, FOR THE FIRST TIME IN JADE SNOW'S memory, it snowed in San Francisco. It was the second experience for Mama; the first time the snows of the bitter winter of 1922 had inspired the name of her newborn daughter: "Snow," the symbol of purity.

The middle name "Jade" was shared by all the Wong sisters. As the name for the most highly prized of precious stones, "jade" was also the symbol for preciousness. In Chinese names, one's family or "last" name appears first, then the middle name, and one's given or "first" name comes last. Again, family is more important than the individual. Curiously enough, a Chinese woman keeps her surname until death; even her tombstone would carry her maiden name. Upon marriage, Jade Snow would become "Wong Shee" or "Mrs. Wong."

The Wong brothers shared a common middle name, "Heaven." This was used not only for Daddy's sons, but also for the sons of his first cousin, to provide a bond between the families. Since Daddy's first cousins were as close to him as brothers, their grandchildren also called Daddy "Grandfather."

However, Chinese family relationships were sharply defined. Relatives on Mama's side were distinguished by altogether different titles from the relatives on Daddy's side. There was no easy escape in calling them all "aunt," "uncle," or "cousin." Any reference to relatives by their correct titles placed them accurately on their side of the family tree and defined their sex and generation without further explanation—a simple and effective method of assuring family order.

As the 1934 snowstorm continued, Jade Snow, with elbows on her window sill, cupped her chin in her palms and stared at the gently falling flakes. The unusual chill in the weather was not so extraordinary as the unaccustomed chill within her heart. For Daddy was sick, very sick; he was in the hospital for the first time that she could recall. The sound of Mama's sobbing came from her bedroom across the narrow hall, rising and diminishing at intervals.

It had started with Daddy's staying up most of the night again. Jade Snow always knew when Daddy was disturbed beyond words, for he would then walk up and down the hundred-foot length of their factory. His pacing back and forth sometimes lasted half through the night, but he preferred to crystallize his thinking and then retire peacefully, rather than to toss about in bed half asleep, half awake all night, and unable to think. Last night he had been disturbed not about his own business, but about the affairs of the hospital in Chinatown, of which he was board chairman. He had been spending considerable time trying to straighten out some administrative matters, not without opposition. In connection with his work, Daddy must have had a very distressing experience—nobody told Jade Snow exactly what. But whatever he had found out last night had outraged him so greatly—and when Daddy was even mildly upset, his eyes flashed fire and the thunder of his voice shook the walls of the building—that it had caused a hemorrhage.

Mama had called Second Older Sister to find an American doctor, who had sent Daddy immediately to the hospital—ironically, to the same hospital that he had been serving. Jade Snow, remembering her last visit there with Grandmother, felt a wordless fear. But what troubled her most was Mama's reaction. Mama stopped working. She hid in the dim interior of her bedroom, crying.

To see Mama suddenly and unprecedentedly lose her poise, to see her with swollen eyes and uncombed hair, without control of the situation, and to hear the words she wailed between sobs, shook to its foundation Jade Snow's sense of security, forged as it had been by the security of her parents themselves.

"I have told your father repeatedly not to run around giving his best to community organizations, at the expense of his own business and personal health. The worst feature of his public work is that he discovers other people's practices to which he cannot subscribe. Then he tries to take a one-man stand on what he believes to be right, and works himself into a frenzy of ill-temper when his stand finds no sympathy.

"And then who suffers? Not only himself, but I and his family!" In Mama's bitter complaint, she abruptly revealed to Jade Snow that the united front, a composite of Daddy and Mama, might not in privacy be so united as it had always appeared.

Emphasizing the consequences of the present situation, she bared to Jade Snow for the first time some of the innermost fears and griefs which filled her private thoughts.

"If your father does not live, what will I do? He is nearly sixty, and you are all yet so small—Forgiveness is only five. Some unkind ones have already taunted me, saying that he will never see our children grown. They say that I know not the customs or language of this country and for survival I will be forced to abandon you and to marry another. I have always ignored them, but now I may have to admit that they are partially correct." Mama's sobs became protesting outcries.

"Desert you children to remarry, I shall not, but with what defense can I comfort myself?"

Jade Snow turned this remark over and over in her mind and tried to control her own increasing fear as she imagined both Mama and Daddy gone, while she and the little ones tried to take care of themselves. Uncomfortable herself, she tried to comfort Mama. Remembering the action of her teacher when she had been hurt in the school yard so long ago, she awkwardly put her arm around Mama's bowed shoulders and timidly patted her. It was so strange —this unexpected and novel closeness to Mama. Here for the first time was a defenseless, criticized, bewildered, intimidated Mama, unburdening herself to her daughter. The Mama who wielded the clothes hanger, the Mama who seldom approved of anything that was fun, the Mama who laid down exacting housework requirements, the Mama who criticized with stern words, was suddenly seen in a new light.

Her appeal stirred in Jade Snow an overwhelming desire to be of concrete assistance. She yearned to carry some of Mama's burden for her. But what could a twelve-year-old, and especially a girl, do? She could not make one promise that would relieve Mama's fears, and she felt dwarfed, ineffective, and helpless.

After a last pat, she bolted to her own room to seek some way to relieve her troubled mind. She could not imagine a world without Daddy as the central strength of their family, however exacting he might be. As other grim possibilities occurred to her, she decided that it would be best not to think of them. After all, the doctor had not said that Daddy would certainly die. She concentrated on what she could do now.

First, she decided that Mama would not desert them, since she cared so much about raising them as clean and educated children and worked so hard for them. This conclusion made Jade Snow so indignant about the unkind things those vague enemies had said to Mama that she resolved to try always to be a credit to both parents. She resolved, too, that when she grew up she would do something to make them take back what they had said. She did not quite know how she was going to achieve this, but she decided to begin by doing well whatever task was at hand, from washing the dishes to studying her lessons.

One concrete service she undertook at once was to fill the gap temporarily left by Daddy in the staff of Sunday-school teachers. She was assigned the beginners' class, to instruct them in group singing and to tell them Bible stories. These twenty or more little Chinese children, with their eagerness to please, their offering of affection reserved for those who sincerely communicated to them, gave Jade Snow a new pleasure and enthusiasm. She poured into her Sunday-school work all the love and energy left over from other duties and she tried her best to create a creditable record for Daddy's inspection when he returned to his church work.

Happily, Daddy was getting better and would soon be able to come home. In the meantime, Older Brother was helping to run the business.

When Daddy eventually did return home, he had to have much more rest than before because he had lost a great deal of weight. And he was even more silent and thoughtful than had been his habit. By Sunday, however, he was eager to go to church again. Agreeably surprised to find that Jade Snow had done well with her class, he at once decided that more young American-Chinese children should receive early guidance in the Kingdom of God under his daughter's direction.

On the first day of the Easter vacation, he told Jade Snow to put on her coat and prepare to spend the day with him recruiting new Sunday-school pupils. Daddy's method was direct and effective. They started at the beginning of a Chinatown block and entered an unfamiliar tenement building. Daddy knocked on each door. Usually it was the mother who answered. Daddy would introduce himself, describe their Sunday-school work, and ask if the household had children under six who could enroll.

"I have a three-year-old boy and a five-year-old girl," the first mother said, "and it does not matter to me whether or not they attend Sunday school. Anyway, they are too small to go alone, and it would be a nuisance for me to bring them and call for them." She began to shut the door in dismissal.

Daddy, however, would not so easily lose two possible followers for Christ, and proposed a measure new to Jade Snow. "Here is my small daughter Jade Snow, who will have charge of this class. She will call for your children each Sunday morning, and will bring them home afterward."

After they secured about thirty recruits, Daddy was satisfied that Jade Snow had a sufficient number to handle in her beginners' class.

Daddy had lost some of his driving energy in his long illness, but he had lost none of his fire; his alertness, dignity, and command were unchanged.

One of the household procedures on which he had always insisted was that all members should be completely dressed before they emerged from their bedrooms, even before they washed up in the bathroom. Everyone dressed immediately upon rising, and retired immediately after they undressed. Therefore, nobody needed slippers in his house. However, slippers had never been specifically forbidden, and when Daddy was in the hospital, Jade Snow had dipped into her carefully saved earnings to buy herself a pair of coveted red mules.

One morning, after his return, Jade Snow trotted out to their living-dining room to have breakfast, wearing her gay new slippers purely to show them off. Daddy noticed them, she thought with satisfaction as he eyed her feet. However, he said nothing until breakfast was over and the dishes had been cleared away.

"Jade Snow, what have you on your feet?"

Jade Snow replied happily, "My new slippers."

Daddy neatly killed her spirits, "And where are slippers supposed to be worn? Have I taught you so inadequately or have you paid so little attention to my teaching that in the short time I was away you can turn the organization of my household into chaos? Little did I dream that I must return to see bedroom attire flaunted publicly in my living room!!"

Jade Snow was dumb with surprise. Such an interpretation should have occurred to her, but it had not. She could only remain silent.

Daddy was not through. "So that you may never forget this lesson you are to go to the public library immediately. Look up the English word for 'slippers' in the unabridged dictionary and report the definition to me," he commanded.

Without question, Jade Snow returned to her room, put on socks and shoes, and walked up the little hill to the library.

She presented an embarrassed face at the loan desk, behind which sat her favorite librarian.

"Please, may I look at your biggest dictionary?" she inquired.

The librarian smiled indulgently, "Now what would a little girl like you want with the 'biggest' dictionary?"

"Please, ma'am, I am very serious," Jade Snow pleaded.

"Very well, I shall find the word for you, as the book is too heavy for you to carry around," was the reply.

"Slippers," Jade Snow said simply.

That was obviously the last word the librarian expected to hear. She stopped, and looked at Jade Snow as if she suspected that she was being teased.

"Well!" she exclaimed testily, "You know what slippers are."

"Yes, I know what they are," Jade Snow said, "But I still have to know exactly what the dictionary says about slippers."

Shaking her head slowly, apparently perplexed by the child's sincerity, the librarian permitted Jade Snow to go behind her desk and obligingly found the definition of "slippers" for her to copy.

Jade Snow thanked her and returned home, clutching her painstakingly acquired information. She found Daddy still reading his morning paper.

He peered over his glasses as she entered the room, "Well, what have you found?"

Jade Snow dutifully read in English, "Slippers: A kind of light shoe, often and typically one which may be slipped on with ease and worn in undress. Often an elaborate one worn with evening dress. One who or that which slips; slipped on or over something. . . ."

"Now translate that into Chinese," Daddy pursued.

Jade Snow obeyed. As she expected, it was the word "undress" that Daddy seized upon from the long definition.

"Undress, I repeat, undress, is not what I expect my eyes to see in my home. It is a state which you must learn—since you apparently have not yet learned—to confine to your private quarters. Now move quickly to wash the dishes, and," concluded Daddy, "I do not wish to speak to you again about such indecorous conduct."

Oldest Sister was preparing to leave for China together with Fourth Older Sister—Oldest Sister to teach school there, and Fourth Older Sister, now about sixteen, was accompanying her to study Chinese.

It was their duty to make a trip to the cemetery before they left. Daddy arranged that on this visit his family should witness the Chinese practice of "gathering bones." When Chinese immigrants had died in the United States, they were considered to be buried here only temporarily. In six or seven years, their family associations automatically arranged to have their bones dug up, boxed, and returned to their closest relatives in China, where they would be permanently reburied in their family grounds. Thus, limited areas of association-owned American ground were freed for burial of subsequent dead.

In preparation for this event, Daddy had purchased a handsome, brown, drum-shaped stoneware jar, about two feet deep. The exterior surface was decorated with the winding design of a watchful dragon. Although the bones of Third Older Sister were not to be sent to China, Daddy felt that while he could attend to such things, her bones should be placed in a sealed container, so that they would never be lost and could be moved eventually.

Death was a subject to which Jade Snow had given little thought. The family's annual trips to the united churches' burial grounds were more or less pleasant outings to take flowers and cut down weeds from the graves of their relatives or friends. On this day, when she arrived with Daddy, older sisters and brother, the grave-digger was already there at work. Jade Snow peered into the opened grave. All she could see was more dirt. The wooden coffin had been rotted away. Daddy climbed in to help search for the bones among the dirt which had covered them. The experienced grave-digger seemed to know well the bones of the human anatomy.

Jade Snow watched wordlessly. Daddy laid a white linen cloth on the ground and placed the bones on it as they were found. Suddenly, he tossed one to her. "Take this, and hold it a moment, and know that it is your sister's arm bone." Jade Snow turned it over gingerly and studied it. It looked more like a chicken bone, it was so small. Unlike her mental picture of white skeletons, these bones were brown from the minerals of the earth.

When all the bones had been found, and they had even recovered the bits of gold jewelry which Daddy remembered had been buried with her, and the dime which had been placed in her mouth in order to prevent her from being orally boisterous in her next incarnation, the items were arranged in order on the cloth, with the skull portion, which was like a piece of soft leather, resting on top. The cloth was knotted up and placed in the ceramic urn. Then Daddy sealed the lid with the cement he had brought. The urn was lowered again into the ground, with the alert eyes of the dragon facing the downward slope of the hill while he guarded his contents and the tombstone behind him.

The procedure took all afternoon. The family was quiet, but no one was upset. Daddy's main concern was that they should not overlook one bone. He concentrated on working efficiently, making sure that his children paid attention. Jade Snow had no moment of fear, no bad dreams that night. The dead were taken so matter-of-factly.

11

WITH EYES ON CHINA

ON JANUARY 21, 1935, JADE SNOW MADE AN ENTRY IN HER FIRST diary, one that Daddy had given her for Christmas. In careful English she wrote:

"Today was my thirteenth birthday. Mama bought me a bowl of 'won-ton' [a filled Chinese paste bathed in chicken soup] for lunch. Daddy gave me fifty cents. Older Brother bought me a chocolate eclair, a chocolate roll, and a small sponge cake with whipped cream. Cousin Kee (who works for Daddy) gave me a quarter, and I spent it for ice cream for the whole family. So ends a beautiful day."

Daddy had given his daughter this diary to encourage her to keep an accurate record of important things. "The mind is quick to forget details," he said, "and records become more valuable as time goes on. I still have copies of the letters I wrote when I first came to America; I have never written a letter without keeping a copy."

As Jade Snow entered her teens, the pattern of family activities changed further and relationships between the young members of the family shifted.

Second Older Sister, after several years of traveling with her husband on business, had returned to San Francisco. Though Jade Snow had corresponded with her through these years, she did not know her very well. But now Second Older Sister and Brother-in-Law, her husband, lived in an apartment only a few blocks away. After a few visits, Jade Snow began to turn to her for the little confidences, companionship, and understanding which Mama and Daddy had never invited. Second Older Sister seemed less formal than Oldest Sister, and was less assertive than Fourth Older Sister, who was nearest to Jade Snow in age. Second Older Sister knew just how one felt, for she too had been brought up one of Daddy's daughters. "Much more strictly than you were," she told Jade Snow.

Another attraction was her abundant larder which offered Jade Snow many unfamiliar foods which their Chinese home diet did not include. Her visits to her sister were surreptitious, for Jade Snow knew that the reason her parents did not invite confidences was that they disapproved of them; they did not encourage companionship because it might undermine respect, or offer understanding because it might conflict with obedience. Besides, Second Older Sister had married into and belonged to another family, and Jade Snow should not be seeking comfort from one who was thus an "outsider."

At home, Jade Precious Stone was growing up with Jade Snow. Younger Sister had always been considered the beauty of the family. From the time her looks had been barely defined at babyhood, visitors had proclaimed her adorable, and had always rushed to pick her up and play with her. She was sweet, cherubic, delicate, and had not a shred of temper.

Whenever the family took snapshots, they found Jade Precious Stone more photogenic than Jade Snow. Younger Sister was fair-skinned, round-faced, and posed gracefully. Fifth Uncle on Daddy's side, who was Cousin Kee's father, said that Jade Precious Stone had the eyebrows of the swan and the eyes of the phoenix, at which Mama beamed with pleasure, for everyone also said that this daughter looked most like her.

On the other hand, Jade Snow was said to resemble her father. Like Daddy, she developed angular features, became dark-complexioned, serious, skinny, sensitive, independent, and not at all adorable. When callers came, Daddy might have this daughter show them how many words she could correctly identify in the Chinese newspaper, and the callers would politely acknowledge her cleverness, but they would be impatient to turn back to Younger Sister.

As a child Younger Sister spent many weeks and sometimes months as an invalid. Three times she was critically ill with pneumonia. But even when she was well, she never had a great deal of energy. Her lack of physical vitality freed Jade Precious Stone from most home responsibilities, which fell therefore on the shoulders of Jade Snow. And because Jade Precious Stone needed rest, she was allowed to discontinue Chinese school at an early age. Their personal differences, which were unimportant to Jade Snow as a child, irritated her increasingly as she approached young womanhood, until finally she began to adopt an attitude of apparent indifference toward her younger sister.

At eleven, Jade Precious Stone was concerned with hairdos, manicures, and make-up, while Jade Snow rejected them as frivolous. As the Wong sisters outgrew their children's Dutch bobs, Mama bought them a Marcel curling iron which had to be heated on a gas burner. The curling iron was Chinatown's latest fad. With its help, straight and coarse black Chinese hair suddenly was transformed into round sausage curls, or done in other fluffy styles, the like of which Jade Snow's ancestors never had seen.

With the curling iron, Jade Precious Stone and Jade Snow made due experiments on one another. To Mama's and Jade Precious Stone's disgust, Jade Snow decided that she preferred to have no further connection with the Marcel process, but Jade Precious Stone used it often.

This decision had caused an explosion when all the Wongs had gathered to have a family picture taken before the departure of the two older sisters for China. Daddy was very fond of family portraits. Before he came to America he had had large portrait photographs made of his father and mother—an unusual proceeding for that place and time.

For this occasion, every female had her hair smartly marcelled; that is, all but Jade Snow, whose hair hung neatly straight to her shoulders. By turns, the family coaxed and ridiculed the recalcitrant member, but Jade Snow grew more grimly stubborn as their pressure became greater. Thus in the one Wong family picture complete with its in-laws, the camera recorded Jade Snow, defiant and tense, with the only head of straight feminine hair in the group of curly-topped, relaxed, smiling faces.

The summer of that year was vacation time for Jade Snow, but it brought her little recreation. Play had long become a dream of the past. When she was eleven, Mama had said, "You are now the oldest daughter at home; you have too much to do to play anymore like a child."

Although the factory was idle all summer, Mama kept busy. She made suits for Little Brother; she knitted sweaters, mended, pieced pillow covers with scraps of pretty silk, and cut out aprons for herself. She was never still a moment.

Jade Snow had to attend Chinese summer school, and it was becoming a tiresome burden. One spent so much time there with so little result. She had yet to tear through a Chinese storybook with the ease with which she could devour *Ivanhoe*, and she still had to struggle to write a Chinese letter with all its elaborate formalities.

After-school hours were mostly spent either in sewing or baking. Jade Snow had been taught the fundamentals of sewing and of making pastries in her high school domestic science courses, and had at once been eager to try out at home what she learned, but there had been no equipment for it. Gradually, however, she bought from her own scant funds, pans, measuring cups, spoons, and the other needed paraphernalia which were no part of a Chinese kitchen. When the two sisters made a trip to the five-and-ten-cent store, Jade Precious Stone would linger at the cosmetics counter examining new shades of nail polish, but Jade Snow would buy a new pie pan.

Mastery over sewing was achieved more easily. Here she had the advantage of professional equipment at home. Daddy had all the tools, space, and different types of machines, and assigned Jade Snow her own electric sewing machine.

At fourteen, her life was on the whole a continuation of the same routine. But it was considerably darkened by the stubborn, unhappy, struggle which began between her and her family.

The difficulty centered around Jade Snow's desire for recognition as an individual. The conflict remained under the surface for nearly two years, because of the Wongs' peculiarity in refusing to recognize or discuss emotional issues. The suppression worked itself out in running diary entries, in confidences to her Second Older Sister and a new-found chum, and in a profound belief in the justice of God.

This chum, the only daughter in a Chinese family of many boys, was a most sympathetic friend. Her parents were even more old-fashioned and traditionally Chinese than the Wongs, and she was alternately teased and protected by her brothers and completely dominated by her mother. Like Jade Snow, Gold Spring had to do most of the housework, with little recognition for her labor. Together, the two girls attended the Chinese school and the Methodist Church, and poured into each other's ears long accounts of their respective trials and tribulations. They were the same age; the greatest difference between them was that Gold Spring had been raised in a small country town and knew very little Chinese, but spoke excellent English. Also, the fact that she had been raised with half a dozen brothers made her a somersaulting tomboy beside sedate Jade Snow. But the troubles that they had in common bound them together closely. Gold Spring listened sympathetically when Jade Snow confided that Mama was usually dissatisfied with her as an older sister to Jade Precious Stone and Forgiveness from Heaven, and was always telling her how well sisters in other families treated the younger children. Jade Snow condoled with Gold Spring when Gold Spring described how her younger brothers took advantage of their mother's favoritism to tease her, while she suffered silently. Then Jade Snow confided the latest distressing incident. Mama would not permit her to go to any social-club activities because she was away from the house all day at school, all evening at school, and at church each weekend, and Jade Snow felt keenly the limitations of this schedule. Then Gold Spring told how her mother wanted to keep her at housework as much as possible so that she would know exactly where she was, and by doing woman's work could perhaps become more feminine and less tomboyish.

Even this friendship was not carried on without difficulty. One evening when Gold Spring came to Jade Snow's house to go with her to Chinese school, Daddy was explaining a Chinese lesson. When Jade Snow jumped up to tell her to wait until she was through, Daddy made her sit right down again. Gold Spring came into the dining room where they were and right then and there Daddy gave her a lecture on "using time." He insisted that she came over to waste Jade Snow's time, and that the two spent their moments unconstructively. Jade Snow was most embarrassed. The next day Daddy forbade Jade Snow ever to go with Gold Spring again, because such companionship absorbed time from more worthwhile pursuits. And when Gold Spring did come to see Jade Snow again, Older Brother shot at her with his BB gun.

At this time, Jade Snow's incompatibility with her Older Brother also caused her real anguish. After she had worked for a week on a new Easter dress, Older Brother commented at length on how unbecoming that shade of blue was; and when the dress was completed he roared with laughter and said, "It looks so funny!" Jade Snow was hurt but thought that probably he was simply teasing, as he usually was. Daddy offered some comfort by saying that it was good cloth. Nevertheless, because Older Brother was an older man who went about in the American world, she also took what he said very seriously.

Older Brother was now a senior at the University of California. Once after she had spent some time trying to decide on her future career, Jade Snow spoke to him. "Older Brother, I'm interested in becoming a dressmaker when I grow up. I like to sew and Daddy has all the different machines and equipment. What do you think?"

Older Brother stared. "A dressmaker? Since you ask me, you'll never be a successful designer. The reason is that you need imagination to design clothes; you need personality to meet people and sell to them, and the trouble with you is that you're so mousy, you lack both of these needed qualities."

"But, Older Brother, I'll go to school and learn better!" Jade Snow protested.

His reply closed the subject and toppled her dream. "Don't be silly, you either have personality and imagination or you don't. You don't acquire them from books."

Jade Snow sat up until two the next morning, trying to study, but she could not put their conversation out of her mind. Completely discouraged she wondered, "Perhaps I could still be a stenographer even without imagination or personality."

It did not comfort Jade Snow to see how Older Brother enjoyed playing with Jade Precious Stone and Younger Brother, or to watch him go out with them to movies while she stayed home to study, or to have him intervening in their quarrels over who should do household chores. He always settled the question in Younger Sister's favor by saying that she was not strong enough for the job.

In her bitterness, Jade Snow made a solemn vow to God as she knelt in bedtime prayer. "To make up for this neglect and prejudice, please help me to do my best in striving to be a person respected and honored by my family when I grow up."

But in this sea of prejudice, Jade Snow retained her deep respect for Daddy. "With all the family picking me to pieces, I notice that Daddy is the only one who shows no partiality between daughters. Tonight, when I came home from Chinese school, Daddy was washing the dishes for me, and he had my dinner warmed for me and everything was hot. Then he helped me fry a lamb chop. I was really touched by this consideration," read a diary entry.

In 1936, money, or Jade Snow's lack of it, became an increasingly pressing problem. She began to need more than her three or four dollars a month could buy, even with the most prudent planning. She wanted a new coat when Mama was not ready to buy her one, and she wanted more expensive sweaters and dresses, to which Mama objected vigorously. Nor would Mama permit her to withdraw any of her bank savings.

Accordingly, since she was not attending Chinese school that summer, Jade Snow decided that she would try to earn some extra money by working for Daddy, besides what she made by doing chores for Mama and Older Brother.

Daddy put her on specialized work—applying bar-tacks to the completed overalls. Bar-tacks were applied at the points of strain to which little boys subject their pants. Jade Snow learned how to operate and maintain the jerky bar-tacking machine. It was built high, which made Jade Snow's left shoulder ache painfully toward the end of the day. Bar-tacking also meant lifting large bundles of overalls to and from the machine; and Jade Snow soon learned why Daddy's workers made a dive for the smallest sizes, sixes and eights. The size sixteens were twice as heavy and more cumbersome to work on.

Sometimes Jade Snow worked on the buttonhole and overlocking machines. The buttonhole machine was noisy and wickedly dangerous; the operator had to be sure to keep her fingers out of reach of the sharp, gleaming, razor-edged blade which chopped down in an unceremonious staccato immediately after the needle encircled the reinforcement for the buttonhole. The overlocking machine, small and compact, was the most difficult to thread, because the underthread had to be tunneled through innumerable bores and eyes for direct feeding from the spool. It had two alternative attachments—one which overlocked seam edges against raveling, and the other which bound the seam edges with bias tape. None of Daddy's overalls or coveralls ever had a raw edge showing, either inside or outside.

For this summer of tiresome, tiring employment, Jade Snow was paid about three or four dollars a week. With another dollar for errands and chores, she made between fifteen and twenty dollars each month. By the end of the summer, she had saved the tremendous and exciting sum of approximately forty dollars!

The following winter and the spring of 1937 were marked by intense academic preparation for graduation from the Chinese school. Chinese studies now emphasized ancient literature (which had to be memorized by heart), contemporary national literature, T'ang poetry, calligraphy, composition, correspondence, and Mandarin. Every evening Jade Snow trudged to school, carrying in her brief case brushes, inkpad, tablets, scratch paper, pencils, all the books for her class subjects, and a dictionary. Because of her conscientiousness in preparing her lessons, she became popular with her classmates, who would cluster around her in the yard before the bell rang, to cull hurriedly the knowledge that Jade Snow had painstakingly acquired through study with Daddy.

Her present instructor's method of teaching Chinese was a departure from anything Jade Snow had previously experienced. Whereas other teachers had begun a new lesson by first reading it to the class, Mr. Lowe assigned a new lesson to the class for preliminary research before he taught it. In taking up the lesson for the first time, he would call upon various members of the class to give the pronunciation and the meaning of a new word, and he would grade them upon their preparation.

Jade Snow, disciplined to be thorough, spent many hours at home in tedious preparation. Armed with her newly assigned lesson and all the Chinese and Chinese-English dictionaries in the house, she would trail Daddy around the factory as he went about his work, the way she had when she was five. Some of these advanced words were new even to Daddy, who had had only five years of formal tutoring; the rest of his considerable vocabulary and his knowledge of Chinese literature he had acquired by himself. Together, father and daughter now studied new words and discussed their interpretations, so that Jade Snow arrived at school fortified with the knowledge of two minds instead of one. This study drew them together in a bond of formal and mutual respect.

Daddy felt that Jade Snow was progressing in her Chinese more rapidly than most other American-Chinese children; he encouraged her to make the mastery of Chinese her main objective; for he wanted her to go to China to study after high school graduation. He thought that a Chinese could realize his optimum achievement only in China.

For that reason Daddy was also making plans to send Older Brother to China to study medicine. Older Brother, who had changed his major subject from engineering to science, was now graduating from the university with a premedical major. Daddy had allowed Older Brother to study whatever he wished, even selling his sewing machines or borrowing money when necessary to pay his expenses. Father and son agreed that the study of medicine in China would prepare Older Brother for his career. Knowing the Chinese language, he could establish himself where medical personnel was greatly needed, and he could strengthen his ancestral ties by visits to Daddy's native village and relatives.

This orientation toward work in China as the proper objective for serious-minded Chinese, even though they were American-Chinese, was further incentive for Jade Snow to apply herself more earnestly to her Chinese studies than to American studies. As graduation time approached, Daddy relieved her from some of the housework chores and she spent many quiet early-morning hours at her desk. One word wrong in an examination meant that her grade would be lowered by 10 per cent, and she was determined to get as high a grade as possible. Occasionally, she studied with other girls in her class. The girls, all in their early teens, had very little in common with the boys, of whom they were painfully conscious, and they made it clear to Jade Snow that they expected her to uphold the honor of their sex by beating the grades of the brightest boy in the class.

Jade Snow's diary ended in June with a record of her graduation from Chinese high school after successfully passing her examinations. Nine years of Chinese study were concluded. In Jade Snow's mind, these were only foundation years. She had still to finish her American studies before she could devote full time to her advanced Chinese education.

12

COUSIN KEE

THERE WAS ONE BRIGHT NEW DEVELOPMENT IN JADE SNOW'S LIFE during this busy year. It was fishing, a wonderful pastime in which Mama became interested through the extravagant fish stories told by their bachelor cousin Kee. Since Cousin Kee was closely related to them, Daddy had given him a job as manager of the factory; but though he sewed expertly and tailored shirts professionally, responsibility annoyed him and he rebelled loudly and openly against Daddy's efforts to steady him. Nevertheless, his sense of humor and generosity both to his friends and to himself made him very likable, and when not unhappy about responsibility, he was the jolliest cousin Jade Snow had. A short, stocky fellow in his thirties who was already rapidly becoming bald, he found escape from the irritation of making a living in gambling, drinking, eating, and fishing—all to excess. His practice and tales of the first three found no sympathy with Mama, but the last struck a response. Cousin Kee talked about spearing perch which were larger than the Wongs' largest platter; he talked about catching five dozen silver smelts in an hour; he talked about netting crabs and hooking sharks; and he talked about how to cook them. In fact, he loved to talk. Besides the sport it offered, fishing apparently brought a most profitable return on a small investment, since a dime's worth of sardines and a quarter's worth of shrimps were all the bait one needed for a supply of fish to last a family for several days.

Mama, who was by nature extremely cautious, especially about spending money, and even more so about initiating any new activity, gave Cousin Kee money and authority to buy fishhooks, crab nets, lines, sinkers, and any other needed equipment. He bought small hooks for small-mouthed smelts, larger ones for perch, and some giant hooks designed to catch striped bass. He also purchased a crab net, heavy sinkers, light sinkers, lines, leaders, bait, and by the time he got through, he had spent nearly two weeks of Mama's earnings. Mama did not complain, however, being confident that the fish and crabs they could catch would offset this large investment.

The family spent the evening before their first fishing trip learning how to prepare fishing lines. Jade Snow was taught how to knot the lines and how to attach the transparent leaders and the sinkers. Mama, Cousin Kee, Jade Precious Stone, and Jade Snow each had his or her own line.

The next day they put up their lunch of sandwiches, oranges, and a thermos bottle of Chinese tea. As they started out, only Cousin Kee carried a long, slender Calcutta pole on his shoulder. He was sure nobody else could handle one. The rest had their lines wound around little wooden cores. After a fifteen-minute walk, they reached a pier which branched out from San Francisco's Embarcadero waterfront. It was called the "Potato Pier," because the slow old barges which carried potatoes and onions down the Sacramento River into San Francisco Bay tied up here to unload. Mountains of onions and potatoes were scattered over the concrete floor under the roof of the pier shed, which stretched for several hundred feet on its pile foundation over the dark waters of the bay. Eventually, the hills of potatoes and onions were worked over by crews of sorters, who put the sound ones into one-hundred- or fifty-pound string or burlap sacks ready for distribution, and discarded the spoiled ones.

Consequently, for Jade Snow fishing became associated with the indescribable blended odors of thousands of yellow onions and new potatoes, waiting in the heat which beat in through the skylight of the shed roof, and the dank odor of spoiled vegetables which had been tossed into dark corners to sprout and rot away forgotten. Others, thrown or dropped into the bay water attracted many fish to the pier.

On this particular morning the group spread out. Cousin Kee arranged them on the sunny southwest corner of the pier, looking out on shallow, quiet water, and showed them how far to let down their light lines with three hooks and a sinker. He said that he was going to brave the sea to cast the crab net and his heavy lines with the large hooks, baited for striped bass. He was going to fish from the farthest tip of the pier which, facing eastward, reached the deep waters of the bay. With open mouths, Mama and her three children, in the shelter of their corner, watched Cousin Kee as he stood firmly against the wind, rolled up his shirt sleeves, picked up a line, whirled it around and around at his side to warm up, and finally sailed it out into the air and landed it in the water. He repeated these motions in casting the crab net. Then he took up the Calcutta pole to fish for perch and smelt. Moving with practiced authority, he was managing three operations.

Jade Snow, with considerably less drama, unwound her little spool of line, baited her small hooks with hunks of raw shrimp, and let the line down slowly into the water.

"Wind one end of your line around that nail sticking out from the pile, or you will lose it altogether," Cousin Kee warned her with conscious importance.

Jade Snow silently complied.

"Now throw the line over your index finger, and when you feel a tug, pull it up.

Jade Snow sat waiting for a long time. She felt no tugs. Jade Precious Stone played a little at fishing, but soon lost interest and went off to play with Forgiveness instead. After a while, Mama got a bite and pulled up a little shiner. Jade Snow was determinedly patient. Cousin Kee called, "Pull up your line, and let's see what's the matter."

Jade Snow pulled up her line and Cousin Kee laughed and laughed. "You have no bait. Ha, Ha! How do you expect to catch fish without bait? Do you want them to come over and tug on your hook to be pulled up?"

Jade Snow was chagrined. How had that happened? She baited her hooks again, this time working the bait in and out twice. Mama was kinder and more constructive.

"Don't use such large pieces, or your fish will nibble on a corner and pull off the bait."

Soon there was an unmistakable tugging. Jade Snow jumped. She jerked the line, and hard. Up she pulled, and saw that she had caught a baby perch, coral and silver-blue in color, fighting and flipping its tail on its way up. With excitement, she removed the struggling, slippery, cold, wet fish from the hook, though distressed to see red blood running from its gills and its eyes popping out. Gingerly, she put the fish into a coffee can, covered it, and set it in the shade.

Cousin Kee, supposedly the old hand at fishing, did not catch enough to pay for Mama's investment. His crab net brought up a few undersized specimens which had to be thrown back into the bay. His striped bass hooks brought up a terrifying leopard shark which weighed sixteen pounds. When this happened, Cousin Kee dramatically whipped out a sharp little dagger from nowhere and plunged it again and again into the leopard shark's head to kill it, while the Wong children clung together and watched this destruction of a man-eating monster in horrified fascination, and from a safe distance.

By afternoon, Jade Snow had gone through a gamut of new experiences. She had felt the keen disappointment of losing a fish after pulling it out of the water; she had known the joy of pulling out two fish at once; she had tingled with exasperation when her line became entangled just as the biting was good, she had found that careless handling of fishhooks resulted in bleeding fingers and snagged clothes; she had decided that it was better to have fish bite and not get hooked than to have them not bite at all, she had known the anxiety of having her line become caught in another's, and she had gloried in seeing a string of her own fish, her very own even if they were little ones, dangling in the water to keep fresh.

Yes, fishing was a pleasure out of this world! There within smell of the salt water, with the bay breezes and the sunshine joining forces to brown one's skin, one could forget about housework, homework, family problems, and all other troubles for at least a part of a day.

After giving up their attempts to catch more fish beyond what was enough for supper, the little group returned home. Cousin Kee did not seem discouraged, and already was planning their next trip to another good "spot." Unexpectedly they came upon Uncle Kwok, restlessly, but still deliberately, pacing back and forth on the pavement in front of their factory.

"Uncle Kwok," Mama cried out in surprise. "What are you doing here? Don't you remember that there was no work today? It is a holiday."

Uncle Kwok looked wounded and regarded the group severely from behind the glasses perched halfway down his nose. "It is fortunate that I forgot and came here, for I found that you had left your front door unlocked!" He pointed to the door with an accusing sweep of his long arm.

Mama still couldn't understand. "Why didn't you lock it, then, and go on your way, instead of waiting past the hour when you should have reported to the apartment house?"

Uncle Kwok, his precious satchel hugged tightly, drew himself up to his full majesty. "Because, Mama, if I had done that, you would never have learned that you left your front door unlocked!"

With these crushing words, he turned from his surprised friends, and with his little satchel ceremoniously clutched in his hand, started off for his janitorial work.

"A crazy man," Cousin Kee muttered as Mama opened the door.

As he cleaned their catch for supper, he regaled them with stories of other great catches he had made. He decided that the fish should be cooked in a favorite Chinese way—by steaming. He arranged the cleaned little shiners with heads and skin on, in a shallow bowl and sprinkled over them slivers of fresh ginger root, a sauce of garlic pounded with sugar and black, salted soybeans, soy sauce, and peanut oil. The dish was placed on a rack and steamed in a kettle until barely done. Fresh green onions were chopped and added after the fish was cooked, which took only about fifteen minutes.

Daddy came into the kitchen. "I like my fish poached in water."

Cousin Kee wasn't bothered. "This is a better way with small fish, as all the juices are kept in the dish and the meat doesn't fall apart."

The fish was delicious, and Cousin Kee expanded his chest in pride. "To think that a few hours ago these fish were still blinking their eyes in the bay and to think that none of you fished before this day. Now your Cousin Kee has educated you and brought you, fishing, and fish together!"

13

A PERSON AS WELL AS A FEMALE

AFTER GRADUATION FROM THE CHINESE SCHOOL, JADE SNOW
seriously sought a solution to her money problem. For two
reasons, she decided that she would try working outside their factory-home. She thought that she could make a little more money,
and even if she didn't, she would at least escape from some of the
continuous family friction. She sought help from the state employment service, which found openings for her in housework. Within
the following six months, Jade Snow worked in seven different
homes and was exposed to a series of candid views of the private
lives of these American families. Jade Snow made her own decisions.
At no time did she consult her family about the various jobs; she
simply told them when her mind was made up.

Daddy and Mama did give her one bit of serious advice when she
started her first job. Mama said, "I have done my best to teach you

to be honest and diligent. Now you are about to emerge on your own. You must follow your best judgment and conscience and, above all, do not be greedy in your work. If you were to see your employer's diamonds and gold pieces lying around, do not covet them."

Daddy was reminded to reminisce a bit: "When my father began his business training as an apprentice, one of the duties assigned to him was to sweep the floor daily. At times, he found a coin on the floor. Without a word, he picked up the coin each time and put it away. After many months, his employer complained. 'I do not know who can be trusted around here. I have been missing some coins.' Whereupon your grandfather calmly went to his quarters and produced all of the salvaged coins, each wrapped carefully in a memorandum dated with the time your grandfather found it. He effectively proved himself to be trustworthy."

Her parents probably did not remember the incident of the peddler specifically but Jade Snow had never forgotten. Aloud, she simply answered, "Yes."

First she worked for the Schmidts, who ran a small soft-drink fountain and poolroom near their home in a residential district of San Francisco. The mother was a big-hearted, merry-eyed, stout woman who worked hard and continuously. She usually cooked one hot dish a day, to be served at the fountain as the luncheon special. Jade Snow helped her with the cooking and the light housework, and quickly became great friends with her employer, who treated her with utmost kindness. There were two things Jade Snow always thought of when she looked back on this job: the perpetually darkened "front room" with its heavy velvet drapes, drawn to keep the sun from fading the plush furniture, and her own weeping eyes as she peeled and ground vast mounds of onions for the endless hamburgers ordered at the fountain.

After a brief period with the Schmidts, Jade Snow moved on to their good friends, the Jeffersons, because young Mrs. Jefferson was ill after an operation. Mrs. Schmidt said that she could manage somehow, but her friend really needed help; she had several small children, and her husband, who operated a service station, was busy all day.

Jade Snow's most persistent memory of her first day in this

new position was a big galvanized pail of string beans set on the back of the kitchen stove. The husband, struggling to work, shop, and care for the children as well as to nurse his wife, had cooked quantities of this vegetable to feed all of them for several days. Perhaps ten pounds of beans were boiling through their second hour. Jade Snow, trained in the Chinese tradition of quick cooking of finely cut vegetables, who had never cooked string beans more than seven or eight minutes, suppressed her surprise and politely asked the reason.

Mr. Jefferson replied, "Where I come from in the South, we don't think a bean is tender until it has been cooked at least two hours!"

However, the Jeffersons good-naturedly let Jade Snow take over their very informal household. For a month, while the mother was getting well, Jade Snow was busy from morning until night with all the familiar home chores; but now she was paid fifty cents an hour, and there was no criticism.

At the end of the summer Jade Snow was a senior in high school, and could take on only part-time work. She decided to try working at several odd jobs so that she would not be tied down completely. By word-of-mouth referrals, she made four contacts which kept her busy. She really liked these odd jobs better, since all that was involved was serving party dinners and washing dishes, which was not so tiring as the entire management of a household.

Mentally she tabulated these four families by type rather than by name—"the horsy family," "the apartment-house family," "the political couple," and the "bridge-playing group."

The "horsy family" was composed of an elderly, mild father who said scarcely a word, an ambitious, tense mother, and two equally ambitious and mutually antagonistic daughters in their thirties, whose chief purpose in life was to be "smart." They were unrelenting in their efforts to get their names on the social page of the local newspapers, and their method was horses. They had their pictures taken in horsy poses, and they gave parties, but only for guests who "mattered." They owned a large house patterned after English cottage architecture, which the mother tried to keep in perfect order as a setting for her daughters' activities. The father, who worked all day, said nothing when he came home, but the daughters argued continuously about the best means to achieve their common goal.

The "political" middle-aged couple gave dinners in honor of up-and-coming young California political figures; there were always many men but few women at these parties. Here, Jade Snow was initiated into a new wrinkle in the American pattern—the off-color story.

Needless to say, the Wong household, if not always gentle, had high standards. Between Confucian decorum and Christian ideals, even unessential or boisterous laughing was dissonant. There an off-color story had never reared its ugly head. However, at this home, toward ten o'clock when everyone had had many cocktails, and the waiting dinner was turning to ruin in the oven, a group of men, including the political star of honor, howling with laughter, would burst into the kitchen to get away from the women in the living room. Here they would start on their gleeful "Have you heard the latest one?" slap each other, and roar with gales of laughter over each tale.

The small, lone female, Jade Snow, must have been to them merely another kitchen fixture for they never recognized her. Stoically she continued her work, trying not to blush at their remarks and double talk and to drive them out of her memory.

What would Daddy and Mama think about this? They never knew that in these months their fifth daughter saw and heard things that broadened and humanized the American world beyond the realm of typewriters and stenographers, which had provided her first and only childhood associations with Caucasians. Needless to say, she never talked about these new experiences at home. Mama and Daddy were comfortable in their knowledge that Jade Snow had found honest work and was performing it satisfactorily. She was making about twenty dollars a month, and now paid for her own lunches, carfare, clothes, and all the other necessities of a fifteen-year-old schoolgirl. She had completed Chinese school, was about to complete the American high school, and was apparently establishing firm habits for earning a living and being a good homemaker, in accordance with the traditional Chinese pattern for women.

The "apartment-house" dwellers had one little girl about three, who was the light of their life. Everything Arleen did or said was the most astounding thing in the world, and had never been done or said so well before. If Arleen threw her dinner at the window of the kitchen door, she was not reproved or punished; she was excused for being "full of spirit." The only reason Jade Snow continued to oblige Arleen's fond parents was that once their angel child was asleep, she could use the evening to study, while being paid.

Finally, there were the Gilberts, or rather, Mrs. Gilbert, who loved bridge parties. The Gilberts' home was large, beautiful, adequately landscaped, and they were very proud of it. Mr. Gilbert liked golf. "Nothing like it in the world for relaxation and public relations," he always said. Every Saturday afternoon which did not see a downpour of rain found him at his favorite activity.

Mrs. Gilbert's passion for bridge demanded every Saturday, rain or shine. On the afternoons when she entertained "the girls" in her own home, Jade Snow helped her. On other Saturdays, she was at "the other girls' " homes.

When Mrs. Gilbert was hostess for a "simple" buffet luncheon, she set her table with her best lace cloth and polished silver. It was Jade Snow's first acquaintance with buffet meals. "The girls," from thirty-five to fifty in years, arrived, gushed, giggled, gossiped, ate, and played bridge all afternoon—and what was most amazing to Jade Snow—all the while with their hats on! It was always the same crowd of faces under different hats. Jade Snow wondered what it would be like to be one of them, to have so much time that you would try to spend it playing bridge, and so much money that you could pay someone to come in and wash the dishes while you played.

Jade Snow now concentrated intensely on her American schoolwork, since there were no more Chinese lessons to divide her energy. As her graduation was approaching, she began inquiries about qualifications for college entrance. She found that she had met the academic requirements for the state university; but the registration and other fees, together with commutation and books, would be beyond her part-time earning capacity, and more than she could possibly save, since she was using all her earnings for current expenses.

But if not college, what was her future?

"Education is your path to freedom," Daddy had said. "In China, you would have had little private tutoring and no free advanced schooling. Make the most of your American opportunity."

"Be a good girl—and study hard," Grandmother had said.

"Daddy thinks that Jade Snow is so intelligent," she had over-heard her older sisters say skeptically, "but let's see if she can bring any honors home to our family."

"I resolve to be a credit to Mama and prove that the unkind predictions about her children were wrong," she had vowed once when Daddy was ill.

"Give me the strength and the ability to prove to my family that they have been unjust and make them prouder of me than anyone else," Jade Snow had pleaded later in unnumbered prayers.

Constantly, she remembered these challenges.

Moreover, she was most curious about college, and eager to learn more about the new worlds which her high school subjects were just opening up to her.

Yes, Jade Snow agreed with Daddy that education was the path to freedom. Forgotten was her early ambition to be a stenographer. She resolved to ask Daddy to help her with the college fees. After all, he had financed Older Brother's education.

Her next free night, when she was alone with Daddy in the dining room after dinner, Jade Snow broached the subject.

"Daddy, I have been studying the state university catalogue, and I should like to continue my education there, but it will cost more than I can manage, even though I still worked all I could. Would you help me to meet the college expenses?"

Daddy reluctantly pulled himself away from his evening paper and settled back in the large, square, straight, black armchair that was his alone. He took off his dark-rimmed reading glasses, and looked thoughtfully but distractedly at the figure standing respect-fully before him. Then he chose his words seriously and deliberately.

"You are quite familiar by now with the fact that it is the sons who perpetuate our ancestral heritage by permanently bearing the Wong family name and transmitting it through their blood line, and therefore the sons must have priority over the daughters when parental provision for advantages must be limited by economic necessity. Generations of sons, bearing our Wong name, are those who make pilgrimages to ancestral burial grounds and preserve them forever. Our daughters leave home at marriage to give sons to their husbands' families to carry on the heritage for other names.

"Jade Snow, you have been given an above-average Chinese education for an American-born Chinese girl. You now have an average education for an American girl. I must still provide with all my powers for your Older Brother's advanced medical training."

"But Daddy, I want to be more than an average Chinese or American girl. If I stay here, I want to be more than average. If I go to China, I shall advance further with an American college degree," Jade Snow pleaded earnestly.

"I have no other means even though you desire to be above average," Daddy replied evenly, and Jade Snow could not detect either regret or sympathy in his statement of fact. She did not know whether his next words were uttered in challenge or in scorn as he added, "If you have the talent, you can provide for your own college education."

Daddy had spoken. He returned to his Chinese paper with finality and clamped on his glasses again. By habit, Jade Snow questioned aloud no more. She had been trained to make inquiry of Daddy with one question, and to accept his answer; she never asked twice. But her mind was full of questions as it echoed his words, "If you have the talent, you can provide for your own college education."

Tonight his statement did not leave Jade Snow with the customary reaction, "Daddy knows better. Daddy is fair. Even though I do not like what he says, he has eaten more salt than I have eaten rice, and in time I shall understand why this is my own problem and must be endured."

No, his answer tonight left Jade Snow with a new and sudden bitterness against the one person whom she had always trusted as fair to her.

"How can Daddy know what an American advanced education can mean to me? Why should Older Brother be alone in enjoying the major benefits of Daddy's toil? There are no ancestral pilgrimages to be made in the United States! I can't help being born a girl. Perhaps, even being a girl, I don't want to marry, *just to* raise sons! Perhaps I have a right to want more than sons! I am a person, besides being a female! Don't the Chinese admit that women also have feelings and minds?"

Jade Snow retreated to her little bedroom, but now she felt imprisoned. She was trapped in a mesh of tradition woven thousands of miles away by ancestors who had had no knowledge that someday one generation of their progeny might be raised in another culture. Acknowledging that she owed her very being and much of her thinking to those ancestors and their tradition, she could not believe that this background was meant to hinder her further development either in America or in China.

Beyond this point, she could not think clearly. Impulsively, she threw on her coat and left the house—the first time that she had done so without notifying Mama.

In a lonely walk, she wandered in the darkness over the San Francisco hills. She went first to the waterfront, saw a few tramps sleeping in empty railroad cars, hid from some drunken brawlers in front of the saloons, climbed up Telegraph Hill, came down and went up again over Russian Hill, to Van Ness Avenue, then back to Chinatown and home.

As she walked, she pushed away her bitterness in order to organize a practical course of action. To begin with, she was not going to give up her education. She felt that it was right to go on with it, and she must try to provide for it alone. She would try to get a scholarship to college.

But Daddy had also said, "If you have the talent. . . ." Jade Snow reasoned: talent is what you were born with—in combination with what you have learned. Did she have talent? Older Brother had said that she had no imagination nor personality, but did she have talent? She reasoned further: she had always tried to make the most of her ability. Often her classmates seemed to get the right answer much more quickly than she did, but she always hung on, and eventually she caught up with them. If she continued to do her very best, and if what she had set her eyes on was the right thing for her to do, she had to believe that the talent part would somehow be taken care of.

She decided as simply as that. She would try her best to do the right things; somehow things would work out, and she would not worry. She was concerned only with doing what was immediately at hand, and putting her best into it. So she continued to keep people's houses clean, exhausted herself studying, ignored her family, got straight A's except in physical education, and left it to God to take care of His share in bringing her college education to reality.

14

GIRL MEETS BOY

THAT WINTER JADE SNOW'S OLDEST SISTER AND FOURTH OLDER sister were bombed out of their home in Canton by the Sino-Japanese war, and were forced to return to San Francisco. Oldest Sister settled in Grass Valley with her husband and son. Fourth Older Sister moved into the Wong household because she decided to work in San Francisco. The folding sofa in the Wong dining room became her bed, and Jade Snow's and Jade Precious Stone's seven-by-twelve bedroom became her room too. This physical crowding added to Jade Snow's increasing feeling of being stifled. The quarters which had served two sisters passably well as children had in five years become too small for still growing and highly individualistic young adults.

One day, after another family disagreement, Fourth Older Sister found Jade Snow weeping in their room. She started to comfort her and suggested: "Why don't you consider getting a job which would give you room and board besides wages, and get out of everyone's way here?"

"Get out of everyone's way"—this was a new idea which seemed like a perfect solution. Through the state employment service again, Jade Snow found a room-and-board job with the Kaisers, a family composed of husband and wife, two children, aged four and six, and a large white dog. They lived in an old house with only the rooms usual in an American home, but it seemed very spacious to Jade Snow. An all-purpose room held sewing equipment, children's playthings, discarded objects, and a narrow couch for her bed. The Kaiser family also had a car, vacuum cleaner, icebox, and washing machine!

Jade Snow's new duties included keeping all the house clean (heavy and light cleaning), all the laundry, with a spotless white shirt every day for Mr. Kaiser, and a fresh, starched cotton dress daily for each of the two girls), the care of linens, all the subsequent ironing, cooking the family breakfasts, helping to prepare dinner under Mrs. Kaiser's supervision, serving, washing all the dishes, caring for the dog, and telling stories to the children who trailed her as she worked, for six and a half days a week. On Sunday, she was allowed a half day off to go to church and to take Mama for a walk, but she had to be back again at four to take care of her employer's Sunday dinner.

Being responsible for the tidy condition of the old house and its occupants meant that Jade Snow's work never seemed to get quite done. But she was often reminded by her employer that not many "school jobs" at that time offered twenty dollars per month in addition to room and board.

Tedious and unending and tiring as the work was, Jade Snow gained more than just room and board and twenty dollars per month. For a considerable period of time, she was an intimate member of an American household, where she observed its occupants early and late, moving in a pattern completely different from her own Chinese background. It was a home where children were heard as well as seen; where parents considered who was right or wrong, rather than who should be respected; where birthday parties were a tradition, complete with lighted birthday cakes, where the husband kissed his wife and the parents kissed their children; where the Christmas holidays meant fruit cake, cookies, presents, and gay parties; where the family was actually concerned with having fun together and going out to play together; where the problems and difficulties of domestic life and children's discipline were untangled, perhaps after tears, but also after explanations; where the husband turned over his pay check to his wife to pay the bills; and where, above all, each member, even down to and including the dog, appeared to have the inalienable right to assert his individuality— in fact, where that was expected—in an atmosphere of natural affection.

The Kaisers were kind to Jade Snow and the children never took advantage of her. After her work was done, she enjoyed the new, rare thrill of being able to close her door and be alone within four walls, in peace and quietness. Yes, it was worth all the hard work to have an opportunity to crystallize her thoughts without having to leave the house, to shed no more tears under the bedcovers, to be free of seething, undefined emotions which must be bottled up because they were not permitted expression.

In the meantime, high-school graduation activities were reaching a climax. Jade Snow bought her senior accessories and participated in the events of her class program, along with her "crowd" of six or seven other Chinese-American girls.

The highlights of this general "rush" were the dances, and in these Jade Snow, to her secret pain, could not readily participate. Daddy had never permitted her to learn to dance. He had nothing but scorn and disapproval for the American pastime of social dancing. To see male and female hugging each other in public was most revolting to him, and he had forbidden his daughters either to learn to dance or to attend dances.

But all the others in Jade Snow's crowd enjoyed dancing. Jade Snow had not even gone out on her first "date," and attending a girls' high school did not help the situation. So she would help the others to organize a dance or decorate the hall, but during the dance itself she was there only to check hats and coats and watch her classmates with their dates all having a good time. It was then that she began to wonder whether getting the highest grades was the most important accomplishment in school after all. She knew that she was missing something obviously very desirable, but she could do nothing about it. At least she thought that she could do nothing until a month before graduation, when a number of first experiences came her way in rapid succession.

The Chinese Students' Club of her high school held one big dance a year, and this year they chose "Cotton Capers" for their theme. The invitation bids in Girls' High colors of gold and white were tufted on the cover with a bit of snowy cotton. The girls were to wear bright cotton dresses. Half a dozen girls in the club who usually did all the planning enlisted the aid of their current boy friends. Jade Snow pitched in and helped make the cardboard cutouts for signs and other gay decorations in cotton materials. The dance hall was decked with streamers of twisted multicolored cotton strips. The cases of "cokes" had to be ordered, and number tags had to be made for checking the guests' belongings.

Jade Snow found time to make herself a new navy-blue coat trimmed with silk ribbon, and a little dress with puffed sleeves, tight bodice, and a full gathered skirt of figured red cotton.

When the evening of the dance arrived, it was Jade Snow's good fortune that because she was now living at the Kaisers', she did not have to ask for parental permission to go to "Cotton Capers." She had only to tell the Kaisers as a matter of routine, and they even wished her a good time!

As usual, Jade Snow busied herself in the cloakroom as soon as she had seen that everything else was in place and running smoothly. The American-Chinese boys who had been helping—Frankie, Wilson, Edward, and Joe—were all there, alternating between dancing and giving the girls a helping hand with the cases of "cokes." Joe, a clean-cut, pleasant fellow, but known to be quite a tease, had worked very hard with them on the dance. Now he brought Jade Snow a "coke," and during a slack period in the flow of coats, struck up a conversation with her.

He was obviously pleased with the results of their handiwork, "Don't you think our sign stands out pretty well with the special lighting effect shining through the cutout letters?"

Jade Snow was rather reticent, "Yes, I think things have worked out pretty well."

This was too moderate a degree of enthusiasm for Joe. "Pretty well? Why, I think it's doing better than any other high school's Chinese Students' Club dance given this year! Have you been to any of the others to see how poor some are?"

Jade Snow felt inadequate. "Well, no, I haven't."

Joe stared. "What's the matter with you—don't you like dances?"

"No. . . ." Jade Snow was miserable. "I don't mean 'No,' I mean, I don't dance. I mean I don't know how to dance."

"Well," Joe seemed relieved, "let's teach you then."

"No," replied Jade Snow again, "you'd better not."

Joe stared again, "You mean you don't want to learn?"

"No, no, it isn't that!" (Oh dear, Jade Snow thought, how am I going to get out of this situation?)

"Oh, I guess you don't want to have me teach you," Joe said quickly, and before the upset girl could muster another "No," he had hailed a passing friend.

"Hey you, Frankie, come here a minute."

Obligingly, Frankie paused and ambled over. He was a thin, olive-skinned young man with a quick smile and shiny, neat black hair.

Joe explained, "Here's a girl who doesn't know how to dance and wants to learn. Do me a favor, will you, and give her a few whirls out there on the floor?"

Jade Snow found her tongue, "Oh, no, no, no," she protested, "I really don't want to learn right now and here. I have to watch the cloakroom, you know. Please go away and leave me alone."

Joe reached in, unlatched and swung open the little Dutch door, and retorted cheerfully, "I don't believe a word you're saying. I'll watch your old coats for you, and I promise that I won't rob the club of its tips. Now don't disappoint poor Frankie."

With Joe pushing her gently but firmly, and Frankie's grip on her arm, Jade Snow was practically pulled to the dance floor by force. She was self-conscious, tense, and terrified, not knowing with which foot to start, nor how to follow, nor even how to keep time to the simple music. After a most unhappy, and it seemed lengthy, period of stumbling around, Franklie laughingly returned her to the cloakroom, where Jade Snow was relieved to pick up her duties again.

Joe teasingly called back over his shoulder as he left, "I was watching you. I think there's some hope of making you a dancer yet!"

After another hour or so, Joe came around again, "Say, someone is asking to see you."

"Who is it?" Jade Snow was mystified.

Joe was noncommittal. "I don't know."

"Oh dear," she thought, "I wonder if it could be Daddy? Maybe he found out about me!" In a silent paralysis of fear, she went reluctantly in the direction Joe indicated.

It was Frankie!

"Come now, no protests." Stopping her before she could express her vexation, he pulled her onto the dance floor, where, by perfect timing, Joe appeared. In a quick second, he had exchanged places with Frankie, who trotted off happily to the "coke" stand.

A breathless "Well!" was all astonished Jade Snow could manage at this quick maneuver.

Joe was unconcerned. "I'm a much better teacher of dancing than Frankie is," he explained modestly. "Now stop struggling and relax," he commanded.

Patiently, Joe initiated Jade Snow into the mysterious principles of dancing, until Jade Snow lost her fear as she gained confidence in Joe, and in wonder, gained confidence in herself.

This time the dance was over all too soon. The two were laughing over her mistakes as Joe took her arm and escorted her back to her post. It was now midnight, the end of the party, and he helped her find the coats for departing guests.

Then he proposed that they all go off for a snack and a ride in his car. Jade Snow, Joe, and two other couples went together for Chinese noodles, and autographed each other's white napkins in ink as permanent souvenirs of a lovely evening. The ride which followed along the bay and ocean coastline was the first time that Jade Snow had been in a mixed crowd of friends without a chaperone. It was all innocent fun with jokes tossed back and forth, and a lot of good-humored teasing of Jade Snow.

Then it was June, 1938, and graduation time. With her classmates, amid a noisy buzz of excitement in the dressing room, Jade Snow put on her white wool academic robe and mortarboard. She sat on the stage with her class, knowing that in the audience somewhere all of her family except Daddy were watching to see her receive her diploma. Daddy was traveling throughout California as a representative of his San Francisco Chinese Family Association, to raise donations from fellow villagers who were scattered on farms and in small towns but who were still obligated to support their association's headquarters.

Family associations took care of personal and business matters for Chinese in America. Controversies without legal status in American courts could be taken up in association meetings; destitute Chinese families or widows who were not American citizens could get immediate assistance; men without relatives could have their funeral arrangements assured. Six such associations whose members were from districts of Canton affiliated to form the Chinese Six Companies, which was a supreme court for Chinese controversies submitted by Cantonese throughout the United States. Yes, it was more important for Daddy to attend to his civic duty than to see his daughter graduate from American high school, even though the graduation program had an asterisk before Jade Snow's name, with the notation, "Elected to life membership in the California Scholarship Federation, in recognition of academic achievement."

The graduation activities ended that week end with a senior ball, to which Jade Snow went with a little confidence gained from the "Cotton Capers." She wore her first American evening gown of white chiffon, new silver sandals, flat-heeled so that she wouldn't seem so tall, and a fur wrap and a sequined evening bag borrowed from two older sisters. She was taken to the dance by Wilson, one of Joe's friends, whom he had persuaded to escort her. It was also Joe, Jade Snow discovered, who had persuaded Wilson to bring her her first orchid corsage of two beautiful blossoms.

Summer vacation began as graduation ended.

Jade Snow continued to work for the Kaisers, but in place of going to school, she filled in the day hours by working for Daddy again at the factory. She was greatly discouraged at this time, because she had not received the long-hoped-for scholarship award from the state university. She had worked and studied so hard, why couldn't she get what she wanted? What should she plan to do now?

During the summer months, Joe telephoned her occasionally to see how she was. After a while, he began to join her on some of her walks. They had to meet secretly on street corners, since Jade Snow dared not let her parents know about her new friend. For friend he was indeed. Joe was easy to talk to, interested in her perplexities, and generously kind. It was a comfort to tuck her arm in his strong one and have him help her over the rough rocks on Telegraph Hill or Russian Hill, where they often wandered, deep in conversation. But Jade Snow noticed that Joe hardly ever wanted to talk about himself, and she wondered about his family and his problems.

On one of these walks, Jade Snow confided to Joe her unhappiness over the notice she had received from the state university Alumni Scholarship Committee: "because of the number of applicants" she did not qualify for a scholarship. It was near the end of the summer; she had to come to a decision. For the first time, Jade Snow told another person all about her family difficulties and felt the relief that comes from revealing to a kindred soul the depths of one's personal troubles. In her mood of despair, she burst out, "Oh, Joe, I am so discouraged! I did so want to go to the university. I thought that if I wanted the right things and tried hard, the right things would happen for me. I can never lift up my head at home again if I have to admit to my parents that in my first independent resolution and endeavor, I've failed in what I sought. Perhaps I've figured things wrong, after all, and I should give up now."

Joe did not agree, "Even if you can't go to the university, that doesn't mean that you have to give up all higher education. There is still the San Francisco Junior College, where you can study for two years without the time and the expense of commuting to Berkeley."

Jade Snow was uncompromising: "If I can't go to the university, I don't want to go to a junior college."

Joe remonstrated with her: "Now you're just being stubborn. What makes you so sure that a junior college can't teach you anything? Isn't it education you are after? I quit college once, and I'll always be sorry about it. Once you stop school, it's hard to go back."

Jade Snow was reluctant. "I suppose it wouldn't hurt to try the junior college. . . ."

"Of course not. Maybe you can even save more money this way, by working during the extra time you will have. Then you won't have to strain yourself so much in the two advanced years and still can get your degree from the university. Remember, half a loaf of bread is better than no bread at all; so don't be so proud about holding out for the whole loaf. I'll bet that some day you'll be glad I told you all this. Promise me that you will try, won't you?"

Jade Snow was deeply touched. Here was someone who really cared about her future and her ideas. The boy whom all the other girls in her crowd found most desirable was bothering with her problems. "I promise you, Joe," she answered softly.

Joe continued, "I'll make a date with you for five years from now, to meet on this same hill; by then you should have graduated from college. I'll bet you'll be thanking me then for talking you into going to junior college."

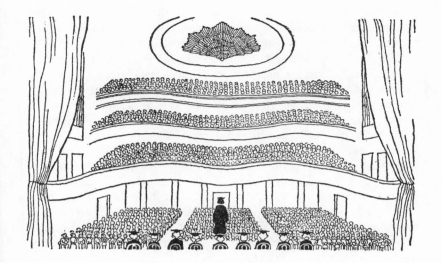

15

A MEASURE OF FREEDOM

So, without much enthusiasm, Jade Snow decided upon junior college. Now it was necessary to inform Mama and Daddy. She chose an evening when the family was at dinner. All of them were in their customary places, and Daddy, typically, was in conversation with Older Brother about the factory:

"Blessing, when do you think Lot Number fifty-one twenty-six will be finished? I want to ask for a check from our jobber so that I can have enough cash for next week's payroll."

To which Older Brother replied, "As soon as Mama is through with the seams in Mrs. Lee's and Mrs. Choy's bundles, the women can finish the hems. Another day, probably."

Mama had not been consulted; therefore she made no comment. Silence descended as the Wongs continued their meal, observing the well-learned precept that talk was not permissible while eating.

Jade Snow considered whether to break the silence. Three times she thought over what she had to say, and still she found it worth saying. This also was according to family precept.

"Daddy," she said, "I have made up my mind to enter junior college here in San Francisco. I will find a steady job to pay my expenses, and by working in the summers I'll try to save enough money to take me through my last two years at the university."

Then she waited. Everyone went on eating. No one said a word. Apparently no one was interested enough to be curious. But at least no one objected. It was settled.

Junior college was at first disappointing in more ways than one. There was none of the glamour usually associated with college because the institution was so young that it had not yet acquired buildings of its own. Classes were held all over the city wherever accommodations were available. The first days were very confusing to Jade Snow, especially when she discovered that she must immediately decide upon a college major.

While waiting to register, she thumbed through the catalogue in search of a clue. English . . . mathematics . . . chemistry. . . . In the last semester of high school she had found chemistry particularly fascinating: so with a feeling of assurance she wrote that as her major on the necessary forms, and went to a sign-up table.

"I wish to take the lecture and laboratory classes for Chemistry 1A," she informed the gray-haired man who presided there.

He looked at her, a trifle impatiently she thought.

"Why?"

"Because I like it." To herself she sounded reasonable.

"But you are no longer in high school. Chemistry here is a difficult subject on a university level, planned for those who are majoring in medicine, engineering, or the serious sciences."

Jade Snow set her chin stubbornly. "I still want to take Chemistry 1A."

Sharply he questioned: "What courses in mathematics have you had? What were your grades?"

Finally Jade Snow's annoyance rose to the surface. "Straight A's. But why must you ask? Do you think I would want to take a course I couldn't pass? Why don't you sign me up and let the instructor be the judge of my ability?"

"Very well," he replied stiffly. "I'll accept you in the class. And for your information, young lady, I am the instructor!"

With this inauspicious start, Jade Snow began her college career. To take care of finances, she now needed to look for work. Through a friend she learned that a Mrs. Simpson needed someone to help with household work. "Can you cook?" was Mrs. Simpson's first question.

Jade Snow considered a moment before answering. Certainly she could cook Chinese food, and she remembered a common Chinese saying, "A Chinese can cook foreign food as well as, if not better than, the foreigners, but a foreigner cannot cook Chinese food fit for the Chinese." On this reasoning it seemed safe to say "Yes."

After some further discussion Jade Snow was hired. Cooking, she discovered, included everything from pastries, puddings, meats, steaks, and vegetables, to sandwiches. In addition, she served the meals, washed dishes, kept the house clean, did the light laundry and ironing for Mr. and Mrs. Simpson and their career daughter— and always appeared in uniform, which she thoroughly disliked. In return she received twenty dollars a month. At night, she did her studying at home, and sometimes after a hard day she was so tired that the walk from the Simpson flat to the streetcar on Chestnut Street was a blessed respite, a time to relax and admire the moon if she could find it, and to gather fresh energy for whatever lay ahead.

Desserts, quite ignored in a Chinese household, were of first importance in the Simpson household. One particular Saturday, Jade Snow was told to bake a special meringue sponge cake with a fancy fruit filling of whipped cream and peeled and seeded grapes. Following a very special recipe of Mrs. Simpson's, she mixed it for the first time and preheated the oven. Mrs. Simpson came into the kitchen, checked and approved the prepared cake batter, and said that she would judge when it was done. Meantime she and her husband and their guests lounged happily in the garden.

Almost an hour passed. The meringue was baking in a slow oven. The recipe said not to open the door, as the cake might fall. An hour and a quarter passed, and the pastry smelled sweetly delicate. Yet Mrs. Simpson did not come. Jade Snow wondered whether or not to call her. But she remembered that her employer disliked being disturbed when entertaining officials of her husband's company.

After an hour and forty-five minutes the cake no longer smelled delicate. Jade Snow was worn out! What could she do? At last, there was a rush of high-heeled footsteps; swish went the kitchen door, and Mrs. Simpson burst in, flushed from the sun or excitement.

"I must look at that meringue cake," she burst out.

The oven door was pulled open, and Jade Snow peered in anxiously over her employer's shoulder. Too late! It had fallen and become a tough, brown mass. Jade Snow was dumb with a crushed heart, inspecting the flattened pancake, mentally reviewing all the processes of whipping, measuring, and sifting that she had gone through for hours to achieve this unpalatable result.

Mrs. Simpson crisply broke through to her anguish, "Well, there's nothing to be done but for you to make another."

That afternoon was a torturous nightmare and a fever of activity —to manage another meringue cake, to get rolls mixed, salad greens cleaned and crisped, vegetables cut, meat broiled, the table set, and all the other details of a "company" dinner attended to. By the time she was at last washing the dishes and tidying the dining room she felt strangely vague. She hadn't taken time to eat her dinner; she was too tired anyway. How she wished that she had been asked to cook a Chinese dinner instead of this interminable American meal, especially that cake!

Of her college courses, Latin was the easiest. This was a surprise, for everyone had told her of its horrors. It was much more logical than French, almost mathematical in its orderliness and precision, and actually a snap after nine years of Chinese.

Chemistry, true to the instructor's promise, was difficult, although the classes were anything but dull. It turned out that he was a very nice person with a keen sense of humor and a gift for enlivening his lectures with stories of his own college days. There were only two girls in a class of more than fifty men—a tense blonde girl from Germany, who always ranked first; and Jade Snow, who usually took second place.

But if Latin was the easiest course and chemistry the most difficult, sociology was the most stimulating. Jade Snow had chosen it without thought, simply to meet a requirement; but that casual decision completely revolutionized her thinking, shattering her Wong-constructed conception of the order of things. This was the way it happened:

After several uneventful weeks during which the class explored the historical origins of the family and examined such terms as "norms," "mores," "folkways," there came a day when the instructor stood before them to discuss the relationship of parents and children. It was a day like many others, with the students listening in varying attitudes of interest or indifference. The instructor was speaking casually of ideas to be accepted as standard. Then suddenly upon Jade Snow's astounded ears there fell this statement:

"There was a period in our American history when parents had children for economic reasons, to put them to work as soon as possible, especially to have them help on the farm. But now we no longer regard children in this way. Today we recognize that children are individuals, and that parents can no longer demand their unquestioning obedience. Parents should do their best to understand their children, because young people also have their rights."

The instructor went on talking, but Jade Snow heard no more, for her mind was echoing and re-echoing this startling thought. "Parents can no longer demand unquestioning obedience from their children. They should do their best to understand. Children also have their rights." For the rest of that day, while she was doing her chores at the Simpsons', while she was standing in the streetcar going home, she was busy translating the idea into terms of her own experience.

"My parents demand unquestioning obedience. Older Brother demands unquestioning obedience. By what right? I am an individual besides being a Chinese daughter. I have rights too."

Could it be that Daddy and Mama, although they were living in San Francisco in the year 1938, actually had not left the Chinese world of thirty years ago? Could it be that they were forgetting that Jade Snow would soon become a woman in a new America, not a woman in old China? In short, was it possible that Daddy and Mama could be wrong?

For days Jade Snow gave thought to little but her devastating discovery that her parents might be subject to error. As it was her habit always to act after reaching a conclusion, she wondered what to do about it. Should she tell Daddy and Mama that they needed to change their ways? One moment she thought she should, the next she thought not. At last she decided to overcome her fear in the interests of education and better understanding. She would at least try to open their minds to modern truths. If she succeeded, good! If not, she was prepared to suffer the consequences.

In this spirit of patient martyrdom she waited for an opportunity to speak.

It came, surprisingly, one Saturday. Ordinarily that was a busy day at the Simpsons', a time for entertaining, so that Jade Snow was not free until too late to go anywhere even had she had a place to go. But on this particular Saturday the Simpsons were away for the weekend, and by three in the afternoon Jade Snow was ready to leave the apartment with unplanned hours ahead of her. She didn't want to spend these rare hours of freedom in any usual way. And she didn't want to spend them alone.

"Shall I call Joe?" she wondered. She had never telephoned to a boy before and she debated whether it would be too forward. But she felt too happy and carefree to worry much, and she was confident that Joe would not misunderstand.

Even before reporting to Mama that she was home, she ran downstairs to the telephone booth and gave the operator Joe's number. His mother answered and then went to call him while Jade Snow waited in embarrassment.

"Joe." She was suddenly tongue-tied. "Joe, I'm already home."

That wasn't at all what she wanted to say. What did she want to say?

"Hello! Hello!" Joe boomed back. "What's the matter with you? Are you all right?"

"Oh, yes, I'm fine. Only, only . . . well, I'm through working for the day." That was really all she had to say, but now it sounded rather pointless.

"Isn't that wonderful? It must have been unexpected." That was what was nice and different about Joe. He always seemed to know without a lot of words. But because his teasing was never far behind his understanding he added quickly, "I suppose you're going to study and go to bed early."

Jade Snow was still not used to teasing and didn't know how to take it. With an effort she swallowed her shyness and disappointment. "I thought we might go for a walk . . . that is, if you have nothing else to do . . . if you would care to . . . if. . . ."

Joe laughed. "I'll go you one better. Suppose I take you to a movie. I'll even get all dressed up for you, and you get dressed up too."

Jade Snow was delighted. Her first movie with Joe! What a wonderful day. In happy anticipation she put on her long silk stockings, lipstick, and the nearest thing to a suit she owned—a hand-me-down jacket and a brown skirt she had made herself. Then with a bright ribbon tying back her long black hair she was ready.

Daddy didn't miss a detail of the preparations as she dashed from room to room. He waited until she was finished before he demanded, "Jade Snow, where are you going?"

"I am going out into the street," she answered.

"Did you ask my permission to go out into the street?"

"No, Daddy."

"Do you have your mother's permission to go out into the street?"

"No, Daddy."

A sudden silence from the kitchen indicated that Mama was listening.

Daddy went on: "Where and when did you learn to be so daring as to leave this house without permission of your parents? You did not learn it under my roof."

It was all very familiar. Jade Snow waited, knowing that Daddy had not finished. In a moment he came to the point.

"And with whom are you going out into the street?"

It took all the courage Jade Snow could muster, remembering her new thinking, to say nothing. It was certain that if she told Daddy that she was going out with a boy whom he did not know, without a chaperone, he would be convinced that she would lose her maidenly purity before the evening was over.

"Very well," Daddy said sharply. "If you will not tell me, I forbid you to go! You are now too old to whip."

That was the moment.

Suppressing all anger, and in a manner that would have done credit to her sociology instructor addressing his freshman class, Jade Snow carefully turned on her mentally rehearsed speech.

"That is something you should think more about. Yes, I am too old to whip. I am too old to be treated as a child. I can now think for myself, and you and Mama should not demand unquestioning obedience from me. You should understand me. There was a time in America when parents raised children to make them work, but now the foreigners regard them as individuals with rights of their own. I have worked too, but now I am an individual besides being your fifth daughter."

It was almost certain that Daddy blinked, but after the briefest pause he gathered himself together.

"Where," he demanded, "did you learn such an unfilial theory?"

Mama had come quietly into the room and slipped into a chair to listen.

"From my teacher," Jade Snow answered triumphantly, "who you taught me is supreme after you, and whose judgment I am not to question."

Daddy was feeling pushed. Thoroughly aroused, he shouted:

"A little learning has gone to your head! How can you permit a foreigner's theory to put aside the practical experience of the Chinese, who for thousands of years have preserved a most superior family pattern? Confucius had already presented an organized philosophy of manners and conduct when the foreigners were unappreciatively persecuting Christ. Who brought you up? Who clothed you, fed you, sheltered you, nursed you? Do you think you were born aged sixteen? You owe honor to us before you satisfy your personal whims."

Daddy thundered on, while Jade Snow kept silent.

"What would happen to the order of this household if each of you four children started to behave like individuals? Would we have one peaceful moment if your personal desires came before your duty? How could we maintain our self-respect if we, your parents, did not know where you were at night and with whom you were keeping company?"

With difficulty Jade Snow kept herself from being swayed by fear and the old familiar arguments. "You can be bad in the daytime as well as at night," she said defensively. "What could happen after eleven that couldn't happen before?"

Daddy was growing more excited. "Do I have to justify my judgment to you? I do not want a daughter of mine to be known as one who walks the streets at night. Have you no thought for our reputations if not for your own? If you start going out with boys, no good man will want to ask you to be his wife. You just do not know as well as we do what is good for you."

Mama fanned Daddy's wrath, "Never having been a mother, you cannot know how much grief it is to bring up a daughter. Of course we will not permit you to run the risk of corrupting your purity before marriage."

"Oh, Mama!" Jade Snow retorted. "This is America, not China. Don't you think I have any judgment? How can you think I would go out with just any man?"

"Men!" Daddy roared. "You don't know a thing about them. I tell you, you can't trust any of them."

Now it was Jade Snow who felt pushed. She delivered the balance of her declaration of independence:

"Both of you should understand that I am growing up to be a woman in a society greatly different from the one you knew in China. You expect me to work my way through college—which would not have been possible in China. You expect me to exercise judgment in choosing my employers and my jobs and in spending my own money in the American world. Then why can't I choose my friends? Of course independence is not safe. But safety isn't the only consideration. You must give me the freedom to find some answers for myself."

Mama found her tongue first. "You think you are too good for us because you have a little foreign book knowledge."

"You will learn the error of your ways after it is too late," Daddy added darkly.

By this Jade Snow knew that her parents had conceded defeat. Hoping to soften the blow, she tried to explain: "If I am to earn my living, I must learn how to get along with many kinds of people, with foreigners as well as Chinese. I intend to start finding out about them now. You must have confidence that I shall remain true to the spirit of your teachings. I shall bring back to you the new knowledge of whatever I learn."

Daddy and Mama did not accept this offer graciously. "It is as useless for you to tell me such ideas as 'The wind blows across a deaf ear.' You have lost your sense of balance," Daddy told her bluntly. "You are shameless. Your skin is yellow. Your features are forever Chinese. We are content with our proven ways. Do not try to force foreign ideas into my home. Go. You will one day tell us sorrowfully that you have been mistaken."

After that there was no further discussion of the matter. Jade Snow came and went without any questions being asked. In spite of her parents' dark predictions, her new freedom in the choice of companions did not result in a rush of undesirables. As a matter of fact, the boys she met at school were more concerned with copying her lecture notes than with anything else.

As for Joe, he remained someone to walk with and talk with. On the evening of Jade Snow's seventeenth birthday he took her up Telegraph Hill and gave her as a remembrance a sparkling grown-up bracelet with a card which read: "Here's to your making Phi Beta Kappa." And there under the stars he gently tilted her face and gave her her first kiss.

Standing straight and awkward in her full-skirted red cotton dress, Jade Snow was caught by surprise and without words. She felt that something should stir and crash within her, in the way books and the movies described, but nothing did. Could it be that she wasn't in love with Joe, in spite of liking and admiring him? After all, he was twenty-three and probably too old for her anyway.

Still she had been kissed at seventeen, which was cause for rejoicing. Laughing happily, they continued their walk.

But while the open rebellion gave Jade Snow a measure of freedom she had not had before, and an outer show of assurance, she was deeply troubled within. It had been simple to have Daddy and Mama tell her what was right and wrong; it was not simple to decide for herself. No matter how critical she was of them, she could not discard all they stood for and accept as a substitute the philosophy of the foreigners. It took very little thought to discover that the foreign philosophy also was subject to criticism, and that for her there had to be a middle way.

In particular, she could not reject the fatalism that was at the core of all Chinese thinking and behavior, the belief that the broad pattern of an individual's life was ordained by fate although within that pattern he was capable of perfecting himself and accumulating a desirable store of good will. Should the individual not benefit by his good works, still the rewards would pass on to his children or his children's children. Epitomized by the proverbs: "I save your life, for your grandson might save mine," and "Heaven does not forget to follow the path a good man walks," this was a fundamental philosophy of Chinese life which Jade Snow found fully as acceptable as some of the so-called scientific reasoning expounded in the sociology class, where heredity and environment were assigned all the responsibility for personal success or failure.

There was good to be gained from both concepts if she could extract and retain her own personally applicable combination. She studied her neighbor in class, Stella Green, for clues. Stella had grown up reading Robert Louis Stevenson, learning to swim and play tennis, developing a taste for roast beef, mashed potatoes, sweets, aspirin tablets, and soda pop, and she looked upon her mother and father as friends. But it was very unlikely that she knew where her great-grandfather was born, or whether or not she was related to another strange Green she might chance to meet. Jade Snow had grown up reading Confucius, learning to embroider and cook rice, developing a taste for steamed fish and bean sprouts, tea, and herbs, and she thought of her parents as people to be obeyed. She not only knew where her ancestors were born but where they were buried, and how many chickens and roast pigs should be brought annually to their graves to feast their spirits. She knew all of the branches of the Wong family, the relation of each to the other, and understood why Daddy must help support the distant cousins in China who bore the sole responsibility of carrying on the family heritage by periodic visits to the burial grounds in Fragrant Mountains. She knew that one could purchase in a Chinese stationery store the printed record of her family tree relating their Wong line and other Wong lines back to the original Wong ancestors. In such a scheme the individual counted for little weighed against the family, and after sixteen years it was not easy to sever roots.

There were, alas, no books or advisers to guide Jade Snow in her search for balance between the pull from two cultures. If she chose neither to reject nor accept *in toto*, she must sift both and make her decisions alone. It would not be an easy search. But pride and determination, which Daddy had given her, prevented any thought of turning back.

By the end of her first year of junior college, she had been so impressed by her sociology course that she changed her major to the social studies. Four years of college no longer seemed interminable. The highlight of her second year was an English course which used literature as a basis for stimulating individual expression through theme writing. At this time Jade Snow still thought in Chinese, although she was acquiring an English vocabulary. In consequence she was slower than her classmates, but her training in keeping a diary gave her an advantage in analyzing and recording personal experiences. She discovered very soon that her grades were consistently higher when she wrote about Chinatown and the people she had known all her life. For the first time she realized the joy of expressing herself in the written word. It surprised her and also stimulated her. She learned that good writing should improve upon the kind of factual reporting she had done in her diaries; it should be created in a spirit of artistry. After this course, if Jade Snow had not mastered these principles, at least she could never again write without remembering them and trying her best to apply them.

Hand in hand with a growing awareness of herself and her personal world, there was developing in her an awareness of and a feeling for the larger world beyond the familiar pattern. At eighteen, when Jade Snow compared herself with a diary record of herself at sixteen, she could see many points of difference. She was now an extremely serious young person, with a whole set of worries which she donned with her clothes each morning. The two years had made her a little wiser in the ways of the world, a little more realistic, less of a dreamer, and she hoped more of a personality. In the interval she had put aside an earlier Americanized dream of a husband, a home, a garden, a dog, and children, and there had grown in its place a desire for more schooling in preparation for a career of service to those less fortunate than herself. Boys put her down as a snob and a bookworm. Well, let them. She was independent. She was also frank—much too frank for many people's liking. She had acquaintances, but no real friends who shared her interests. Even Joe had stopped seeing her, having left school to begin his career. Their friendship had given her many things, including confidence in herself as a person at a time when she needed it. It had left with her the habit of walking, and in moments of loneliness she found comfort and sometimes the answers to problems by wandering through odd parts of San Francisco, a city she loved with an ever increasing affection.

On this eighteenth birthday, instead of the birthday cake which Americans considered appropriate, Daddy brought home a fresh-killed chicken which Mama cooked their favorite way by plunging it into a covered pot of boiling water, moving it off the flame and letting it stand for one hour, turning it once. Brushed with oil and sprinkled with shredded fresh green onions, it retained its sweet flavor with all its juices, for it was barely cooked and never dry. It was the Wongs usual birthday dish. Naturally, the birthday of a daughter did not call for the honor due a parent. There was a birthday tea ritual calling for elaborate preparation when Mama's and Daddy's anniversaries came around. Still, to be a girl and eighteen was exciting.

The rest of the year rushed to an end. The years at junior college had been rewarding. Now several happy surprises climaxed them. First there was the satisfaction of election to membership in Alpha Gamma Sigma, an honorary state scholastic organization. On the advice of her English instructor, this precipitated an exchange of letters with an executive of the society concerning a possible scholarship to the university.

In the meantime, overtiredness and overwork brought on recurring back pains which confined Jade Snow to bed for several days. Against her will because she could not afford it, she had been driven to see a doctor, who told her to put a board under her mattress for back support, and gave her two prescriptions to be filled for relief of pain. But there was no money for medicine. She asked

Daddy and Mama, who said that they could not afford to pay for it either. So Jade Snow went miserably to bed to stay until the pain should end of its own accord.

She had been there two days when Older Brother entered casually and tossed a letter on her bed. It was from the scholarship chairman of Alpha Gamma Sigma, enclosing a check for fifty dollars. It was an award to her as the most outstanding woman student of the junior colleges in California. Jade Snow's emotions were mixed. What she had wanted and needed was a full scholarship. On the other hand, recognition was sweet—a proof that God had not forgotten her.

On the heels of this letter came another from her faculty adviser, inviting her as one of the ten top-ranking students to compete for position as commencement speaker. "If you care to try out," it concluded, "appear at Room 312 on April 11 at ten o'clock."

Should she or should she not? She had never made a speech in public, and the thought was panic. But had she a right to refuse? Might not this be an opportunity to answer effectively all the "Richards" of the world who screamed "Chinky, Chinky, Chinaman" at her and other Chinese? Might it not be further evidence to offer her family that her decision had not been wrong?

It seemed obvious that the right thing to do was to try, and equally obvious that she should talk about what was most familiar to her: the values which she as an American-Chinese had found in two years of junior college.

At the try-out, in a dry voice, she coaxed out her prepared thesis and fled, not knowing whether she had been good or bad, and not caring. She was glad just to be done. A few days later came formal notification that she would be the salutatorian at graduation. She was terrified as she envisioned the stage at the elegant San Francisco War Memorial Opera House, with its tremendous sparkling chandelier and overpowering tiers of seats. Now she wished that she could escape.

The reality was as frightening as the anticipation when on June 7, 1940, she stood before the graduation audience, listening to her own voice coming over the loudspeaker. All her family were there among the neat rows of faces before her. What did they think, hearing her say, "The Junior College has developed our initiative, fair play, and self-expression, and has given us tools for thinking and analyzing. But it seems to me that the most effective application that American-Chinese can make of their education would be in China, which needs all the Chinese talent she can muster."

Thus Jade Snow—shaped by her father's and mother's unceasing loyalty toward their mother country, impressed with China's needs by speakers who visited Chinatown, revolutionized by American ideas, fired with enthusiasm for social service—thought that she had quite independently arrived at the perfect solution for the future of all thinking and conscientious young Chinese, including herself. Did her audience agree with her conclusion?

At last it was over, the speeches and applause, the weeping and excited exchange of congratulations. According to plan, Jade Snow met her family on the steps of the Opera House, where they were joined shortly by her faculty adviser and her English professor. Conversation proceeded haltingly, as Daddy and Mama spoke only Chinese.

Mama took the initiative: "Thank your teachers for me for all the kind assistance they have given you. Ask them to excuse my not being able to speak English."

"Yes, indeed," Daddy added. "A fine teacher is very rare."

When Jade Snow had duly translated the remarks, she took advantage of a pause to inquire casually, "How was my speech?"

Mama was noncommittal. "I can't understand English."

"You talked too fast at first," was Older Brother's opinion.

Daddy was more encouraging: "It could be considered passable. For your first speech, that was about it."

The subject was closed. Daddy had spoken. But there was a surprise in store.

"Will you ask your teachers to join us for late supper at a Chinese restaurant?" Daddy suggested.

"What restaurant?" Jade Snow wanted to know, bewildered.

"Tao-Tao on Jackson Street. I have made reservations and ordered food."

Hardly able to credit her senses, Jade Snow trailed after the party. At first she was apprehensive, feeling it her responsibility to make the guests comfortable and at ease in the strange surroundings. But her fears were unfounded. The guests genuinely enjoyed the novel experience of breaking bread with the Wongs. It was a thoroughly happy and relaxed time for everyone as they sat feasting on delicious stuffed-melon soup, Peking duck, steamed thousand-layer buns, and tasty crisp greens.

The whole day had been remarkable, but most remarkable of all was the fact that for the first time since her break with her parents, Mama and Daddy had granted her a measure of recognition and acceptance. For the first time they had met on common ground with her American associates. It was a sign that they were at last tolerant of her effort to search for her own pattern of life.

16

MARRIAGE OLD AND NEW STYLE

EARLY ONE MORNING, FOURTH OLDER SISTER, STILL IN HER
bathrobe, burst into the room that Jade Snow and Jade Precious Stone shared. Before their surprised eyes she flashed a large
diamond ring and excitedly announced that she was engaged!

Later she told this news to Daddy, and made an appointment for
Prosperous State, her beloved, to come and call. Then Daddy returned the visit to his father, who was well established in the
Chinese community in San Francisco. According to Fourth Older
Sister, at one time he had been the mayor of Canton in China. Jade
Snow was not told all the details, but the negotiations carried on
directly between the two fathers resulted in a mutual agreement
as to the number of special bridal cakes and roast pigs that the
groom's family would supply. These small cakes and sections of
roast pork would be delivered in packages among family friends to
serve as announcement of the wedding.

When everything had been satisfactorily arranged, Prosperous State came to the Wong home with a five-pound box of chocolates from his family in order to "sweeten" relations with their future in-laws.

Of course, the arrangements did not exactly follow the old-fashioned Chinese marriage etiquette. From Mama and Daddy, Jade Snow had already learned that when they lived in China, a young woman would not be personally courted by her future husband. Marriage was a family affair, arranged by a matchmaker between parents of both families. The eligible young girl was inspected by the matchmaker, who might or might not be accompanied by the boy's parents. There were such considerations as the size of her feet, and whether or not her long, hanging braids of silky hair swayed from side to side when she walked. By bargaining, the matchmaker determined such essential details as the size of the trousseau, the amount of jewelry, the number of wedding announcement cakes, the quantity of roast pig, and the sum of "good luck" money that the groom's family was willing to give the bride's parents to repay them for taking away the daughter whom they had raised. The Chinese considered it much less embarrassing to have the matchmaker or middleman reconcile differences, in marriage plans as well as in other business negotiations.

In old China, the wedding date for a Chinese wedding was decided by a professional master of necromancy and astrology, so that the nuptial activities would harmonize with spiritual forces and heavenly constellations.

Besides this general pattern of approach to a Chinese marriage, numerous other fine points must be observed, the variations depending largely on local customs. In the village of Jade Snow's parents, the bride always hid in her room and wailed aloud for days to show the public her grief at leaving her parental home. Afterward, while relatives and friends from near and far gathered to make merry and feast for days, the bride, grieving, silent, and later veiled, played a role characterized by passivity and delicacy.

The weddings of American-Chinese young women followed modifications of this pattern. Although Daddy had sometimes acted as matchmaker for young people who were too shy or too proper to find their own mates, he had never been able to arrange a marriage for any of his own quite independent children. Jade Snow's other older sisters as well as Fourth Older Sister had met their husbands without Daddy's or a matchmaker's help.

Jade Snow was just now getting better acquainted with her Fourth Older Sister, since they had lived apart so much of their lives. In living with Oldest Sister, Fourth Older Sister had had more freedom in social activities than Daddy would have allowed her. She also differed from her younger sister in her love of fun and parties; she delighted in colorful clothes which set off her neat figure, and now she was perpetually bubbling over with happiness. Jade Snow looked upon this older sister with awestruck eyes. She was the center of the largest wedding yet held in the Wong family. For one thing, she planned an American church wedding at the Chinese Methodist chapel. The family was persuaded to make great preparations, including engraved invitations American-style, custom-made bridesmaids' gowns and white bridal attire, and all the excitement and ceremonies of a traditional American church ritual. In furious activity, the Wongs bustled around, rehearsed their roles, and on the appointed day appeared before the public gathering with the bride in white satin, the bridesmaids in blue and pink lace with matching flower coronets, and Daddy in a rented tuxedo! With carefully measured steps the bridal party proceeded to the altar to the strains of the *Lohengrin* wedding march. While cameras flashed busily, crowds of relatives and friends witnessed Fourth Older Sister's marriage to Prosperous State in a Protestant ceremony, and sent the bride off in a limousine amid a shower of rice.

But the wedding celebration was by no means over.

Jade Snow, the maid of honor, and Jade Precious Stone, bridesmaid, were driven across San Francisco Bay bridge to Fourth Older Sister's future home with her in-laws in Berkeley. As attendants of the bride, the younger sisters were allowed to peer into her new life, but Daddy and Mama and the rest of the family did not enjoy this privilege. In fact, after the wedding day, the bride was not permitted to see her family again for three days, when she might return home for a short visit. Fourth Older Sister was no longer a Wong daughter; she was a member of Prosperous State Lee's family. At her new home, the bride changed from her American wedding dress and veil to a modern ankle-length Chinese wedding gown of apple-green satin, and a knee-length, front-buttoned black satin coat, all handmade and hand-bound, embroidered with rainbow-colored blossoms, birds, and butterflies. Prosperous State still wore his American bridegroom attire, and with his Chinese-dressed bride knelt at his father's and mother's feet in their living room. The young couple had poured ceremonial tea, and now with bowed heads they offered it to the seated parents. Before witnesses, it was a gesture of deference and a promise of filial submission. In return, the new mother-in-law rewarded Fourth Older Sister with some handsome gold and jade jewelry and some money wrapped in red paper as a good-luck start toward their nest egg.

Jade Snow, silently watching her sister's bowed back, reacted mentally against the kneeling. She remembered Daddy's teaching that she was never to kneel before anyone but God. What a novel discovery! There were other Chinese more old-fashioned than Daddy in their observance of Chinese traditions! What if someday her own in-laws were to ask her to kneel? She must think about this new problem.

After the tea ceremony, they witnessed the cutting of a decidedly American, many-tiered, white-frosted wedding cake. "They" included all of Prosperous State's family and close friends, who were enjoying everything immensely. They, as part of the merrymaking, had also organized a few traditional Chinese stunts to tease the bride, while the bride according to convention remained demure and apprehensively docile. Between the sheets of the bridal bed they were now putting peanuts, oranges, Chinese dates, and lichee nuts. These were all fruits or seeds, symbolic of new life, and introduced the theme of fertility. But what an untidy sight it made for the new bride!

After everyone had had his share of giggles at the bride's expense, the guests relaxed for a while to look at the wedding presents, which included such modern American household conveniences as electric toasters, percolators, and waffle irons. Wedding presents were always sent to the groom. According to some customs, the bride would be on hand to witness the opening of their presents in the company of relatives and close friends. But she was not allowed to open them. After being passed around, the presents reached her last for examination and she was required to retie each one with red cord for good luck.

Then they strolled through the garden in the pleasant afternoon sun, while Prosperous State took kodachrome movies of the colorfully dressed women. Now he was "Older Brother Prosperous State" to Jade Snow, and like Older Sister, she addressed his parents as "Mother-in-law" and "Father-in-law."

By six o'clock, it was time to return to San Francisco for the evening's festivities. The wedding banquet was held on the top floor of Chinatown's famous oldest restaurant, which was architecturally patterned after the tea houses in China. The stairway spiraled up three stories and ended abruptly in a lobby. Here on this evening a Chinese orchestra was seated comfortably. Every time a guest arrived, the music was punctuated by huge brass cymbals which clanged to announce him. From this lobby, two large halls branched off, one on either side. The larger one to the right was reserved for men, while one to the left and back was for the women and children. The bridal party and their immediate families, irrespective of sex, banqueted in the men's dining hall.

As the guests arrived, someone checked off their names on a long red master list. Invitations to this occasion, which were separate from the wedding invitations, had been engraved in gold on red cards and delivered by messenger. The guest responded first by sending the wedding gift. If he were head of a household, he was entitled to bring his entire family to the banquet after he sent his gift. He sent a more handsome gift if he had a large family to bring. After his gift was received, the groom's family sent him another gold engraved red card, with one large simple square character of acceptance, "Thanks." The Chinese bride never had to write thank-you notes.

The bride in her Chinese costume stood on exhibition near the lobby, and from a tray of filled cups she offered tea to arriving guests. It was only a gesture, as the guest seldom drank the tea. If he or she were married, however, he responded to this gesture by leaving on the tea tray some good-luck money wrapped in red paper. If he were single, leaving good-luck money was not obligatory.

Approximately three hundred and fifty guests were invited for six o'clock. But no Chinese banquet was expected to begin on time or even within an hour of the given time. This evening it was past nine-thirty before the food appeared on the table. Some of Older

Sister's American friends who had come on time without knowing the Chinese custom were almost starved. But the Chinese guests had eaten a light snack at home. During the period of waiting, friends chatted, as many of them met only on these festive occasions, children played tag, and the guests generally conducted themselves as Americans would after dinner. At the round tables set for ten, everyone sat on stools. Thus in a minimum space, a large number of people could be comfortably accommodated.

Shortly before the food was served there were speeches by an official representing the Chinese consulate and by other representatives from various civic organizations and family associations to which the father-in-law belonged. All expressed about the same sentiments in different words and dialects, such as: Jade Ornament and Prosperous State were wonderfully matched. . . . The speaker was happy to be included in Mr. Lee's hospitality. . . . He hoped that in another year they would all be together again to celebrate Mr. Lee's first grandchild. . . . This particular party might seem a little out of tempo with the general mourning which all patriotic Chinese then shared over China's conflict with Japan, but let it be known that to justify this extravagance during China's hour of need, Mr. Lee was making a most generous donation to the funds for China war relief.

After these speeches, the food began to arrive in quantities. There was much too much to eat, including mushrooms from China, uncountable plump ducks, delicate sea-food soups, whole squabs and chickens cooked in different styles, lobsters and prawns with vegetables in new disguises.

But the bride did not eat at her own banquet. In the first place, she was not expected to do so. In the second place, she was kept too busy. While the guests were dining, Mother-in-law, Jade Snow, and Jade Precious Stone accompanied Older Sister around to each table, carrying a tray containing more cups of tea. The guests again made a gesture of drinking the proffered tea, and again the married ones left red packets of good-luck money on the tray. The little party made the rounds in the men's dining room and then in the women's dining room. The male guests were dressed in ordinary American business suits, but the women were much more colorful, mostly in Chinese dress, and their children wore their gayest costumes, both Chinese and American. Pausing in the doorway, Jade Snow heard a din of conversation and laughter, and saw the room alive with beautiful sheens and vibrant colors. Velvets and damasks in reds, pinks, fuchsias, pale greens, royal blues; embroidered satins in blending shades—all were favorites with Chinese women. Moreover, the guests were glittering with Chinese gold jewelry set with precious opals and jades, or more modern designs with rubies and diamonds. The poorest Chinese woman might wear coarse cottons, but she always treasured some bit of real, precious, handwrought jewelry of twenty-four carat pure gold set with high quality gems.

After this round of tea offering and the collection of good-luck money, Older Sister changed into different dresses about every twenty minutes in order to show her extensive trousseau. So that none would have hurt feelings, she wore all the jewelry given to her as wedding presents. Consequently, both arms were covered with bracelets, and a chain around her neck was laden with rings. Her chest was covered with a shining array of brooches and pendants.

The bridegroom's duties were much fewer. With his brother, father, and an escort, carrying trays of whisky instead of tea, he went to each table and drank with the men. Prosperous State had wisely put apple cider in his own glass, for it was a known fact that many bridegrooms passed out cold on their wedding night after sipping whisky with the guests at more than a hundred tables.

Then the newly-united parents, Mama, Daddy, Father-in-law, Mother-in-law, went around to toast and thank each table of guests for honoring the occasion with their presence.

In less than an hour after the food was served, the guests finished their dinner and began to leave. The hosts stood at the head of the stairs, thanking the guests for coming, while the guests thanked the hosts in return. At a Chinese banquet, all the conversation took place before dinner, and after dinner everyone immediately put on his coat and hat, bade farewell, and departed.

Jade Snow, although keenly interested, did not really feel like a participant in the evening's festivities. She was more like a critical spectator. The guests enjoyed themselves, but appeared to take more interest in the food than in the bride. They were entitled to attend the banquet as long as their wedding present had been sent to the bridegroom and accepted by his family. But hardly anyone talked to the bride; they all talked to the parents. They congratulated the Lees on their newly acquired daughter-in-law, but they did not wish the bride happiness. The bride was merely a sort of decorative, noneating, nondrinking, nonspeaking accessory to the wedding celebration.

As the Wongs walked home after it was over, Jade Snow expressed her wonder to Mama and Daddy, and recounted some of the events which had occurred at Older Sister's new home earlier that afternoon, events which puzzled and troubled her.

Daddy replied, "Chinese legendary symbolism has been passed on by word of mouth from generation to generation until the origins and true meanings have become lost. Superstition combined with economic reasons account for many of the formalities you witnessed today, but because most Chinese do not analyze or question symbols, they are blind followers of tradition. Only those who have become Christians have the courage to question forms of action."

While Jade Snow tried to digest this philosophical explanation, Mama added, "If you think from what you have seen today that the bride is not recognized sufficiently by Chinese custom and is excessively teased, you should know how she is treated in China. Teasing the bride does not stop with putting things in her marriage bed. She is shut up in her bedroom with the chaperone who has been hired to accompany her, and then long strings of bursting firecrackers are thrown into her room to jump and explode uncontrolled. I have seen the chaperone burned so severely in trying to protect the bride that she had to be carried away on a stretcher!"

Mystified, her daughter asked, "But why do they abuse the bride so?"

Mama answered, "As your father explained to you, they do not interpret it according to our ideas. The loud noise is supposed to scare away the evil spirits. Therefore firecrackers are enthusiastically thrown into the bridal room to drive all evil from the new couple's life, not to abuse the bride. What new wife would want to start her marriage without being sure that the evil spirits were frightened away?

"Of course, there is probably another practical purpose also. It is to prepare the bride for her new role of submission. She has married to serve her mother-in-law first and then her husband. Her personality will be completely submerged. Husband and wife are strictly decorous and formal in public, always deferring to the parents or grandparents. There must be no intimate whispers or exchange of laughter, much less the holding of hands, beyond their bedroom door."

Daddy offered further explanation: "In our village, the bridegroom is accompanied by an older man who advises and escorts him. This friend must be a mature man of superior intellect and wisdom, a close friend whom the family chooses to honor by this request. He helps the young man with his toilet, including the arrangement of his long queue, and all the while he quietly advises the bridegroom on his married responsibilities. Because the bride does not eat in public, this friend sees to it that when the couple retire to their room after the festivities, a tray of food and drink is brought in to them. The bridal bed is usually a huge, handsome piece of furniture, with posters and an all-enveloping drop curtain. The new husband and wife retreat behind their curtain in privacy after being blessed by the adviser friend. There the husband is finally alone with his bride to become acquainted with her, and he affectionately feeds her from their own special tray."

Mama added a final word: "However much you may complain about our Chinese 'blind marriage' tradition, just remember that we never hear of divorces in China, and that our Chinese family affairs have been conducted in an orderly fashion for centuries, increasing rather than diminishing the family strength. Women are brought up knowing what to expect, and knowing that their marriage to a suitable man will be assured by their parents. They take a long, patient view of life, and if they are uncomfortable as brides, they know that they will one day be mothers of sons, and one day be mothers-in-law. Then they will be able to sit back in comfort to enjoy the position they have earned which no one can deny them."

17

AN UNEXPECTED OFFER—AND A DECISION

By the end of June, Jade Snow's entire fortune stood at $167.68. A year ago she had opened her first savings account with a deposit of three dollars. After paying for her junior college education, she had by her labors for the Simpsons saved exactly $117.50. This sum was swelled by the $50 scholarship prize and eighteen cents of bank interest. After graduation, Jade Snow took stock of her resources, and pondered the chances of realizing her dream and completing her college education at the state university now that she had been denied a scholarship.

She estimated that she could manage to keep abreast of daily expenses by working in the campus town of Berkeley for room and board and a small salary. Her savings and another summer's full-time job would just pay registration and other fees and buy essential books. So, with mixed feelings of happy fulfillment and apprehension, she had the transcript of her junior college record sent to the state university, together with her application. During that summer, she worked only at the regular Simpson job so that she would have time to make new clothes for herself, for she was determined to be appropriately outfitted for those hoped-for dates and the social whirl which had been woven into the fabric of her college dreams.

Meanwhile her interests and aspirations had become the concern of the Simpsons, who after two years wholly accepted her as part of their family household. Mrs. Simpson was more articulate in expressing encouragement than Mama ever was, and she gave more attention to what was happening within Jade Snow. It was the Simpsons' interest in her college education which prevented her from attending the university after all.

One day Miss Martha, Mrs. Simpson's daughter, said to Jade Snow: "My friend, Peggy Becker, who met you here one evening is a student at Mills College in Oakland, and she knows its president, Dr. Reinhardt, quite well. Peggy remembered her talk with you and told the president about your longing for a college education. Dr. Reinhardt will help you if you are interested in going to Mills because she has had a lifelong interest in the Oriental people."

Mills? Jade Snow had read about Mills College in the social page of the newspapers, and had seen pictures of pretty young girls, pert in riding habits, or lovely in dreamy dance dresses; but she had certainly never thought of this fashionable private women's college in connection with herself. Now she didn't need to think long before deciding against an audience with its president. It would be a waste of time, because she didn't want to go to an exclusive school to acquire American social graces. Of what use would such training be for her, living in a Chinese community? She had her mind set only on intellectual development.

But Mrs. Simpson did not abandon the subject so easily. "Dr. Reinhardt is accepted as a brilliant woman," she told Jade Snow earnestly. "When a person of her reputation has expressed a willingness to interview you, you should at least return the courtesy by going. Besides, you may not again have the privilege of making such an acquaintance."

Reluctantly, Jade Snow wrote for an appointment. When she

told Daddy that she was to see the president of Mills College, he surprised her by saying that Oldest Sister had worked her way through that college for a degree when Jade Snow was a mere baby. He therefore instructed Jade Snow to take a gift of tea as a token of his appreciation, and to tell Dr. Reinhardt that after some fifteen years he still remembered her with gratitude.

One June day Jade Snow reached the Mills campus and wandered through its entrance, Richards Gate, for the first time. The peaceful grounds were deserted during this vacation period. The planting didn't have the formal, orderly look which she had noted at the university, nor were the buildings as impressive, but this informality combined friendly charm with dignity and grace.

At the president's office, Jade Snow waited briefly before a handsomely carved desk until an erect and commanding figure sailed in, a lady of positive action and tone who introduced herself as "Mrs. Reinhardt."

"From what I hear, you are an unusually determined young lady," Dr. Reinhardt began. "Tell me about yourself."

Jade Snow searched for words in correct English to summarize some of the desires dearest to her heart. She also tried to say politely that Mills was not the right college for her. But Dr. Reinhardt was only concerned with how Jade Snow could finance her way through Mills. Her questions were asked with kindness, and she made Jade Snow feel that for the moment hers was the most important problem in the world. Jade Snow was fascinated, for she had never heard words uttered with such assurance, nor seen them punctuated with such extraordinarily spirited motions. Dr. Reinhardt was the most expressively alive person Jade Snow had ever met, exuberant in her love of humanity.

However, when Jade Snow learned of the tuition fee and the cost of room and board, she was sure that she could not afford to enroll at Mills. Dr. Reinhardt refused to believe that money could be a final obstacle. After a long interview with a searching discussion of finances she declared, "I am going to introduce you to another person who can explain the details of students' self-help plans. She is the dean of undergraduate students, who knows all about entrance qualifications, scholarships, and other gifts."

The dean was as sincerely interested as the president. She asked Jade Snow about her major interests and her grades.

"What work have you done to help finance yourself?" she also wanted to know.

Jade Snow answered simply, "Housework." The dean looked surprised. Taking advantage of the moment's pause, Jade Snow asked a question herself: "Is Mills a better school than the university?" This surprised the dean even more.

She chose her reply carefully. "Well, Mills is a much smaller institution than the university, and can concentrate on educating you into a well-integrated individual. The classes here are small, giving you the opportunity to know your instructors and for them to know you. We also balance our school work with many educational and social extracurricular activities. Because of your interest in preparing for social service work, I should think you would find excellent development here. I can arrange to have you meet a faculty member from our school of social studies."

Dr. Reinhardt interrupted, "Don't you think that we can get this girl a room grant, and perhaps other help to cover her tuition? Then if she works thirty hours a week waiting on residence hall tables in exchange for her board, she might be able to manage all her expenses." As the dean offered no objection, she concluded: "There you are. We should like very much to welcome you to the Mills student body next semester." And the president withdrew.

But Jade Snow still had to make her own decision. At home that evening, she decided to break the silence she had maintained concerning her plans for further schooling. She found courage to do so because of Daddy's high opinion of Dr. Reinhardt. So with the pretext of reporting on his gift she sought him at his desk where he was figuring the weekly payroll on the abacus.

"Daddy, I delivered your gift today, and when you have some leisure I should like to tell you what Dr. Reinhardt said."

Daddy raised his head from his thick, blue, cotton-covered, red-bound Chinese ledgers and replied, "I never have any leisure, but I shall stop and hear what you have to report." He arose, turned off his old-fashioned green-shaded desk light, and moved toward the room which was the scene of all family conferences—the dining room.

After he had settled himself in his own chair, Jade Snow told him briefly of the afternoon's interview. As in any conversation with Daddy, it was not pertinent to express a personal opinion; only the facts were required. So she did not say that the campus was delightful, the personnel was friendly, or that the President and Dean were sincere in their interest. She merely reported what had been said, and by whom.

Daddy listened with no expression of disapproval, and Jade Snow rejoiced quietly at the difference between this conversation and the stormy discussion of two years ago in this very room! However, before Daddy gave his opinion, he said, "I want your mother to hear this too."

Obediently, Jade Snow went downstairs to fetch Mama from her seaming machine. As usual, Mama went right on working as her daughter approached. "Daddy desires you to come to the dining room."

Without question or comment, Mama finished her seam, turned off her light, and went upstairs, with Jade Snow trailing along behind. When they entered the dining room Daddy explained, "Jade Snow tells me that she has a possibility of entering Mills College instead of the state university. The administration is willing to secure sufficient financial aid for the major costs of tuition and room. Jade Snow can wait on tables for board, but she must still have some money for fees, books, and personal expenses. She thinks that what she has saved will help defray these expenses in the coming academic year, and she may be able to earn enough next summer for the following year. But should her earnings prove insufficient, she may ask us to help meet the deficit."

Mama, to whom Mills was just another college, and to whom money was a matter of major concern, replied promptly without any expression of emotion, "The costs of this education are so great that if in her senior year the aid she is promised for this year is not continued, it would be absolutely impossible for us to assist her. By comparison, the small tuition fees of the state university are not beyond our means if she were unable to pay them. Besides, if she is satisfied to go to the university, she could finance her way even without our money."

Clearly Mama preferred to have one less financial problem, and was reluctant to commit herself to another possible, and to her unnecessary, expense. Again it was application of the principle Jade Snow had learned when they shopped for a new coat—to buy within their means without dipping into savings. While in one respect she was discouraged but not surprised by the lack of co-operation, she was nevertheless overcome with pleasure at this indirect hint of Mama's willingness to help if aid were absolutely necessary and of reasonable proportions.

Daddy—he and Mama always agreed with each other before their children—turned to Jade Snow. "You have heard what your mother said. Make your decision as you see best."

The freedom to make up her own mind, thus unceremoniously granted, was quite bewildering. Mama went back to her work and Daddy to his desk. The subject was not reopened in the following days while Jade Snow privately debated the best course to take.

One fact was clear: she could not be sure that she could complete two years at Mills by her own efforts, even with the promised gifts. Besides, it did not seem right to depend on others' generosity. It would be more honest to work without assistance for a lesser prize at the university, and so buy within her budget as Mama had always taught. On these grounds she wrote to decline the college offer.

The letter mailed, Jade Snow gave a sigh for what might have been and dismissed Mills from her mind. In due time, she again turned her thoughts to becoming a coed at the university.

However, another letter came from Mills College. This was from the dean of undergraduate students, who offered an alternative plan of a four-hundred-dollar scholarship to cover most of the tuition, and a position in the dean's household which would give room and board in return for daily work. The plan did away with the need of a subsidy from strangers and reopened the subject of Mills. Admitting its attraction, Jade Snow again figured the dollars and cents, but found the problem still unsolved. Where would she get the extra fifty dollars to make up the total tuition?

Again she wrote, regretting that she could not say "Yes." During these summer months she was living alone at the Simpson home while the family was vacationing, so she had no opportunity to consult with anyone. A second time she erased Mills from her mind.

But another letter came from the dean offering a full tuition scholarship, with work as before at the dean's house and a supplementary clerical job at her office. This letter changed the situation from the impossible to the possible. Jade Snow would have to provide only about fifty dollars for miscellaneous fees.

Now that Mills was as financially practical as the university, she must consider whether a private women's college would give her more or less than a large coeducational institution. So she wrote her junior college sociology teacher to ask his opinion. For days she received no reply. Knowing that she must not delay longer in answering the dean, still in a paralysis of indecision, she sought Joe.

On the telephone, he sounded uninvitingly cold. "What do you want?"

"Oh, Joe, I have to talk to you! All I ask is one evening. I won't be long, and I don't want to be a pest. But you know more than anyone else how long I have wanted to go to the university. Now suddenly there is another alternative and I want your advice."

There was a moment of silence. Jade Snow did not suffer now as she would have two years ago, but she anxiously hoped for an affirmative answer.

A gruff and ungracious "O.K." was the response.

Relieved, Jade Snow proposed, "I can meet you for a walk, or I am sure the Simpsons wouldn't mind your coming up to see me here." She gave him the address, and he replied, "I can come tonight."

When he arrived, Jade Snow didn't ask what he had been doing, or why she hadn't seen anything of him for over a year and a half. Joe acted stiffly impersonal, as she gave him an objective recital of the whole Mills incident.

It was not difficult for him to decide. He was not concerned with whether or not Mills would provide a good foundation for a social service major. In his direct, practical way, he analyzed quickly.

"I don't know the relative academic merits of the two schools, but I do know that for you Mills would be a distinguished education as compared to one at the university. If you want to shine in your family, Mills will polish you to a more brilliant light. Even if you don't learn any more nor as much, you are being offered an expensive package at no more cost than an inexpensive one, just because the people running the place seem to think enough of you to do that."

Jade Snow countered, "But I don't know that an expensive package is the one most suited to me."

Joe threw up his hands in disgust, "Do I have to draw pictures to make you understand? Must an expensive package mean that it is no good? After all, you can still transfer for your senior year if you find your junior year at Mills not up to your standards, or if you decide that you would rather receive your sheepskin from the university.

That sounded reasonable. What would she lose by trying Mills for a year? It would be interesting to attend a private women's college, though she might not be a wholehearted participant. She answered, "I guess you're right, Joe. You always seem to see another side. Thank you."

"O.K. Was that all that was on your mind?" Joe asked with finality, as he rose to leave.

How could she tell him all that was on her mind? Reservedly, she said, "Yes, Joe, that was all."

"Well, I have other things to do. Must be on my way." That was all. Jade Snow trailed him to the front door. There he turned with a sudden kind look on his face.

"Besides, I think it would be fine for you to go to a girls' school without any boys to distract you, either with their need to pick your brains, or to make you act silly over them." Then with a slight wave of his hand in salute, he added, "Good luck, kid; take care of yourself. Here's to your making Phi Beta Kappa yet!"

Jade Snow watched Joe go down the steps, and heard his footsteps die away; shutting the door, she leaned against it a long time, puzzling over what he had said.

In the next day's mail came at last a letter from her former sociology teacher, advising her to try Mills. The letter ended: "With your ability, you will probably sooner or later become fairly successful. But no matter how successful you may become never forget the fight you must make for racial equality. When an individual from a minority group personally succeeds, he too often turns his back on his own group."

Jade Snow was grateful for this expression of a teacher's confidence. This unexpected little note, like the Alpha Gamma Sigma award, the salutatorian honor, the interest of the Mills College faculty, and the response of Joe, was a flash relieving an otherwise quiet, steady, weary push alone into a dark unknown, and marked it as worth the pushing, after all. Paradoxically, when her family voiced doubts or objections, she always mustered supreme self-confidence both to defend herself and to forge ahead. But at other times, when nothing seemed to stand in her way, she cried out in loneliness, questioning why she should have embarked on such an endless quest for individual freedom.

Not one of her American-Chinese high school classmates was trying for a college degree; few even cared to complete two years of junior college. Whether their parents wanted them to attend college or objected to their attending did not matter; they felt no personal compulsion to do so.

For Jade Snow, there was something about having started a course of action which demanded its completion. What had she to lose in the next two years? She was now halfway to her goal, and the two remaining years of college promised to offer further satisfaction. So she wrote a final acceptance to the college of her choice.

18

"LEARNING CAN NEVER BE POOR OR EXHAUSTED"
—Chinese Proverb

JADE SNOW'S YEARS AT MILLS COLLEGE WERE INSEPARABLY COLORED by living at "Kapiolani," the dean's little brown-shingled home. This simple structure located on a hillside road wore a charming crown: a garden of gaily colored fuchsias, bamboo, camellias, azaleas, and species of geraniums and pelargoniums—all thriving in pots bordering the flat roof. At night, the mellow glow from a string of electrically lighted Japanese lanterns extended the tropical setting into evening enjoyment.

On one corner of this roof garden was a miniature penthouse room, surrounded by a ribbon of windows. These pleasant quarters gave Jade Snow her first complete privacy in studying and in personal living, and at last gave her inner peace.

The various rooms of the house downstairs were like the exterior, simple and without clutter. Jade Snow helped operate the house and manage the meals to enable the dean and herself to carry on their respective campus responsibilities and activities with maximum dispatch. Sometimes, she also helped attend to the house or dinner guests. But though these duties filled her days with busyness, she never felt too rushed and she never felt herself to be merely a servant. All who lived in that home, including a pair of cocker spaniels named Pupuli and Papaia, a black cat named Bessie, and Jade Snow, were recipients of the dean's kindness and consideration.

Unexpectedly, life shone with a new glow. Jade Snow returned home each day to a friend who was never too tired to think through a problem with her, who could explain the many new experiences peculiar to a residential women's college, and who shed a mature light on the art of living. With humor, honesty, and affection, Jade Snow was given guidance and comfort without judgment pronounced, and by daily example she was impressed with the marvel of inner spiritual strength and the meaning of gentleness.

Now, living became fun! The fun was partly in being able to participate in the home activities of one of the campus' central figures. At their house, there were teas for parents of students, apple and doughnut parties for seniors, breakfasts for residence-hall mothers, and a host of other unorganized, impromptu, but memorable little gatherings. Here Jade Snow met celebrated musicians, scholars, and speakers who visited the college.

Another kind of fun was initiated and encouraged by the dean, who was often away for dinner and worried that Jade Snow had to eat alone three or four nights a week.

"Why don't you invite some of your friends up here for dinner soon? You must have met some girls you like well enough to want to know them better," the dean said one evening as she was preparing to go out.

"I feel fine alone," Jade Snow replied truthfully, for she was enjoying the novel experience of opportunity for unhurried study.

The dean in her usual straightforward manner rejected this reason, "But it's not good for you to be alone as much as you are." Then, always tactful, she added, "Besides, I'd like to meet your friends, and I imagine they may enjoy coming up here."

Jade Snow agreed to invite some new acquaintances to dinner. New acquaintances were many because everyone said "Hello" to everyone else on the campus. She had also discovered immediately, and to her great surprise, that she was accepted as an equal wherever she went. There were no sororities here—only the five residence halls. There were class loyalties and hall loyalties, but no loyalty in which money figured as an asset. After all that she had heard about Mills being a rich girls' school, Jade Snow could not find who the rich girls were, for the student body dressed simply in sweaters, blouses, skirts, or wash dresses. It would have been the height of bad taste here either to ask, or for anyone to declare, who had money. Mills living was democratic living in the truest sense; the emphasis was entirely on how you used what you had within you.

Although Jade Snow could not participate in residence-hall living, she was invited to affiliate with a hall. She chose Mills Hall, a large, colonial structure still standing from the first Mills days of ninety years ago. This building housed over a hundred girls, and its kitchen staff was entirely Chinese, some of them descendants of the first Chinese kitchen help who worked for the founders of the college. In this hall, conveniently located between Kapiolani and the administration building and library, Jade Snow found her new friends.

There was Wan-Lien, a native of China, athletic, alert, direct, and intensely interested in chemistry. There was a granddaughter of Sun Yat-sen who had founded the Republic of China, sweet, friendly, and charmingly feminine. There was Betty Quon, a quiet, shy Chinese from Honolulu, a music major; Teruko, a Japanese girl from Tokyo, members of whose family were affiliated with the royalty of Japan; and Harriet, an American girl from the state of Washington who mingled with them as much as with her Caucasian friends. For all of these girls, Mills was a novel experience. All were away from home for the first time; all were transfer or new students who were not returning to an already established circle of friendships.

One Sunday noon after chapel service Jade Snow dropped into Mills Hall and made her way to Harriet's room, which seemed to be a congregation center. As usual, Teruko was there already. These two became Jade Snow's best friends.

Hesitantly Jade Snow broached the subject. "Harriet, the dean thinks I am alone too much. She would like to meet some of my friends, and suggested that I invite you to the house. Do you think that you can stand some of my cooking for a change? That is, can you and Teruko come up for some simple food next Tuesday?"

Loud outcries of delight and surprise greeted this proposal.

"Would we like your cooking!" declared Harriet. "If you only knew how tired we get of hall food. Sometimes, just to get a change, we run down to the corner drugstore for hamburgers."

Teruko did not hesitate. "Could we have Chinese food? I have been so homesick for Oriental food."

Now Jade Snow was surprised, "Why, I hadn't planned Chinese food. I've never cooked a Chinese dinner away from home before, but if you're willing to share what I can find, I'll try something."

Both girls were suddenly apprehensive about invading the dean's home.

"I wouldn't know how to behave," Teruko said dubiously.

"We'll have to stand the dean's inspection, won't we?" asked Harriet.

Jade Snow reassured them, "Don't worry; this was her idea anyway. Besides, the dean isn't really what you think a 'deanish' person should be."

As Jade Snow left, she ran into Wan-Lien in the narrow, high-ceilinged hall. Impulsively she began, "Harriet and Teruko are coming up to the house for a Chinese dinner next week. Would you care to join us for some simple rice?"

Wan Lien exploded enthusiastically in their common Cantonese tongue, "I haven't had Chinese home cooking since I came to America. I would do anything you say to be worthy of a Chinese dinner. Thank you, really thank you. You certainly have a good heart!"

Within half an hour, her comrades had raised Jade Snow high in their estimation. To be worthy of this new trust, Jade Snow racked her brains to decide what dishes she could cook without a Chinese larder.

After class on Tuesday, she came back from the neighborhood

grocery store and meat market with the following items: a pound and a half of ripe tomatoes, a pound of yellow onions, a bunch of green onions, a large green pepper, a head of celery, a dozen eggs, a bottle of dark soy sauce which had been bottled for American consumption, a half-pound slice of raw ham, a pound of flank steak, and a box of small-sized long-grain white rice. The rice and soy sauce were chosen after weighty misgivings, but they had to do. The other items were for a minimum menu; even for an ordinary dinner, Chinese cooking involved small quantities of several different meats and vegetables.

In the Kapiolani kitchen, Jade Snow ransacked the cabinets for numerous small bowls to hold the chopped vegetables, a proper pot with tight-fitting lid in which to cook the rice, a sturdy, ample chopping board, and a sharp, strong knife. These, together with a large, heavy frying pan, and a pair of chopsticks—which she did not have—were the minimum equipment for cooking. At home, she had taken the existence of these utensils for granted.

Besides the rice, she was planning only two dishes—egg foo young and tomato-beef. She started her preparations. Chinese dishes were always assembled from similar-sized particles. Vegetables were definitely diced, or shredded, or in chunks, depending on the nature of the meat with which they would be keeping company. They were chosen to give balanced crisp and soft textures and contrasting colors to a dish.

For the egg foo young, everything was shredded for quick cooking. So two onions were sliced thin, and a cup of celery slivered on a bias. The ham was cut into long shreds about one-eighth inch thick. Proceeding with the precooking, Jade Snow fried the onions slightly in the frying pan, and added the ham until both were barely cooked through. Lifting out this mixture, she put in the celery with a little water and covered it until that was barely cooked through, but still crisp. Two or three minutes only were given each vegetable. Then these three ingredients were beaten up with enough eggs—about six—to bind them together. A little soy sauce and chopped green onions were added for flavor and color, and the dish was ready for final cooking later on. Any firm meat could have been used in place of the ham—shredded or leftover chicken, roast pork, shrimp, or crab, but never beef, which would have been too juicy.

A few cooked peas or bean sprouts could have been added to or substituted for the celery and onions. There were no specific proportions to Chinese cooking; just imagination according to personal preference, common sense, and knowledge of basic principles were necessary.

The tomato-beef followed a somewhat different method of preparation. She sliced, marinated, and quickly browned the beef with garlic and oil over very high flames as she had seen Mama do. Since the tomatoes had to be cut in quarters or eighths to preserve their identity after cooking, the large yellow onion and green pepper were also cut in chunks to go with the tomatoes properly. When an hour had passed, there was an array of colorfully filled bowls set out on the kitchen table: the yellow egg mixture dotted with pink and green, a bowl of red tomatoes, one of onions, another of green pepper, and one of browned beef. This freshly cut and precooked food sent delicate and exotic aromas through the house.

In addition, there were two bowls of gravy mixes. One, a basic brown sauce, was made with a tablespoon each of soy sauce and cornstarch mixed with a cup of water. The other was the basic sweet-and-sour sauce for the tomato-beef dish. To make this sauce, a little more cornstarch was used for a thicker consistency. For a cup or so of sauce, two spoonfuls of vinegar and four rounded tablespoons of brown sugar were added. Sometimes more sugar or more vinegar was used—the proportions depending on the dish. Since the tomatoes were likely to be sour, Jade Snow was using more sugar and less vinegar than she would use for spareribs, sweet and sour.

The dean popped into the kitchen to inspect the activities, sniffed the odors, and declared, "I wish I were staying for dinner. Promise me that you'll cook me a Chinese dinner too, sometime. Have a nice evening—build a fire and make yourselves at home."

Soon a chatter of voices announced the coming of the guests, who trooped through the back door, and declared their eagerness to help. While they set the table in the living room, Jade Snow proceeded with the final cooking. As only one frying pan was available, she first fried the egg foo young gently in patties like pancakes, using just enough peanut oil to keep them from sticking, and as they became browned she set them in the warm oven and covered them.

She then started the tomato-beef dish by browning the onion wedges. She added tomatoes and green peppers, and let the mixture come to a boil for a couple of minutes to cook the tomatoes. Pouring on the sweet and sour sauce, she waited until it had turned clear. Then the flame was turned off, and the beef was added last. She dished up the tomato-beef, and used the pan to cook the other brown soy gravy to pour over the egg foo young.

Such a simple dinner these dishes made, but how the girls appreciated it. They enjoyed the fire, the candlelight, and the gaiety and confidences, as only four college girls with a sense of fellowship can do during a free evening.

The girls in their turn invited Jade Snow to dine at their hall, and from these beginnings there sprang a pleasant interchange of visits between Jade Snow at Kapiolani and her friends at Mills Hall. True, she couldn't list among her college experiences many of the usual student activities; but it was a unique pleasure, whenever she could sandwich time between work and studies, or when she returned to the campus with Chinese groceries from San Francisco, to invite someone to tea or dinner. Jade Snow found that the girls were perpetually curious about her Chinese background and Chinese ideologies, and for the first time she began to formulate in her mind the constructive and delightful aspects of the Chinese culture to present to non-Chinese.

It was this sense of serene and broadened living that enabled Jade Snow to reach out for the full measure of value from her academic studies. The average number in her classes was fifteen, and in many special economics and sociology courses, which now were her major, there were only four or five students. The intimacy of these classes was a complete departure from Jade Snow's earlier experiences.

One class of half-a-dozen students studying the history of the Orient was taught by a serious scholar who believed that his class could learn the early history of China best by studying the development of her art, which documented foreign and religious influences. Since the instructor wrote and spoke Chinese, it was most enjoyable to Jade Snow to learn about her ancestral culture with the aid of two languages for an exchange of ideas.

What was disturbing in the first weeks at Mills was that her lifelong perfected system of learning failed her. At the end of several weeks, she had only a handful of lecture notes. The instructor of the labor course, a brilliant and direct man as interested in the practical workings of theory as in the theory itself, taught by encouraging questions. But at the end of every never-dull class period, Jade Snow did not have one lecture note.

How was she going to study without notes? Accustomed to specific assignments in orderly fashion, and habitually thorough, she became concerned by the vagueness of these subjects which defeated her ability to memorize—an ability carefully perfected by her Chinese studies and which had heretofore always worked.

Impressed by the informality and approachability of her professors, she gathered her courage to speak to her labor instructor. "I have a problem in not being able to take any lecture notes from you. At junior college, we were given definite outlines to follow and study for examinations."

Her instructor seemed amused. "Why do you think that you learn only from lecture notes?"

Jade Snow had no answer to this unexpected question.

He continued, "Here we want to know each one individually. Instead of reading a set of prepared notes, I study my students' minds and ideas. By the conversational method, I try to develop your minds, not give you sets of facts. Don't you know that you can always go to the library to look up facts?"

Jade Snow could not immediately grasp this new concept of individual training. She had never thought of the purpose of academic training as being anything else than that of disseminating superior information.

All she could say in defense was, "But I learned a lot from junior college."

The instructor came back neatly, "Sure, you learned a lot. But now I am trying to teach you to think!"

Jade Snow, at a complete loss, mumbled a "Thank you" and trailed off in a state of mental indigestion.

The first midterm gave ample exercise in how to think. Jade Snow arrived at class in a fog of memorized dates, names, and places, and found that one essay question comprised the entire midterm. It was: "You are (choose any one) a Palestinian potter; an Anatolian farmer; an Athenian shoemaker; a Carthaginian clerk; a

Roman cook; a West-Saxon weaver; an Italian goldsmith. You are transferred, buckrogerswise, to Oakland in 1940, and try to get a job in your trade. What problems do you face?"

A buzz of excitement went around the astounded class. Incredulous and confused, Jade Snow reread the question and floundered miserably to find a passably imaginative answer. After spending half an hour figuring what trade to select, she chose the Palestinian potter simply because it was the first one listed, but she didn't know a thing about pottery, let alone Palestinian pottery. In the ensuing hour, her heretofore unshaken faith in the effectiveness of the Chinese study method collapsed completely.

Gradually, through successive examinations and successive classroom discussions, she learned the true meaning of her instructor's remarks, and at the end of a year's study she found that from slow beginnings she was learning to analyze and to evaluate what she heard and read, and to express more readily in English what she thought. She found that her curious mind was being disciplined to work quickly and to find relationships between problems.

She was being led gradually to reverse her lifelong practice, enforced by her parents, of keeping to herself what she thought. Her mind sprang from its tightly bound concern with facts and the Chinese absolute order of things, to concern with the reasons behind the facts, their interpretations, and the imminence of continuous change.

This release did not mean that her imagination soared to new heights on unfurled wings, but it did cause her to search for new answers, to fail painfully before classmates, to grope inwardly for the right expression and find herself and try again—because sometimes in her eagerness with this new-found freedom she said only the wrong thing.

The labor-problems course included a number of field trips. First, the class attended some real union meetings. Next, the instructor—learning that Jade Snow's father owned a small garment factory—interrupted a conversation about piecework factories and workers to ask her one day:

"Do you think that our class might visit your father's factory?"

Jade Snow was startled. "I don't know."

"If you will arrange for a visit to your father's factory," he continued, "I'll arrange for a visit to a large factory manufacturing a famous national brand of overalls and we can compare notes on the two."

"I'll ask my father," Jade Snow promised.

That evening she telephoned Daddy. Not wasting words on pleasantries, she began, "Daddy, one of my instructors would like our class to visit our factory as a field-trip project."

Daddy was disconcerting. "What is there remarkable to see in my factory?"

Jade Snow explained, "The teacher says that he wishes to contrast your factory with a large one. Most of the class members have never seen garment manufacturing in progress."

Daddy asked, "What kind of a person is your teacher?"

"Why, it's hard to say exactly. . . . He is honest and has humility. . . ." and then she was inspired by remembering some biographical facts, "His father was a missionary in China, where he was born. He is, moreover, a Ph.D. in Religion and a Methodist."

In response came a favorable and thoughtful "Is that so?" Then, "Be sure to give me adequate notice before you come, so that the floor will be newly swept."

"Good, Daddy." Chinese parents and children seldom thanked each other in so many words.

At the arranged time, the class toured Daddy's factory, while Jade Snow explained the different processes, familiar to her since childhood. All the while, the Chinese women workers stared at the young, healthy Caucasian girls just as curiously as the students stared at the native costumes and the Chinese babies who played and napped comfortably as their mothers worked.

Jade Snow also showed the class through their living quarters, where Mama and Daddy were waiting for them. In warm greeting Daddy extended his hand and a big smile to the instructor, while Mama hovered shyly but keenly observant in the background. In the Chinese spirit of hospitality, she had made extra tea besides the quart in the thermos bottle which was always on hand to greet unexpected callers, quench thirst, or pacify fright. Now she invited everyone to have tea and tea cakes in the dining room. The girls had their tea standing, and gazed curiously at the numerous photographs of cousins and ancestral graves in China, which Daddy was proud to hang on all the walls. Daddy sat in his customary chair. Although everyone seemed more or less at home, the parents as well as guests, Jade Snow suddenly felt estranged, for while she was translating conversation between instructor and parents, she was observing the scene with two pairs of eyes—Fifth Daughter's, and those of a college junior.

The subsequent trip to the American factory at least twenty times larger than Daddy's brought the contrast sharply home to her. This firm, unlike Daddy's, marketed as well as manufactured its own brand of jeans. The most striking difference to Jade Snow, however, was not merely the size of operations, which impressed her fellow class members. It was the intensity of the Caucasian men and women pieceworkers, who did not chat or stop one moment. No one looked around, ready to laugh and relieve his boredom. A baby would have been unhappy and entirely out of place there. What a difference between the relaxed attitude of the Chinese pieceworkers and the frantic preoccupation of the Caucasians! Instead of thinking of the economic significance of a big business as against Daddy's small one, Jade Snow was thinking that the boss of this vast establishment could not give his personal attention to train each apprentice to correct habits, nor could he repair a basinette for a tired worker's baby; nor could his wife sew alongside his employees and invite a hungry worker to have some soup in her factory kitchen.

Field trips like these were infrequent, but one requirement common to all courses was the term paper, the quality of which tipped the final grade of a course tremendously. It was an opportunity for the individual student to do a unified piece of original thinking at her own pace, but no student seemed to appreciate such an opportunity. Groans, not cries of delight, greeted the instructor's reminder that term papers were expected or due.

Fortunately Jade Snow found that her previous practice in creative writing helped now in preparing a term paper for a year's course in the English novel. Her subject, "The Chinese Novel," offered opportunity for comparing the English and Chinese treatment of novels. At last, she had an opportunity to link her past and present learning.

Coincidentally with her work on this paper came the publication of an English translation of the historically famous Chinese classic novel, *Chin Ping Mei*, written anonymously in the sixteenth century. Jade Snow was therefore able to review a typical Chinese novel, to prove her thesis that the Chinese novel differed completely from the English or Continental novel in its development, form, and purpose.

Jade Snow thought hard, wove her best Chinese and English knowledge into the paper, and felt satisfied with her work. Her English professor was also satisfied. He told her that he had chosen the paper for reading at an English conference to be held at the college, where representatives from three other bay area colleges and universities would gather.

Jade Snow heard this announcement, smiled, but could find no words to answer when her classmates congratulated her. How could she tell them that for a year she had been watching and listening with wonder to catch every movement and sound of these Caucasian girls who participated so easily in the college scene, who absorbed and contributed while she remained a mere spectator? Now at last she too could claim to be a participant.

19

MUSICIANS ON AND OFF STAGE

AT THE END OF HER JUNIOR YEAR, JADE SNOW RECEIVED NOTICE that she was among the ten top students of her class, and her scholarship was renewed in full.

There was one cloud. The Office of Record reminded her that her senior standing was still "provisional" because she lacked a year in fine arts, a requirement for graduation.

She consulted the dean in distress. "I don't know what to do! I have so many courses now necessary to fulfill my major requirement."

"Let me think about it," was all the dean said.

Next morning, as Jade Snow sleepily put on the water for coffee, the dean triumphantly showed her a page of the college catalogue. It said, "Transfer students may be excepted from certain of these requirements after petition to and approval by the Board of Conˑerence."

To Jade Snow's great relief, the board, after due consideration, did excuse her from taking the fine-arts course.

The happy living and stimulation from liberal academic thinking of a wholly Western pattern were the most significant rewards of this year's schooling. Eager to protect them as fully as possible, she clung to the campus except for infrequent visits home.

Home was only about forty-five minutes distant by bus from East Oakland. On the rare occasions when she arrived there with her little overnight case, she first looked for Mama to report to her, then Daddy, as she had been taught to do since childhood. Now, as always in the past, they would look up from whatever they were doing and remark simply without expression, "So you are home again."

No one ever smiled; no one asked how she was; no one was curious about her studies—obviously no one missed her in the crowded and busy factory-home. The only conversation touching her new life concerned the dean. Mama and Daddy felt that their own place in Jade Snow's life was temporarily occupied by her "teacher" so they always respectfully asked after the dean's well-being and quizzed their daughter on how well she was fulfilling her duties there. Thus, the Wongs were better informed about the dean, her activities and ideas, than they were about Jade Snow, with whom they maintained traditional reserve.

Jade Snow no longer attempted to bring the new Western learning into her Oriental home. When she entered the Wong household, she slipped into her old pattern of withdrawal, and she performed her usual daughterly duties—shopping for Mama, household chores, writing business letters in English for Daddy—in the role of an obedient Chinese girl. But now she no longer felt stifled or dissatisfied, for she could return to another life in which she fitted as an individual.

When she was home over a Sunday, she would accompany Mama to church as usual. But seldom did they go together as a family any more. Younger Brother, now thirteen years old, was indifferent to accompany them. Younger Sister, with her own high school and Sunday school circle of friends, was spending a great deal of time on her studies. She was doing well at school. She never failed to make the honor roll and was well liked by her teachers. When Jade Snow was home, Jade Precious Stone would quiz her good-naturedly about technical points of English grammar, and often Jade Snow was caught without the right answers.

The chasm between her changing interests and those of her family was further widened by a new experience in the arts.

During the summer vacation that year Jade Snow worked to augment her income. Instead of part-time clerical duties, she was now doing specialized research, and the job for the summer was to assign arriving freshmen to their residence halls. This was not simple. Each girl's entrance application, which included information as to what she liked to read, her hobbies, character recommendations, and a photograph, was carefully reviewed and the student was placed with a view to balancing the composition of each hall. Jade Snow worked closely with the dean in this project, which called for careful decisions, as they had the power of influencing the lives of almost two hundred people.

During the academic year, work, studies, and a little recreation had occupied all of Jade Snow's waking hours. For uncountable nights she had sat up with black coffee while she struggled to hold on to the tail of an idea for a term paper, or crammed for examinations. Although she knew of the many concerts, dramatic events, and art lectures offered at Mills, she didn't go to them for the same reason that she hadn't gone to the student sports—she didn't have time to do all the things well. She had therefore cut out completely what seemed least important to her educational objective.

But this summer was different. Without the press of studies, work was really done at the end of the day. Shortly after the summer session began, the dean said to Jade Snow, "A world-famous string quartet is playing in the chamber music hall every Sunday afternoon and Wednesday night. Why don't you go? You have time now."

"Well, I don't really understand that kind of music," Jade Snow admitted. "I've never been to a concert and I don't think I'll go right now."

"These are the most celebrated quartet musicians in the United States. People come from neighboring cities and great distances to listen to them. It is part of your education to hear good music, which is one of the important emphases of a liberal-arts college."

"I realize that, but. . . ."

The dean interposed quickly, "If you will water my roof garden for me every day, I'll buy you a season ticket to all the concerts this summer."

It was a command, not a suggestion.

So Jade Snow watered the roof garden regularly for six weeks, and regularly she sat with the audience listening to chamber music. At first, she didn't understand a thing—an "opus," a "movement" —they were strange unknowns. It was like listening for two hours to a foreign conversation without understanding or participating in it. Sometimes she got restless, and sometimes sleepy. But as the weeks progressed she discovered some pattern in what she heard. Gradually she lost her distress to become interested, and finally toward the end of the season she experienced a joyful thrill as she felt a novel inner emotional response to a superb performance of Beethoven's Opus 131.

After these weeks of watching the inscrutably dignified expressions of the musicians and listening in awe to them, Jade Snow was somewhat terrified by the dean's proposal that they give a large party for the quartet—not just a conventional party, but a different one. In fact, it would include Chinese food, of which the quartet was extremely fond. There was no doubt as to who would cook the dinner! When Jade Snow began to protest, the dean said, "Just cook one of those dinners you usually give your girl friends. All you have to do is cook enough for more people. We don't expect anything fancy, and I'll help you all I can."

Jade Snow agreed and went home to consult with Mama and Daddy. If it had been her own idea, she would never have had the courage to seek their assistance, but this was not her idea—it was her "teacher's."

To her parents, Jade Snow explained, "My teacher would like to give a party for some musicians." She could not possibly explain what a string quartet was. "I am asked to cook Chinese food, and I am willing to do it, but what shall I cook, and how can I cook so much? Do you think I should try?"

The Wongs conferred. Daddy announced, "There is a saying:

'He who does not revenge a wrong cannot claim to be a man; he who does not repay a debt of gratitude cannot claim to be princely.' You owe your teacher this dinner. So this is what you should do. . . ."

Then he became a director of operations. First Mama and he decided on a simple menu. Jade Snow was to cook two dishes: sweet-and-sour pineapple pork, and bean sprouts with beef. These would be supplemented by rice and a Chinese melon soup.

Since the stock for the soup would be the most difficult item, Daddy promised to get freshly prepared chicken soup stock from a restaurant for which he had made the cooks' aprons. Mama reviewed with Jade Snow the cooking procedures for the other dishes —she still didn't think that Jade Snow knew much about Chinese cooking.

"Be sure to pour boiling water over the bean sprouts or else they will taste too green, but also be sure not to overcook them until they are limp, as that will make them stringy."

Daddy instructed, "You had better shop in our Chinatown for all the supplies you need, as you may not be able to get what you want in Oakland."

"Yes, but how am I going to manage to get all the packages and the soup stock over to Mills?"

"I have a plan," Daddy explained. "Like anything worth doing at all, this affair must be carried out well. You must get not only the right ingredients to cook, but you must have the proper equipment. Take our large kettles, the frying pan, a cleaver, chopsticks, a large colander to drain the bean sprouts, and an ample, heavy chopping board. Do not worry about transporting these, for I am going to send your older brother in his new car to take the groceries and kitchen equipment to you. I will also send your younger sister to assist in the kitchen."

Daddy's plans, always carefully considered, always worked, and this one was no exception. The whole family became interested in the party and for the first time threw their support into one of Jade Snow's projects. At the appointed hour of the appointed day, Jade Snow and Jade Precious Stone were carrying out the steps in preparation for the dinner as rehearsed with Mama, using the ample pots and pans and other equipment assembled by Daddy and transported by Older Brother.

The guests began to arrive: faculty members, administrative officers, head residents, and the quartet members with their wives. Jade Snow had almost expected to see the musicians appear in white palm-beach suits, carrying their stringed instruments. But now they were dressed informally; there was nothing of the serious, flawless performers about them. In short order, they fitted into the party as modest, good-natured, warm, informal human beings, all deeply interested in Chinese food and the cooks, the Wong sisters.

The food was served buffet style on the roof garden, where the guests were gathered in the warm, summer evening air. But the quartet hardly stayed on the roof; they were continually drifting downstairs to inspect the cooking, ask questions, and get better acquainted with the cook. On one of these trips, the violist drifted into the living room and spied a genuine Russian brass samovar. With delighted cries he captured it from its shelf and declared to his hostess and fellow guests that he and his wife would boil the water for the Chinese tea in a Russian samovar. They wanted no assistance. From the woodshed on the back porch they brought in some kindling, but—alas—the smallest sticks were still too large to fit under the samovar!

The violist ran into the kitchen excitedly, looking for an ax. His wife entreated, "Be careful of your hands!"

He wasn't worried about hurting his priceless hands—he worried only for lack of a suitable ax. Suddenly he spied Jade Snow's cleaver on the sinkboard, the one she had borrowed from Mama. Gleefully he seized it. "This is just the thing."

And that was how the Wong cleaver, which had for many years sliced such innocent fare as vegetables and meat, or chopped up chickens and ducks, for the first and only time in its utilitarian life split kindling to heat a Russian samovar, to help make Chinese tea for a party honoring a string quartet.

That was a wonderful evening, which Jade Snow thoroughly enjoyed, and not only because Jade Precious Stone helped until the last dish was dried. For the first time Jade Snow felt an important participant in the role of hostess. Because of everyone's interest in the kitchen preparations, she soon lost her shyness in the presence of celebrities and acted naturally. There was no talk about music, only about Chinese food. And Jade Snow ceased thinking of famous people as "those" in a world apart. She had a glimpse of the truth, that the great people of any race are unpretentious, genuinely honest, and nonpatronizing in their interest in other human beings.

20

SHE FINDS HER HANDS

THE HAPPY OUTCOME OF HER FIRST EXPERIENCE WITH MUSIC MADE Jade Snow more interested in and receptive to the other fine arts. In her senior year, she wrung out enough time to go to the college theatricals, and to her first modern-dance concert. Unlike the muddled impressions her first concert evoked, the modern dance struck her immediately with its significance. After she had adjusted herself to the shock of seeing figures dancing with bare feet and flying hair, she became absorbed in the movements, the choreographic pattern, the simplicity and color of the costumes. Her emotional response was also different from her response to concert music. It was a sympathetic response to visual form and motion, directly expressed. This discovery of the effectiveness of understatement and abstracted simplicity opened another door to enlarge her world.

The stunning impact of this first modern-dance performance was duplicated later when an entirely different form of visual art penetrated her consciousness. Since her social service courses had been chosen to prepare her for service in her community, especially with young American-Chinese, Jade Snow began a year's course in group work and practical, recreational leadership for girls. It included a number of activities, such as physical games, paper games, study projects, and craft work. Jade Snow liked them all, but craft work was the most interesting. Needle and thread and materials had been part of her life since early childhood days, so it was great fun to knit, sew, or make linoleum blocks for college credits.

The physical education teacher of the course was a colorfully warm and alive person who expressed her belief in the humor of life not only by her twinkling eyes and gay voice, but even in her movements. The laughter, however, did not interfere with her discriminating judgment. Sometimes Jade Snow was invited to her house for simple suppers, and they would talk at length about people, art, or cookery. Sometimes they had salad and hamburgers; sometimes they cooked Chinese food; sometimes with guests, at times alone. They became close and fast friends, more than teacher and student.

This woman was directly responsible for bringing Jade Snow another form of art experience—her first personal creative expression. At the end of the semester, when she brought in her completed craft projects for grading, the instructor examined them and said, "You have above-average ability with your hands. Why don't you take a course 'Tools and Materials' offered next semester for the first time by the Art Department? You will learn the principles of woodworking, weaving, metal work, and ceramics, and the proper use of shop tools. You should develop your ability with your hands, if only for your greater personal enjoyment in life."

Jade Snow was dubious. "I like to work with my hands very much, but I doubt that I will be allowed to take an art course for credit now. You see, I thought that I was not interested in Western art, and I petitioned to be released from the fine-arts requirement."

The instructor suggested, "Well, don't just say 'No.' Give it some thought."

On investigation, Jade Snow discovered that the course was

scheduled for evening, which would leave days free for her major subjects; so she arranged to take it. It proved a happy discovery, for it gave her entire college curriculum new pleasure and meaning. Instead of setting a new pace for her mind, it set a new pace for her hands.

The instructor was a quiet-mannered man, with amazing capabilities in all the crafts. More than anyone else Jade Snow had met, he knew the nature and use of materials from the reeds of the fields to precious silver and gold. But instead of giving his students ready answers to their numerous questions, he would encourage them to work out problems for themselves by saying, "I don't know." Indeed, in handworking materials as Jade Snow found, too, no one can ever know the final answer and form at the very beginning of any project. This method made learning slow and painful, for it meant that students made mistakes, but in the end they learned better and more, and they developed individual ingenuity.

The course started with woodworking, and Jade Snow made a bookcase; proceeded to paints and pigments, and she painted the bookcase with linseed oil and pigment which she herself had ground together; metal work, and she slaved to snip off a round of copper, anneal and pound it into an ashtray; weaving, and she made herself a primitive loom from an old berry crate; paper work, and she made her own paste and paper dolls and decorated paper beads. Finally there was work in clay, emphasizing ceramic sculpture and pottery.

One day, the class transferred to the pottery studio which was little more than a gray shack underneath some lovely cork elm trees. In this small room, about ten by twenty feet, were a sink, one electric, and three foot-treadled potter's wheels, many shelves and one cabinet. Two auxiliary rooms held a firing kiln, an old pie oven for drying green ware, glazes and glazing equipment. Fine clay dust had settled over everything. But what marvels the shelves in the main room held! The instructor told them to wander around and get acquainted with the place, but to be careful of breakage.

On some shelves were drying, half-completed forms. Others held finished work, and when Jade Snow's eyes lighted on them she felt shocked excitement. The articles were reaching out and speaking to her! She couldn't herself understand the stimulation and response. Among these completed examples of student pottery were pitchers, vases, cups, bowls. Some were imperfect, thick, warped, or crude. But they were all glazed in beautiful, clear, and unfamiliar shades of blues, greens, and yellows. Some were delicate, and some virile, but they all had that hand quality which was the stamp of a creator's love of his craft. It was a provoking awakening, a discovery of another new thing in the world at which to wonder and marvel.

This wonder and marvel of pottery never ceased for Jade Snow. The instructor now gave them simple lectures on the nature of clay, what they should and should not do with it, on glazes and firings, and then left them alone with their hands and the materials. As the class hours were short, Jade Snow would return at odd times, on week ends and evenings, to make little bowls or to trim or glaze pots. She played with simple forms, decorations, and textures, and the hours, like the fishing trips during her childhood, would simply fly while all troubles were forgotten in the joy of creating. The clay forms became a satisfying reflection of personal will and skill.

One day after class hours, Jade Snow said to the instructor: "This is a craft course and not an art course; most people speak of them as separate knowledges. I wish now that I had taken an art course. Perhaps I would know more about what forms I am making. Where does art begin and craft end?"

The usual and expected "I don't know" was not forthcoming this time. Instead, the instructor burst out, "That's just an eighteenth-century idea—the division between art and craft. The good artist must first be a good craftsman, and a good craftsman who works in good taste is an artist in his work. As you work and accumulate knowledge in a craft, you develop as an artist, and an artist cannot be considered a good artist unless he is skilled in the techniques of his craft. In fact, I found that theoretical study of art did not mean much to me until I began to work with my hands in crafts; then, I appreciated and understood the limitations and achievements of art forms."

"Then I don't need to take art courses to make good pottery?" Jade Snow asked wonderingly.

"You work and work with your materials, and you will find that with experience your eyes and hands will help you make better pottery than any theoretical analysis of form."

So Jade Snow worked with her hands, eyes, and mind in the pottery studio where she felt completely at home. She never found time to read any books on pottery making.

In crafts, she found, one learned more by seeing and feeling for oneself than by instruction. She did not ask her instructor for much personal help, but all about her in various stages of completion were his own pottery forms and colors to serve as silent standards of criticism. He himself seemed a tireless worker, maintaining the best possible equipment and stock of materials for his students, and constantly re-establishing new and higher requirements for making pottery. Whenever he had perfected one technique or form he progressed to another unknown. Whatever formulas he discovered and all his voluminous notes on experiments, were at the disposal of his students. Through innumerable informal talks with him as each worked separately, Jade Snow developed a "feeling" for art, an inspiration for good pottery, and the knowledge that sober, hard work was the most important quality of all.

Her first products were certainly bad or mediocre. While inspired by the work of others, her pottery was nevertheless her own creation, a combination of the clay she chose, the form she achieved, and the glazes she used. They reflected the quality of her workmanship and the impulses of her heart more than any other material she had used. The final satisfaction was that they were physical remembrances of certain personal moments in time which could never be considered lost so long as the pottery was not broken beyond repair. Jade Snow made as many pieces as time and energy would allow in the short month remaining before graduation, and while she regretted that she had discovered the fascination of clay so late in her college days, she rejoiced that at least she had discovered it.

Graduation was growing nearer with its need for future plans. Jade Snow had assumed that she would continue graduate work for a master's degree in social work. She had thought of trying to get a scholarship from an Eastern college to widen her experience. But Pearl Harbor had been bombed and the students, like everyone else, were caught in the war fever. In common with all her friends, Jade Snow felt the urgent call to make some contribution. She decided to get a war job and at the same time try to save enough money so that for once she might attend school without having to work.

Graduation offered little excitement. She wasn't going to the senior prom, or take part in the other social activities of the pre-commencement period. She was just enjoying the thought of not having to study again for a long, long time, although trying not to dwell on the fact that she might be leaving the good college life forever.

She was also carrying a family secret of stupendous implications —Mama was going to have another child!

This meant that Mama would not be able to see Jade Snow graduate. When she went home with the formal, engraved invitations, Mama took her aside and cautioned her. "Your father must know the exact arrangements about the time and meeting place. When one of your older sisters graduated she did not have a clear understanding with him about where and when to meet, and when he could not find his way he turned around and took the next train home without seeing the exercises."

So on the important day, while Mama stayed home, Older Brother drove the rest of the family to the appointed meeting place at Kapiolani. It was a happy day as well as important. Daddy brought his little Brownie box camera and took pictures of his brood against a variety of campus backgrounds. And as one of the day's high lights Jade Snow took him to the art gallery to see the student exhibit in handicrafts. There, among paintings and sculpture by other classes, was her set of shelves, on which were arranged the best of the pottery she had made, a woven belt, and the copper bowl.

Daddy could hardly believe the evidence of his eyes and ears. "Did you do these by yourself?"

"I did, and I am especially interested in the clay work."

He turned the articles over appreciatively, carefully examining them. "You may not know this," he said, "but my father, your grandfather, was artistically inclined and very interested in hand-work. He always said that a person who knew a craft trade would be a better person, for he would have the assurance of never starving. When I was only a young boy he made me apprentice in a slipper shop for three years to learn to sew on slipper soles by hand, to be sure that I knew at least one handcraft well. I received no wages but paid fourteen dollars a year for instructions. Your grand-father thought that slippers would be an item always in public demand. He would have been happy to see your work."

It was not becoming for a daughter to say "Thank you" in return for an indirect compliment, so Jade Snow merely said, "Is that so?" But in her heart she felt that these few articles which Daddy could visually understand were more meaningful to him than her hard-earned Phi Beta Kappa key.

That afternoon, she fastened on her black cap and gown, and walked with her family toward the academic procession. There, the Wong party met the college president. Even with the press of the hour ahead, Dr. Reinhardt unhurriedly turned to Jade Snow. "Is this your family?" she asked smilingly.

Daddy beamed. With an expression of respect and joy, he ex-tended his hand to return her greeting. Then he asked Jade Snow in Chinese: "Do you think that your president would permit me to take a picture of you two together?"

"She is so busy now, I hate to ask her," Jade Snow countered, also in Chinese.

The president interrupted, "What is your father saying?"

Embarrassed, Jade Snow replied, "He wants a picture of us to-gether!"

Dr. Reinhardt took over the management—the first woman ever to do so with Daddy. "Now, Mr. Wong, you take your camera over there, and your daughter and I will remain here under the tree, in conversation."

To Jade Snow she said, "Let us be talking so that this little snap-shot scene will be a natural one."

In a moment, Daddy had taken some very natural pictures of the two in academic dress, smiling and talking pleasantly.

After the graduation exercises, Jade Snow held in her hand her diploma and a program with notations about herself: "Awarded to Membership in Phi Beta Kappa," and "Graduated with Honor and Distinction in Economics and Sociology."

She also carried her cap, gown, and bachelor's hood of gold satin and white velvet, for she was returning home to accomplish one more mission for that day. At home she looked for Mama, working away at her overall seams in the lowest factory level. Jade Snow again put on her academic dress, and silently walked up and down for Mama to see her. Mama said not a word, just watched, with tears in her eyes.

For Jade Snow the moment of triumph had come. She had proved that Mama could raise her children to be a credit to the Wongs. She had shown her father and mother that without a penny from them, she could balance her own budget and graduate from college, not in debt, but with one hundred of the original hundred and seventy-four dollars still in the bank.

But now, in her moment of triumph, she could find no sense of conquest or superiority. There was an overwhelming flood of happiness and release, and the great comfort that a supreme achievement secretly brings, but she could feel no resentment against the two who had no words of congratulation—Daddy, who wanted so much to record a picture of her and her college president, nor Mama, working with tears of mingled joy and sadness in her eyes.

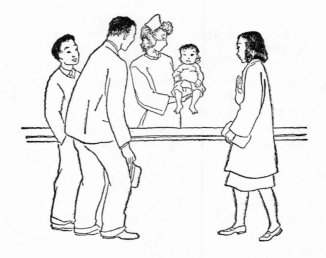

21

A SUMMER OF EXCITEMENTS

Shortly after graduation activities the dean announced her engagement, news which had been confided to Jade Snow several weeks earlier. Soon Kapiolani was permeated by the atmosphere which accompanies wedding preparations.

Among the many visitors was one who introduced herself as a Mills alumna. As she left she said to Jade Snow, "You've been quite a help to the dean here, haven't you? It's too bad though, that you have graduated without having had the experience of residence-hall life."

"Oh, but I wouldn't have traded my life at Kapiolani for anything!"

The alumna did not drop the subject there. "Why don't you remain here for summer session, and then you will have the experience of residence-hall life?"

Jade Snow couldn't explain to a stranger that she couldn't afford summer session; so she replied, "No, I already have other plans."

"If I made it possible for you to attend summer session, couldn't you change your plans and find something interesting to study?"

Astonished, Jade Snow could not grasp her exact meaning. "Why do you say, if you made it possible for me? Why should you make it possible?"

The answer was, "I love this college and, as I have told you, the dean has given a great deal of herself to it, and I know that you have helped her. It would make me happy to do this for you. I would take care of all your expenses. Surely you can change your plans to enjoy six weeks of summer session?"

"Oh, this means that I can go on and take a course in pottery! Thank you very much," was all that Jade Snow could think to say in appreciation. As she watched the woman walk slowly down to the road, her heart was bursting with excitement at this unexpected gift. She looked up to the sky, and murmured another humble "Thank you" to the One to whom she had addressed so many questions, doubts, and requests.

The remaining weeks were busy, spent in sorting out belongings which were to be transported home and those she would use for the summer, helping the dean with her arrangements, shopping for a baby layette for Mama, and finally, helping the family to move.

There had first been talk about, and finally action in choosing certain properties in Chinatown for a Federal housing project. This property included the factory-home where the Wongs lived. Daddy foresaw that whenever the housing authority decided to condemn the property, he would lose his entire investment in improvements in the store and would be left with only his movable machinery.

To ensure the future of his business, he hunted diligently until he found another location. It had been a sewing factory, and was located four blocks from Chinatown, toward the waterfront. Once more the Wongs began to fix up a home. This new place was a second-story loft with sun and air coming through skylights. They partitioned off the entire front for bedrooms, leaving the middle part of the loft for installation of sewing machines and cutting boards. As the building was half a block long and extended to a street behind, the large kitchen in the back had both sun and air.

All the children shared in painting and plastering, and Jade Snow and Jade Precious Stone did their own room. They chose coral-colored, plain wallpaper and white, ruffled curtains, and bought white bedspreads, harmonizing linoleum, and a group of unfinished furniture which they painted eggshell white to match the woodwork.

At last Daddy and Mama were able to construct adjoining separate rooms, where Daddy could keep his clutter of accumulated possessions undisturbed, and Mama could be as neat as she wished without throwing away any of Daddy's belongings.

Older Brother, who had quietly gotten married without fuss or formality, fixed a room for himself and his bride, and helped with the painting and cabinetwork in the rest of the house.

And even though there was no notice as yet to vacate the old location, the Wongs, for the first time in their lives separated family living from the factory life and moved to their new home. When it proved necessary, the factory could be moved too.

Mama did as much work as she had always done. She did not feel that she required either special attention or special mention. Like Daddy, she had always been aghast at the American habit of announcing an expected child by mouth or by letter, sometimes months before its coming. Married love was expected, but it was also a private affair. Mama always said, "You can share a common bed in the privacy of your room, but that does not mean that you should hold hands in public." Children, Mama also said, were expected results of marriage relations to complete a family, and should not be anticipated with excitement. The birth of a child was time enough for others to know about it.

When Jade Snow had first noticed her mother's physical condition, she had by a cautious question confirmed her suspicions, but after that she said nothing. Mama expressed no emotion and made no special preparations for the expected event. She went right on working and lifting, and she ate and slept as before. Whatever was in her mind, whatever the feelings that Mama and Daddy shared about another child expected now fourteen years after the last one had been born, Jade Snow was not told, and she felt no right to pry. But now, as a young woman of twenty, she suddenly felt pity for another woman who was working away her life almost by compulsion, who was receiving little affection from the very children for whose welfare she was working, because affection had not been part of her training, and she did not give it in training her own. As if a veil separating her from her mother were lifted for a moment, Jade Snow saw clearly that at this time Mama did not need from her grown daughter the respect which she had fostered in all her children so much as she needed the companionship which only one woman can give another.

So Jade Snow asked gently, "Mama, have you been getting medical care?"

Mama didn't look at her daughter. She replied defensively, "I did not have prenatal care for any of you, and I had no trouble."

Jade Snow ventured some advice, expecting almost any reply. "I think that you need some attention now, because you are quite a bit older, and your body is different. I will be glad to take you to a doctor as often as necessary."

Mama consented without a struggle. Jade Snow sensed that beneath her dignity and calm, Mama could be a troubled and frightened woman.

The moving was accomplished and preparations completed just in time for the dean's wedding. Then, the day before the ceremony, Daddy telephoned across the bay to Jade Snow, something which rarely happened. His voice was grave. "I think your mother's time has come. She should go to the hospital, and the doctor should be notified."

"I shall be home immediately," Jade Snow assured him.

At home, she piled Mama and Daddy into a taxi in short order. Mama hadn't wanted to go to the Chinese hospital where most of Chinatown's residents went. Since Grandmother died there, Mama had never felt comfortable even visiting the place. So now she was taken to the French hospital. As she was not painfully uncomfortable yet, Jade Snow returned to Oakland. The next day, as soon as the wedding at the college chapel was over, she dashed back to the hospital where Daddy was still waiting with Younger Brother.

Mama was now in intense pain. Jade Snow saw her writhing on her bed, stripped of pretense or reserve. Awkwardly trying to comfort her, Jade Snow bent over to catch Mama's whisper, "Do not let your father see me in this shameful condition."

Jade Snow did not argue. "Yes, Mama, but you know that he is outside if you wish to see him." She wrung out wet cloths to cool her mother's forehead, and stayed at her side silently.

The staff doctor, a woman of Swedish ancestry, was kind and soothing. "It is always so much harder for an older woman," she said sympathetically. "Where is the father?"

"Oh," Jade Snow hurried to reply, "Mama doesn't want him to see."

"Of course, he should see. I think a man little realizes what pain a woman endures." The doctor went into the hall and brought Daddy in.

Jade Snow felt out of place and backed quietly into the corner as the doctor left.

Daddy and Mama said nothing to each other. Mama turned away her face and cried out fitfully. In a gesture she had never before witnessed, Jade Snow saw Daddy take Mama's hand in both of his, and a tear dropped on her coverlet. Then he turned and went out.

Anxiously the family of three waited in the hall. With so much time to think, Jade Snow, suffering from dry throat and anxious heart, began to realize that, after all, growing up was not a happy release from domination, but could be serious and painful with responsibility. It was a disconcerting shock to see Daddy and Mama no longer as respected dignitaries directing affairs from a world apart, but as human man and woman with problems for which they were now beginning to need her adult aid.

An hour after Mama had been taken to the delivery room, Daddy could stand the suspense no longer; Younger Brother succeeded in persuading him to go around the corner for an ice cream and some funny books, luxuries in which Daddy almost never indulged a child. They had no sooner left than Jade Snow saw Mama, still unconscious, trundled back to her room. "It's a boy," said the doctor, "Your mother and he are both doing fine!"

Jade Snow tore out, caught Daddy and Younger Brother on the hospital steps, and relayed the good news. Daddy's reaction was very close to dancing. He caught her hand and shook it. Beaming, he turned to Younger Brother and said excitedly, "Did you hear that? Now you have a Younger Brother and you are a Big Brother."

Then, right on the hospital steps, he bowed his head and offered prayer fervently, "Thank you, my God above, for blessing the Wong family with another male heir, and for his mother's safe recovery."

The infant—a little red screaming bundle, reportedly two inches longer than the average baby, a little Wong already with an inch of black hair, ears close to his head, a high forehead, and a well-formed body—opened one eye and looked out at them before shutting it again. The child was duly named Prosperity from Heaven.

That was a day not to be forgotten in Jade Snow's memory book.

On the tail of all the excitement of a new home, a bride, and a baby, summer session began. Jade Snow spent all her spare hours on her pottery and thoroughly enjoyed the six weeks, which were more like relaxed play than studying. She understood why the kind alumna thought that she should experience carefree residence-hall life; it was a taste of community living. She became friends with the quartet members, who were also summer residents of that hall, and she enjoyed dining, swimming, and playing with them. Several evenings they spent together making a basinette for the new baby from a big clothes basket and some light-blue denim from Daddy's factory.

The end of this summer found Jade Snow with a considerable collection of pottery; she was tanned, rested, happy, and ready for a full-time job.

22

SENDING THE SHIPS TO WAR

S HE SOUGHT EMPLOYMENT ADVICE FROM THE COLLEGE PLACEMENT
office but received little help, since that office had more re-
sources for placing teachers than for placing office workers. As Jade
Snow rose after the interview, she remarked, "I came only because
you sent us seniors a letter to be sure to report to you for advice
before seeking a job. I guess I'm not going to get any from you."

"Oh yes, I can give you some good advice," her interviewer
retorted. "If you are smart, you will look for a job only among your
Chinese firms. You cannot expect to get anywhere in American
business houses. After all, I am sure you are conscious that racial
prejudice on the Pacific Coast will be a great handicap to you."

Stung and speechless, Jade Snow felt as if she had been struck on
both cheeks. The numbness gave way to the first anger she had
felt against any of the college staff. She had been told that because

she was Chinese, she could not go into equal competition with Caucasians. Her knowledge that racial prejudice existed had never interfered with her personal goals. She had, on the contrary, found that being Chinese had created a great deal of favorable interest, and because of its cultural enrichment of her life she would not have traded her Chinese ancestry for any other.

No, this was one piece of advice she was not going to follow, so opposed was it to her experience and belief. She was more determined to get a job with an American firm.

By this time the trek to the shipyards was well under way. The patriotic fever to build as many ships as possible, together with the boom wages, combined to attract people from all types of occupations. Lawyers, artists, housewives, and street derelicts were seeking either skilled or unskilled work in the shipyards. Jade Snow joined the trek and sought work at the nearest new yard in Marin County, across the bay from San Francisco. Jade Precious Stone, who had unusual ability with her long fingers, had left college to take evening courses in ship-drafting and she was already established in a good position at the same yard. Reunited after having lived apart for two years, she and Jade Snow were close companions again and adolescent differences were now forgotten.

In a crowded reception hall, Jade Snow filled out questionnaires, and waited for hours until her turn for an interview was called. The crisp interviewer, a brownish woman in about her middle fifties, asked her what kind of work she was seeking.

"Any kind of office work—I don't think that I would be any good at physical work."

The woman peered over her horn-rimmed glasses, "We have very few clerical office openings, and a long waiting list besides. Too bad you're not a stenographer. Well, if anything turns up, I'll let you know."

"You can't tell me when that will be?"

"Really! I can't say. It may be an hour or a week! I can't predict when requisitions will come in."

Jade Snow left discouraged, choosing to believe that these words were statements of fact, rather than confirmation of what the college placement officer had said. It took only about twenty-four hours to prove herself right. A telephone call came: "Miss Wong, you are fortunate. When you were in my office yesterday, a requisition was brought in personally by a secretary in one of our departments. She saw you and has asked for you to fill that job."

"What kind of a job is it?"

"Typist-clerk; just what you wanted. One hundred and sixty dollars a month; forty-eight-hour week."

"That sounds like what I was looking for. But what department is it and for whom will I work?"

"Really, Miss Wong, I'm a very busy person. I can't answer so many questions. You don't know how lucky you are not to have to wait your turn, or even be subject to approval by interview. Now, do you or do you not want the job?"

"Oh, of course I do. I just wanted to know. . . ."

"Very well. . . . Be here tomorrow to hire in."

The next day Jade Snow was hired.

Thus began a new schedule of living, working, and learning. The day shift, starting at eight in the morning, did not seem so bad until Jade Snow realized that to punch the time clock at that hour she had to rise at five-thirty, dress, have breakfast, grab a put-up lunch from the refrigerator, and walk or run down to the station to board shortly after six the provokingly slow ferryboat which made a leisurely trip to the shipyard.

With great anticipation of a new day dawning, she dressed with care the next morning in what she thought the smart career girl should wear: her new gray tweed suit, a gift from Older Brother, a freshly pressed white shirt, shiny alligator shoes and brown bag, all of them graduation presents. She even wore precious nylons and spotless white gloves. With Jade Precious Stone she hurried along the commercial fruit district to get to the Embarcadero.

At this early hour, the Italian produce merchants were at the peak of their activity. The workers trundling their hand trucks or dollies were jolly and certainly informal. A continuous stream of "Hi's" trailed after the sisters as they rushed past the piles of crisp orange carrots, crates of fragrant melons, greens, and citrus fruits.

It was the first time that Jade Snow had been on a ferryboat since a trip with Daddy once as a little girl. Boarding the boat with eagerness, she was dismayed to find it filled mostly with dirty and unkempt men. The few women were also dirty and unkempt. Men crowded the benches—unceremoniously stretched out asleep, or reading, or sitting stoically silent. Others were scrambling around in a circle on the floor, playing games of chance. Each one had pinned on his chest his badge of admittance, and each wore another universal badge of the shipyard worker—the dome-shaped hard hat.

It was a weird scene; dawn was barely breaking and a half moon still gleamed on the gray waters. Pruned by Chinese discipline, fresh from the stimulation and inspiration of a women's college, Jade Snow was going to work; and the first adjustment to make was to accept three hours a day in a dirty ferryboat, the target of open stares from curious men. The dark, stained floor was littered with rubbish and the atmosphere was permeated with the indescribable blend of liquored breaths, stale tobacco, and sweat-soaked garments, odors unique in their eloquence.

Jade Precious Stone, already familiar with the workings of the shipyard, "tipped off" her sister on the way over. "You must always wear your badge or they won't let you in. Military secret, or something like that. And you had better not be late one minute. If the clock is punched any later than eight on the dot, you get docked for the first quarter of the hour at time and a half. You've got to punch in, punch out. Your life will be tyrannized by your badge and the time clock."

As Jade Snow entered the yard, she felt drowned by the humanity rushing around and dwarfed by the giant machinery and steel sections. The welders' torches flared unexpectedly, and the loud continuous rat-a-tat-tat of the chippers was nerve-racking. Sometimes, she ducked as tools flew through the air without warning. No wonder the yard workers wore hard hats!

The sisters walked to the mold loft, where the younger one worked upstairs in the drafting room. Jade Snow found her office, a small room without windows. There she was greeted by the secretary, a woman of distracted manner and heavy step, whose acute nervousness was either relieved or intensified by heavy smoking. She sat Jade Snow down at the corner of a work table and gave her a stack of literature to read. Only now did Jade Snow discover what kind of work this office did. It was called the "War Production Drive," supervised by the War Production Board in Washington, D. C. It was one of a national network of offices located in major war plants.

Its purpose was to increase production; its method was to solicit suggestions from the workers as to ideas for improving production techniques; and it was implemented by a labor-management committee, which met regularly.

Workers deposited their ideas into conveniently located suggestion boxes and Jade Snow's job was to type them into coherent form and acknowledge them, pending definite action. Two of their men were assigned to investigate the merits of suggestions and report their findings to the boss. The boss checked on the feasibility of the suggestions, and studied ways to improve upon them. Each month, the ten most constructive suggestions won war bonds for their originators, and the office would send a detailed report on them to Washington so that the best of their thinking could be shared with other shipyards.

The secretary considered herself the office manager.

"If you want to know anything, ask me. Don't bother the boss. You know, he's really a famous architect, educated in France and everything like that. He's a very busy man and hates office details."

"Yes, ma'am," Jade Snow answered. She certainly wouldn't break any rules, even though this position was a far cry from her imagined role of white-collar girl.

The boss was a big hearty man with a happy smile. Jade Snow learned that he didn't like to stay in a business suit at his desk, but spent all the time he could in khakis out in the yard. She also found that he had a keen sense of humor, and could match in wit the "smart" suggestions which were calculated to stump him for an answer.

After several months of this clerical work, Jade Snow felt lost in a morass of detail and monotonous copy-typing. She found comfort only in the thought that in a small way she contributed to the war effort, and that she was saving for her postgraduate education. Otherwise, there was little personal compensation in the tiring daily twelve-hour struggle.

The monotony was relieved in one respect by learning about the American work world—commonly known as "a man's world." Until now American men were to Jade Snow a strange and unknown species of the human race. Now she was literally rubbing elbows with them day after day. She was wide-eyed and wide-eared to discover how they thought, talked, and worked. The yard was tumultuous, not only with construction, but with rough-and-tumble, swearing, pushing men, ready to criticize management and eager to send out the Liberty Ships faster and faster.

Then, one morning when the secretary was absent because of illness, the monotony was broken for Jade Snow. She had finished her work, and didn't know what to do next. Preferring to break a rule rather than to waste precious time, she asked the boss if she could do anything for him.

"Sit down here a minute and tell me something," he answered. "I don't think that you really like what you're doing. What would you prefer to do?"

It was like a story you might read, a question like that. She had no ready, brilliant answer, only the truth. "Why, I haven't done any other work except research in college. I used to do my best in study projects and term papers, but of course those are rather remote from our problems here."

The boss replied, "Well, we're not exactly a college. But what would you do if you had your way?"

Jade Snow caught at her chance. "I have been noticing that many suggestions come in about giving the workers cold vaccines to reduce time lost because of colds. We haven't been able to give satisfactory answers, and I'd like to find out how practical cold vaccines would be."

"O. K. It's all yours. Put on your hat and coat and go find out. I'll take care of your time card."

Somewhat bewildered by this turn of affairs, and while the other girls were dumb with astonishment, Jade Snow clapped on her rain hat and coat and rubber boots, and went out.

On the bus returning to San Francisco, she decided on a course of action. She went to the main library and spent the day reading pertinent material on the subject. Any material which the library allowed to be withdrawn she took to the yard the next day. Now, instead of typing suggestions, she read and made notes, ignoring the daggered innuendoes of the secretary. Then she arranged for interviews with the staffs of the Army, Navy, and bay area university medical departments.

After several weeks, she completed a paper analyzing the prob-

lem, giving the experiences of other war industries and the recommendations of the medical experts. In conclusion she pointed out
that it was impractical to administer vaccines on a mass scale to
the workers, who could not be given medical examinations; that
vitamins were recommended as the most effective means of building resistance to colds and should be made available to the workers
at low cost.

The boss sent the paper to upper management and in a short
while low-cost, multiple-vitamin capsules appeared for sale at all
lunch canteens. After this arrangement, which proved that management heeded their cry, the workers did not make further suggestions about vaccines.

From then on, Jade Snow's work was mainly concerned with
research projects. She studied the workers' need for more lunch
canteens, the value and effects of morale in increasing production.
Then, in early 1943, the nation raised a hue and cry against absenteeism which was sabotaging work schedules. Suggestions poured in,
and Jade Snow undertook to find out why absenteeism existed.

Meantime, the boss was promoted and took Jade Snow with him to
his new position. As secretary, her work included personnel duties.
By studying a book, she learned shorthand. But the research was
pushed aside, for in the following six months her boss was superintendent over eleven hundred people distributed throughout all
three shifts of the yard's twenty-four-hour operation.

During these months, Jade Snow developed confidence in deal-
ing and working with the men. The lesser supervisors came in and
out of the office with their problems. Sometimes she gave advice;
sometimes she ignored them; sometimes she brought questions to
the boss' attention. Often they teased her because she took everything so seriously, but gradually she learned their way of talking and
lost her timidity. She found dignity and respect accorded her in
the shipyard. Sometimes at conferences she would be the only
woman present in a room full of men. At first these experiences
found her uneasy, but she continued her work quietly, and she soon
learned to maintain her equilibrium in almost any situation.

At the yard, it seemed that everything should have been done
two minutes ago, and the two telephones, which were ringing
almost every moment of the day, were indispensable in expediting

action. She learned the first rule of the shipyard, "Never trust the other person to get something done. Keep on checking yourself." It became her main job to see that all the "red tape" required of their department by the head office was handled with dispatch and accuracy. Jade Snow liked the responsibility of her job. Her boss was kind, and except for his expressions of interest in the Chinese culture, she was never made conscious of her ancestry. Certainly she had no reason to consider it a handicap.

Despite these busy months, Jade Snow's longest and most careful piece of research on "Absenteeism—Its Causes and Cures" was completed, but the copies sent to upper management were ignored. Of course, the recommended action was not so simple to carry out as the purchase of vitamins, for it was based on the theory that labor and management should lay aside their differences. She made specific suggestions for getting together and solving the basic problem of mass morale.

As war industries strained to produce and to deliver more military supplies faster, absenteeism reached such acute national proportions that a San Francisco newspaper sponsored a coastwide essay contest to find the best way of coping with the problem. The prizes were the privilege of christening a Liberty Ship, and a war bond—both offered by bay area shipyards other than the one in which Jade Snow worked.

On the ferry she read the morning paper and came to the office with it. Playfully she asked her boss, "How do you think I would look launching a ship?"

Not giving her the satisfaction of even flickering an eyelash in curiosity, he replied casually, "I think you would look fine!"

Jade Snow explained about the contest. "Apparently the management of this yard has just filed or buried my written report. You wouldn't object if I sent in a revised copy to the contest? I'll polish it up and edit parts on my own time. Perhaps somebody else may see it who will read it!"

With her boss' blessing, she carried out her idea and promptly forgot about it. Many weeks later, she received a telephone call at home. It was from the editor of the absenteeism contest. She had been chosen the winner! Her essay was being incorporated into a congressional report to the President of the United States, and they wanted pictures and a story immediately.

The next few weeks were filled with excitement. Letters of congratulations poured in from individuals, business firms, and the War Production Board in Washington. Jade Snow was asked to speak on the radio, to broadcast overseas. Her picture was printed, not only in the contest-sponsoring newspaper, but in all the Chinese papers, which carried translations of the main points of her essay. For the first time, Daddy and Mama had the opportunity of understanding how their fifth daughter's mind worked. They received some inkling of how she related theoretical knowledge to practical action. They were surprised and thoughtful by turn.

Now, even Chinatown felt a burst of pride that one of their female citizens had won a contest in competition against Caucasian-Americans. The community excitement even penetrated to Daddy, and caused him to come home one evening in a rare, happy glow.

As the Wong family sat down to their dinner table—Mama, Daddy, Older Brother, Sister-in-Law, Jade Snow, Jade Precious Stone, Younger Brother, and eight-months-old Prosperity playing in his high chair—Daddy stood to say grace. Still in a happy glow when he had finished, he continued standing and announced, "Everywhere I went to purchase groceries today, my fellow countrymen were congratulating me, and saying, 'We are reading in the papers that your fifth daughter has won great honor in the American world. You must be very satisfied to have your family name so glorified by a female.' I tell them that you have done it all yourself. But even I must now add my congratulations to those you have already received!"

And for the first time, Daddy held out his hand in a sincere gesture of respect for his daughter. Jade Snow arose, as speechless as the rest of the family, and received her father's hand in an American handshake. The congratulations of others would soon be forgotten, but she knew that she would never forget the most distinguished handshake she had ever been privileged to receive.

The excitement was not yet over, for the shipyard which had offered the prize telephoned and asked, "Would you like to sponsor our next Liberty Ship, the *William A. Jones*, this coming Sunday?"

"I would love it!" Jade Snow accepted with enthusiasm.

The public relations director of the yard gave Jade Snow all the pointers on the etiquette of a ship launching. She gave him a guest list of people to be invited by telegram, including Chinatown officials who Daddy said should not be overlooked.

Dawn of April 16, 1943, was a beautiful forecast of the day to come, as Jade Snow dressed in an embroidered Chinese coat. Jade Precious Stone, who was to attend her sister, wore a matching robe. Both were of black satin, handmade in China, one embroidered with peacocks and peonies, the other with the phoenix and peach blossoms, all in bright, variegated colors. Daddy was dressed in his best business suit, Mama in a pale-blue Chinese gown, and baby Prosperity spanking clean in a white wool suit and cap. Then an immaculate blue limousine, chauffeured by a liveried driver, called at the Wongs' front door.

On arriving at the yard, they were greeted by the officials near the launching platform, and there they met Jade Snow's boss and his family. His little blonde, pink-cheeked four-year-old daughter, dressed in white fur coat and cap, was flower girl. It was almost like a wedding!

Chinese music was being broadcast over the loudspeakers, and the platform was already filled with guests and curious workmen. As the Wongs settled themselves in the seats of honor, corsages were pinned on all the ladies. Jade Snow received two huge, delicate-colored orchids.

After her one-minute speech, her arms laden with roses, Jade Snow approached the ship.

The order was given for the workmen to cut away the remaining plates which held the ship's hull lightly in place. "Burn One!" someone called out.

"Burn One!" they echoed from below the ship's bow.

"Burn Two!"

As the last number was called, and the last hole was burned through, the ship trembled momentarily and gave a great shudder.

"Now!" the command was to Jade Snow.

"I christen thee the *William A. Jones!*" she called, and struck the bow with the champagne bottle wrapped gaily in ribbons of the national colors. Simultaneously, the ship rumbled down the way with a thunderous roar. The crowd clustered around and watched as it slid into the water with a great splash.

After Jade Snow was presented with a sterling platter for a souvenir and congratulations were over, the waiting limousine drove the Wong family back to Chinatown. In keeping with the unusual festivity of the day, Daddy proposed what was to him the height of extravagance—that his family have lunch at a Chinese restaurant.

As it was still early for Chinatown, especially for a Sunday morning, most restaurants were not yet open. But Daddy found an old friend who was willing to serve the party in a private dining room, where the balcony window overlooked the clean and picturesque shelter of St. Mary's Square.

Without hesitancy, Daddy had invited their chauffeur of the day to take lunch with them. Regarding him as a friend who was doing them a favor, Daddy lost no time in getting acquainted. In his limited English, he managed to learn about the man's wife and children, his dog, and his working conditions.

Daddy ordered the best of everything—delicate soup, barbecued squab, and a wonderful big Canton platter full of crab. This shellfish had been broken and cooked in its shell with a tomato-curry sauce, and soon the group lost all formality in eating with fingers and sucking its juices. Their chauffeur guest was tasting his first real Chinese food, and enjoying it without difficulty.

It was a day filled to overflowing with happiness. Not one dissonant note occurred to mar the harmony. Although there was no Chinese word in her vocabulary which corresponded to the American word "proud," this was the first occasion when the entire Wong family was assembled in pride of the fifth daughter.

23

"A LITTLE CHILD SHALL LEAD THEM"

T HE FIRST YEAR OUT OF COLLEGE FOUND JADE SNOW SEARCHING for her own niche in Chinatown again. She called on her former American-Chinese girl friends. For several reasons, they opened their doors but not their hearts to her. Many of them had married instead of going to college, and now their interests differed sharply.

Jade Snow made a few attempts to adjust herself to their pattern of activities, but after two years away from them and from Chinatown, she now felt more like a spectator than a participant in her own community. Finally she accepted the fact that with them she just couldn't "pick up where she left off."

For companionship she turned to those who would share the interests that she had found in the Western world. There was an attractive Caucasian girl about her age whom she had met at the pottery class during summer session. They explored dinner places around San Francisco, especially spots serving foreign foods, and especially Chinese restaurants, for the girl liked Chinese food and they could get better food in the good restaurants where native Chinese ate at a price suited to working girls' budgets. This friend was also a secretary, working for the Navy Department, and the two had fun getting acquainted.

On these evenings Jade Snow met her friend on some street corner, for she had not yet brought her Caucasian acquaintances to her home; her parents had never suggested it, and she knew that they would be made ill at ease with their different customs and the inability to converse in a common tongue. But she kept no secrets from them. From childhood habit, she always told Mama whom she was meeting, when she would leave, and when she would return. Her parents no longer interfered, but were mildly interested in her choice of friends. Making the right friends, they now said, was important. "If you are to walk in the company of two others; first observe their qualities. Find the superior one and follow him; decide who is inferior and cast him aside."

Mama was more interested in what Western people were like than in what they did; the first she could understand, but the other was beyond her experience. To Jade Snow, it seemed only reasonable that a mother living in a country foreign to her, whose daughter spoke the strange language and participated in activities incomprehensible to her, should at least like to know how the child's associates measured in terms of human values. Whatever Mama heard from Jade Snow was related to Daddy in privacy, so that even though Daddy was at his factory all day, he could depend on a pretty accurate, if Mama-colored picture, of his children's activities.

After some months, Mama had heard enough about Jade Snow's new friend to convince her that the girl was sincerely interested in everything Chinese. Mama then made a magnanimous gesture and invited her to visit their home for some simple Chinese home cooking. It was a first experience for both the Wongs and the girl. The family extended hospitality to her exactly as they would to a Chinese guest, even to passing her rice and tea with both hands. Without speaking a common language, they communicated their mutual friendliness. Daddy expanded, and tried to converse in his imperfect English, while Jade Snow translated whenever necessary.

The conversation came around to the Chinese use of names and their significance. Daddy explained the importance of names as symbols. Impulsively, their guest asked, "Would you be willing to give me a Chinese name, Mr. Wong?"

Surprised and pleased, Daddy went to his room to get his voluminous Chinese dictionary. In a burst of good humor and gratification, he decided to welcome this guest into his family by giving her his daughters' middle name, "Jade." He asked her what her main interest was, and when she replied "music," he turned to that section of his reference book.

Mama commented, "I picked the names of all my girls, while he named the boys; but now he will have the opportunity to select a girl's name!"

For moments Daddy searched and mentally debated. Not once did he think aloud, "Let's see now. How about this, or that?" Instead, when he was ready he announced conclusively, "Harp, the symbol of music, has been used since ancient days."

Jade Snow interpreted this into English. Then Daddy wrote the Chinese characters "Jade Harp" on a piece of paper and presented it to their new friend. Thereafter, whenever the Wongs referred to her, they no longer struggled to remember her by her American name, but simply called her "Jade Harp."

Jade Harp fitted in perfectly as a guest in the Wong kitchen where they always ate. She especially liked the salmon steamed with garlic and soybean sauce. She was interested in the many glass jars filled with Chinese brown sugar, dried mushrooms, dried duck gizzards, lemoned-ginger, dried red dates, dried lotus blossoms, all imported from China. Mama kept them in a neat and convenient row on an open shelf. Their guest was gracious and polite and made a great to-do over little Prosperity from Heaven, who was now a healthy bundle of energy. He responded to Jade Harp by stretching his hands in fascination to grab the first Caucasian nose within his reach.

Prosperity from Heaven had now become the greatest unifying factor in the family. At the age of six months or so, he began to respond differently to each one. The first concern of anyone upon reaching home was to look for him.

To Jade Snow home was primarily a place to go and come from

work and other activities. Here the Chinese rules she had learned so well were still observed, but she no longer had stormy sessions with her parents, although they often quoted to her old proverbs on the ethics of living. It was a rather uneventful life. Sometimes she gardened on the roof or sewed; often she baked for the cooky jar, which was the most popular item in her office. It was not unusual, at a tense moment in a business conference, for her boss to break a charged silence by saying "Have a cooky!" The men were surprised out of their defensive nervousness as they munched.

So a dual pattern, combining the new interests and the old familiar comforts, was established. The shipyard work, which permitted no vacations, kept her too busy and exhausted for discontentment. By now, the Chinatown community had lost all of its fit young male population. The first crop of sons born in America to Daddy's contemporaries had enlisted in the armed services. Dances and other usual boy-girl activities were discouraged.

As life jogged along evenly if not satisfyingly, Fate suddenly slapped Jade Snow hard.

Her back had been bothering her for some time, first with pain which was relieved by a hard bed and osteopathic manipulation, and then by attacks which could not be relieved by any drug but would confine her to bed for indefinite periods. As these attacks occurred with closer regularity, she began a series of X-rays, medical consultations, and laboratory tests for a correct diagnosis. The last consultant was an orthopedic surgeon.

The first thing he said was, "Isn't it strange that we should be sitting here in my San Francisco office, when I was born in China, and you were born here!" He continued, "My father was a missionary in Tientsin, and I spoke only Chinese until I was thirteen, when I came to America."

When he had made an examination, checked her bone measurements, listened to her case history, and studied the laboratory tests, he gave his diagnosis.

"You have an incomplete bridge in your right sacro-iliac joint and the leg on that side is shorter. It has caused a continuous strain on your lower back, and something—we don't know exactly what— is destroying that joint. It will never be well until we operate."

Jade Snow, without preparation for such a verdict, felt a clutching fear. "What does an operation mean?"

"Three weeks in the hospital, flat on your back, and at least another three weeks without walking. You should plan to be out of work for at least two months."

Jade Snow could find no words to utter. She walked to the window and looked down into the sunshine, where the people were moving normally on the streets below. In a way, everything looked the same, but it was no longer the same. A dark shadow had descended over her. She lifted her eyes above the roof lines of the city buildings, and asked the heavens why this misfortune should happen to her.

"It is not a matter of life and death," the doctor was saying, "but you will have more frequent unpredictable attacks until that joint is fused."

"How much will it cost?" she asked.

The surgeon's fee, incidentals, and hospitalization would run close to a thousand dollars.

A thousand dollars! That meant all her savings for graduate studies. Her heart welled with bitterness, and tears came, stinging her eyes. But what alternative was there? For a long moment she kept silent. "The Heavens do not heed, and the Earth does not answer," she remembered a Chinese proverb.

The surgeon broke the silence: "Would you like to talk this over with your parents first?"

"No," she answered. "No, it would be no use. It is my own decision to make, my own obligation to pay."

"Do you want to think about it?"

Jade Snow gathered her courage. "No, I'll do it."

She reported to her family briefly that she was entering the hospital in a few days, and the reason for it. Nobody seemed upset. Older Brother offered to drive over and visit her. Mama's reaction was, "If it has to be done, it has to be done." Daddy was most sympathetic. He shook his head. "Too bad!" he said in English. He gave her a notebook to print plainly for him the name of the hospital and the date of the operation. "I'll come and be with you until you wake up from the anesthetic."

Jade Snow was touched. "No, I'll have good care, and your business may be inconvenienced by your coming."

Daddy reiterated firmly, "I shall be with you. That is the right thing to do."

Mama added, "Have a telephone put in your room, and I won't have to come to see you; you can phone if you want anything."

So Jade Snow packed her little bag, took a taxi to the hospital, and underwent the operation. Sure enough, Daddy was there to comfort her when she awoke, feeling bound and stiff and dull in her bandages. Then she fell into a long sleep again.

The next day, when she was more aware of activities about her, Daddy came again, purposely more cheerful than she usually saw him. He carried a pot of nutritious Chinese chicken-and-herb soup, which he had made himself, and a porcelain spoon and bowl. He knelt by her bed, said a prayer for her recovery, and had her turn her head so that he could spoon-feed her. With his bamboo chopsticks, he fed her mushrooms and red dates from the soup. It was one of the few times when father and daughter had been alone together, and Jade Snow felt warmly grateful for this brief and affectionate companionship.

She tried to be light. "I haven't been such a baby since I had my tonsils out, and you waited with me until I woke up. I guess I haven't been fed like this since then."

Daddy's response was unexpectedly tender, although he tried to sound matter-of-fact. "I didn't personally feed you enough as a baby, and now I am patching up the hurt!"

On some days, Older Brother was a visitor, bringing a Chinese dish that Mama had fixed, of greens or carrots enriched with meat or liver to replenish her blood. One day Daddy brought her a bunch of red roses, the first she had received from him. The workers at the shipyard joined together and sent her a gigantic bouquet in a box five feet long, with candy, books, records and a get-well card signed by over fifty contributors. This illness surprised her with a knowledge of who really loved and cared for her.

The boring weeks of recovery, brightened by unexpected visits from co-workers, at last led to the day when an ambulance took her home for convalescence. As the attendants carried her upstairs on a stretcher, she caught a glimpse of little two-year-old Prosperity, dressed in a bright new jersey suit in honor of her homecoming. But he immediately scampered away and hid under her desk in fright when he caught a glimpse of the two "foreigners." Jade Snow couldn't help smiling when she saw in her little brother a picture of her own frightened self as a child when "foreign" technicians or salesmen called on her father.

Often she coaxed him to climb up on her rented high hospital bed, to play with her and help pass away the long hours of inactivity. The sensitive little boy was a great conversationalist, for being youngest in a household of seven senior members, he was unusually mature and articulate. Jade Snow and he soon established a close tie. They understood each other perfectly, and each called the other a very American term of endearment, "Honey."

Little Prosperity was most sympathetic and cautious in climbing around her bed. "Hurt?" he would query in Chinese, each time he moved about hard. When it was dinner time, he prepared to get down.

"Before you slide off my bed, get your shoes. I must put them on you first."

Instantly, Prosperity's straight brows lifted slightly, and he corrected his sister gravely, "No, first you must seek the Kingdom of God! That is what Daddy says."

Not wanting to undermine Daddy's teachings, Jade Snow good-naturedly complied: "All right, first seek the Kingdom of God. But you know, Mama also said that you must never run around without your shoes, or you'll get splinters from the factory floor."

"O.K.!" was the cheerful American retort.

Jade Snow, old enough to be her brother's mother, began a program of interpreting, enforcing, and supplementing her parents' teaching, to bridge a gap of over half a century between parents and son. Remembering her own youthful confusions, she hoped to save him unnecessary hurts.

For the next four weeks Prosperity devoted his life to Jade Snow's comfort, relieving the gloom of solitary convalescence. Sometimes she told him American stories of "Little Black Sambo" and "The Three Bears" in Chinese translation. Daddy insisted that his baby learn only Chinese until he went to American kindergarten, but Jade Snow wanted him to know some common American folk tales.

When she became well enough to learn to walk again, however, and hobbled along to re-educate her leg muscles while clinging to Mama's shoulder for support, Prosperity became upset and jealous. This was not the correct order of things! He had never seen Big

Sister and Mama with their arms around each other! After patient explaining, Mama put her arms around him too, and he was finally pacified. Then he fell into the spirit of things, and gave Honey his hand on her other side.

It was surprising how the child had already absorbed the family creed of the Correct Order of Things. As soon as he learned to toddle, he would shut dresser drawers and doors left open by careless users. Later, having followed around after each member of the household, he knew better than anyone else just where things belonged and whose they were. To protect himself from blame, he made himself custodian of individual property rights, and protested bitterly if anyone used another's possession. Daddy's creed of "Each one to his own pair of scissors" was being literally enforced, and even if beloved Older Sister Jade Snow used Mama's pair of scissors by permission, he would scream his distress.

Prosperity had already formulated his policy concerning each family member, for although he was free to seek comfort and a good time from anyone, he was by the same token subject to the whims and discipline of many elders.

Oldest Brother's dexterity with tools and machinery fascinated him. If a drain clogged, a switch failed, the child would announce the fact immediately upon Oldest Brother's arrival home. "Big Brother can fix anything," he was sure. When the fixing was in progress, Prosperity was an absorbed audience. As a result, standard baby toys didn't interest him, but tools did. In lieu of scissors, he already had his very own hammer, and he loved to nail pieces of wood together.

Prosperity was devoted to Jade Precious Stone's wardrobe, among which were frilly or frou-frou hats, and her toilet articles, including make-up and sultry perfumes. When Prosperity was in a mood to masquerade, he would seek Jade Precious Stone's co-operation in applying lipstick, perfume, and hand lotion, and top himself off with a little black-lace-and-roses hat; then he ran around the house to be admired.

During the day, when the other children were either at school or at work, Prosperity relied on Mama for care and companionship. Her discipline with him was unrelaxed, and he already had learned to fear the clothes hanger. He might in a moment of abandonment start to push the contents off a table, and counter Mama's warning with, "But baby *must* sweep," but the sight of a clothes hanger instantly arrested him.

However, it was not just discipline that he received from his mother, for she was also giving him a thorough Chinese education. After her housework was done, Mama still sewed seams. Older Brother brought home the overalls in his automobile, and returned them to Daddy's factory when sewn, so that all the overalls Daddy made still went through Mama's hands. As Mama worked, her son would be perched on a table near by or on a corner of her machine. Through long hours, Mama patiently taught him a repertoire of Chinese children's rhymes, from four to fifty lines long. These were part of the folklore handed down from generation to generation by word of mouth in her native Cantonese village. Jade Snow, hearing them, was reminded that she learned exactly the same lines when she was a baby.

Prosperity clung to Daddy, whom he saw for comparatively brief moments, because he found that Daddy indulged him almost completely. When the family chastised their smallest member for naughtiness, and he was unusually naughty when Daddy was at home, their father would say, "You should not be severe with a little child but should rejoice that he has an inquiring mind!"

Prosperity's training was, in one way, exactly the same as Jade Snow's at the same age; but in another way it was different. Daddy and Mama, who claimed that they brought up all their children with the same discipline, had nevertheless mellowed a great deal, and they were much more affectionate with this child. He might just as well have been an only child with three times as many parents as the average child. The fact that he was unusually endearing helped; also the fact that their economic struggles had been greatly relieved by now, since former dependents had grown into wage earners who contributed to the family budget.

Thus Prosperity was comparatively daring in the liberties he took with his father. Once, when Daddy crawled under a machine to fix its belt, he reached for the tools he had left there. Finding none, he gave an outraged roar. His son with "the inquiring mind" had picked them up to repair a machine himself!

"Prosperity, bring back my tools and go away. Get OUT!"

Prosperity made no move, but quietly asked, "Daddy . . . do you still love me?"

Daddy, slightly confused and completely softened, answered, "Yes, I still love you. . . . But I want my tools!"

Reassured, Prosperity retorted in English, "O.K.," and scampered to fetch them. He earnestly explained, "You said, 'Get out' as you would order a horse!"

Daddy gave his youngest son a good foundation in Biblical hymns, quotations, and Christian philosophy, all of which enraptured the child. He especially liked the hymns, and sometimes would pick up the telephone to call Daddy at his factory, in order to sing a hymn with him, although the resulting harmony left much to be desired.

While Mama took care of his academic training, Daddy took care of his practical education. When an epidemic of mice struck their home, Daddy brought from the factory his favorite black cat, Forever Fragrant. Prosperity loved to chase the cat in play, but after a few weeks at home he noticed that the cat was swelling out in her belly. "Why is our cat in such a condition?" he demanded.

Mama looked significantly at Daddy, and said nothing. The older brothers and sisters caught the look and refrained from answering. Some things were for their father and mother to decide about their own child.

"Why is our cat in such a condition?" Prosperity demanded again.

Daddy assumed the responsibility of answering him. "I shall tell you privately, after dinner."

After dinner the father, nearing seventy, and the son, nearing three, went hand in hand to Daddy's room. The door was shut during their private conference. They emerged later, both looking grave. Prosperity said nothing about their conversation. The kittens were born, and after a few days Forever Fragrant brought them out. She lay in the sunshine that came down from the skylight, and blinked her eyes as she nursed her babies. Prosperity studied the scene at great length, but said nothing. It was clear that, whatever Daddy had told him, he was profoundly impressed.

When the older sisters and brothers-in-law came home to visit occasionally, Prosperity called them by customary title, "Oldest

Sister" or "Older Brother." This form of salutation created amusing situations, as when he addressed Oldest Sister's strapping teenage son. "Hello, Big Nephew," Prosperity would say. "Hello, Little Uncle," his nephew would respond.

Although he called the in-laws "Brother" and "Sister," he was not exactly sure about their proper relationship. One day, when Prosperous State took him for a walk, Prosperity asked him, "Older Brother Prosperous State, are you one of 'our people,' or are you not one of 'our people'?"

Prosperous State was amused. "What do you mean? Why, of course I am one of your people."

Prosperity was delighted and relieved. "That is fine. Mama says that I am not to ask anybody to buy me candy or toys unless he is one of 'our people.' Now I can ask you to buy me something and she can't scold me!"

In the areas where she was sure that there would be no conflict with the policies of Mama and Daddy, Jade Snow tried to supplement Prosperity's early training with exposures which she had missed as a child. She wanted this little brother to encounter people and experiences of the Occidental world, so that for him there would never be the shock of sudden adjustment when it was time for him to mingle outside his own home. Therefore, whenever possible, she took him to call on friends, to shop, to walk and visit the parks—outings which would bring him into the realm of Western habits and customs. Since he spoke no English, he depended upon Jade Snow to interpret both language and the meaning of these new experiences.

At their first party where the other children were fair-skinned Caucasian youngsters, Prosperity silently clung to his older sister, not missing a thing, but not participating. Finally, when another little boy just his age approached him, Jade Snow curiously asked, "Now what do you think of this cute little boy?"

Prosperity reserved judgment. "Does he have to wear diapers like me?"

Caucasians to him looked different from the people in his familiar environment, but he had begun to look for certain fundamental likenesses.

For Jade Snow, Prosperity was almost like a son of her own. He was always delighted when, on their trips together, strangers mistook her for his mother. As he phrased it, "Mama is my inside mother at home, but Honey is my outside mother."

24

REDISCOVERING CHINATOWN

J ADE SNOW WAS MOVING WITH INCREASING CONFIDENCE AND PLEASURE in the Western world, but she was also taking pleasure in redis- covering her Chinese community. Chinatown had, of course, changed greatly since the war began. War restrictions on commer- cial shipping had prevented further imports of all the wares and foods upon which Chinatown had depended, both as business for the stores, and for daily living. Enterprising merchants sought sub- stitutes, some of which were fairly satisfactory. These included Texas Patna rice, domestic soy and mung beans (for soy sauce and bean sprouts), Monterey's dried squid and salt fish, and Chinatown's own cured sausage, pressed duck, and preserved duck eggs.

Others were quite unsatisfactory. Among these were plastic spoons which curled up when used for hot soup, bright and heavy domestic pottery to replace Chinese porcelain, strong English-type teas in place of delicate Chinese bouquets.

The mellow look in Chinese store windows gave way to a bazaar aspect as display gaps were filled with Mexican pottery and glass, glittering costume jewelry, flimsy baskets, and humorous souvenirs. But the eager tourists with the flush pockets of 1944 created enough of a demand to make Chinatown an economically prosperous community.

Jade Snow never entered the novelty bazaars, except when visiting friends insisted. She shopped for most of her needs in the American department stores or specialty shops. But there were a few services which she liked to have done near home when time was at a premium. Among the craftsmen in Chinatown were several of the older generation who took great pride in their work.

The shoe-repair man operated a tiny factory, just big enough to hold his machinery, a counter, and two chairs. His front window was filled with plants, and the shop itself was not wide enough to allow more than two people to walk abreast. A cheesecloth curtain separated the front business portion from the living quarters in back. The proprietor held a war job during the day and repaired shoes at night. His wife had the first-generation look—feet which had once been bound, long black cotton Chinese skirt and blouse, straight all-black hair knotted into a bun, and an ageless plain face like Jade Snow's grandmother.

When the bell jangled to announce that a customer had entered, the wife came out from her living quarters, sometimes wiping her hands dry from housework, and took the shoes for repair or found shoes being called for. She was not talkative, but she knew the business, could determine prices and when work would be ready. She made change from money she kept behind the curtain.

Her husband was a mild, gray-haired man, of smaller build than she. In spite of the fact that shoe repairing was not a clean occupation, Jade Snow never found him with a spot on his clothes, or a hair out of place, or a shiny nose. He was most shy, worked meticulously and pridefully, and always shined shoes free with every job.

Jade Snow might never have come to know him except that his begonia looked pale and sickly. Impulsively she asked, "What do you feed your plants?"

The man was surprised and reluctant to open a conversation. "I don't know," he said.

"I have some fertilizer that is good for acid-loving plants," she volunteered, knowing full well that it was not very polite for a young Chinese woman to be so forward with a stranger.

"Acid plant?" He didn't seem to understand.

Jade Snow launched into a discussion of plants and their habits, and found that the shoe-repair man loved plants, but didn't know what to do for them. When she called for her shoes after a few days, she brought with her some of the chemicals she had mentioned and doctored his plants. He no longer hesitated to talk, but he was embarrassed to know how to thank her. From that day he gave her first priority, and her shipyard-scuffed shoes were always well cared for in the days of shoe rationing when every pair was precious.

A watch-repair man was equally interesting. His store was on Grant Avenue, the main thoroughfare of Chinatown. Rows of clocks ticked busily in the window. Inside, a short man, as wide as he was tall, sat stooped and hunched over his work, with a magnifying glass perpetually fitted over one eye. Like the shoe-repair man, his was a one-man business also, his desk was meticulously in order, and the shop was just big enough to allow two people to pass.

Jade Snow first brought him a very tiny wrist watch which had simply stopped running. He looked at it and declared, "No use to fix this."

"Why not?"

Unlike the shoe-repair man, he was loud, positive, and temperamental. "Why not? This is like a tiny frying pan heated beyond its normal temperature and without oil. It's just no good any more."

Jade Snow didn't try to argue with him. Daddy let her have one of his old watches, and she brought this to him to be oiled and checked.

"All right, all right," he said this time. "It will be seven-fifty and you can have it next week. Now write your name in Chinese in this book, and I will enter the serial number so that you may be sure when you call for it that I have not traded your watch."

As Jade Snow wrote the Chinese characters, he said, "I am surprised that you know how to write Chinese. These Chinese girls born here usually have less interest in education than in boys." He examined the characters. "Hm . . . they are fairly good—square and straight."

A few months later, the watch was ailing.

"Does this watch need fixing again?" he asked. "Let me see if it is no good, or whether you have strained it. I remember that I fixed it well, and not very long ago either." And to her amazement he gave Jade Snow the exact month of repair.

He opened it up and looked through his magnifying glass. "Where do you work?" he asked indignantly.

Mystified, Jade Snow replied, "The shipyard."

"No wonder it is so filled with fine metallic dust. Good thing you have a man's watch. You can never wear a delicate woman's watch."

Jade Snow wrote her name again in the little notebook.

"Ah, so you work in the shipyard. In China, I worked in a shipyard, too. I have been doing work with my hands all my life."

Jade Snow, who had never heard of a shipyard in China, asked him some questions, and he answered with interesting particulars about working conditions. She hazarded another question, "You don't happen to know anything about pottery work in China, do you?"

Surprisingly, he did. "I grew up near the stoneware kilns in China. I used to watch the Chinese potters work. They kicked their wheels with their feet, and when big pots had to be made, one man did the kicking and the other did the shaping."

Seeing Jade Snow's interest, he expanded, "But I think that was pretty crude stuff. Only peasants used that handthrown pottery with the earthy look. The big crocks were used for shipping preserved food or for cooking and kitchen purposes. No metal containers, you know."

Jade Snow disagreed with his low opinion of handthrown Chinese stoneware, "Here in this country it is greatly in demand, and it is expensive."

He was scornful, "Oh, the foreigners here; there are always a few who like to be different, if they can afford it. But you know that the majority use those nice, shiny, smooth, bright dishes, reasonably priced at stores everywhere. I really admire American expertness with machines. You can place the cheapest little dish on a polished table and it will be so smooth it won't scratch. But you take the most expensive piece of Chinese porcelain—its foot will be so gritty that you can use it as a sharpening stone for knives!"

Jade Snow no longer tried to argue. But she never failed to have an interesting conversation with him whenever she brought in her watch or the watches of her friends. Sometimes they talked about Chinese pottery-firing kilns; sometimes they talked about shipyards; sometimes they talked about watches; and sometimes just about people. But the philosophical proprietor of the watch-repair shop never failed to have an opinion about everything, and never failed to express it forcefully.

The Chinese opera was one of the experiences Jade Harp shared with Jade Snow. As a child, Jade Snow had been to the theater once or twice, but she didn't have any real understanding of the opera and the language of the stage was not their daily Cantonese. However, she delighted in the brilliant costumes, the bizarre make-up, snow-white or jet-black artificial hair and beards, and jeweled headdresses.

Now, returning as an adult, she was able to pick out the plot and to see the audience as well as the performance with new eyes.

The girls arrived one evening a few minutes after the opera had begun, but they alone were the audience. The players were singing solos, without apparent effort or thought. They stared curiously at the two girls, until Jade Snow felt that they instead of the play were under observation. The property man wandered around on the stage unconcernedly, straightened a pillow or a chair here and there, and joined the actors in staring at the punctual members of their audience. One of several standard sets of painted scenery formed the stage background. Now it was the interior of a home. To the left, a five-piece orchestra played on the stage; one of the traditional string instruments had been replaced by a violin, which echoed the others in Chinese harmony. Brass cymbals broke into loud clanging whenever a character was about to enter the scene.

About half an hour after the performance had begun, a few old Chinese women drifted in to join the girls and the ushers. Some of these older inhabitants of Chinatown came regularly every night, for the opera was the center of their social life. For another hour, more people drifted in and sat anywhere they wished in the almost-empty theater. Those who recognized friends went over to chat with them. Children who didn't have tickets gathered together, first in the boxes. Then, as ticket holders of those seats came, they ran to front seats on the main floor, and later as these seats were claimed, they went to the balcony. Sometimes, they chased the cats which wandered about in leisurely fashion. People freely left their seats to purchase peanuts, soda pop, or candy. The cracking of melon seeds was a distinctive minor note. Mothers nursed babies with bottles and fathers read Chinese newspapers. A few young girls, whispered about as flirts, paraded up and down the aisles in new form-fitting silk Chinese dresses, which covered them completely except where the high side slits revealed shapely limbs as they walked. The older men gave them appreciative glances. It was a relaxed gathering, with everyone in high spirits. The seats were only half filled an hour and a half after the performance had begun, and the actors and actresses were still playing their roles with half a heart. Small wonder, for no one could tell that the audience was paying any attention.

Then it was nine-thirty, and a horde of people swarmed in sud-denly to fill all the unused seats, which went for reduced prices at this hour. Some came because of the lower prices, others to see the better acting. For now both performers and audience settled down to the business of the evening. The actors gave a quick résumé of what had happened, and then worked toward the climax. Whenever a scene of importance was beginning, the cymbals obligingly announced it with a great flourish. The men quickly folded their papers and the women turned from their babies and visiting to pay undivided attention. Like the Chinese novel, the opera, which was based on great Chinese legends, offered many side excursions and indulged in subplots which it never intended to finish. As a matter of fact, the last hour was really the best and most exciting.

Jade Snow interpreted to Jade Harp and explained the profuse use of symbolism: the little wand with varicolored tassels which indicated a horse, the pacing back and forth on the front part of the stage which indicated a journey, the women who were acting as men, the men who were acting as women, and the costumes which were the key to the positions of the actors—a nobleman, a warrior, a scholar, a princess, a servant girl, a messenger.

The play was a bedroom farce, wherein a beautiful young wife, rebelling against her "blind" marriage to an old wealthy landowner, surreptitiously carried on an affair with a handsome young scholar whom she met at her garden wall. Rightfully, she was trapped in her unfaithfulness by her husband. The climax was reached when the downcast sinner was chastised in the privacy of their bedroom by her wrathful spouse. He strode up and down indignantly, hurling scornful denunciations, with his hands tucked importantly in his elaborate belt. The audience now paid undivided attention.

Then a most terrible fate was announced by the husband: "You deserve the action I am going to take—I shall report this to your honorable father!"

So the curtain dropped on the triumphant husband and the pleading, weeping wife, who could not have heard a more severe and disgraceful sentence. The audience nodded in approval. Then, at a quarter to one in the morning, the crowd prepared to leave for a midnight snack or to return home.

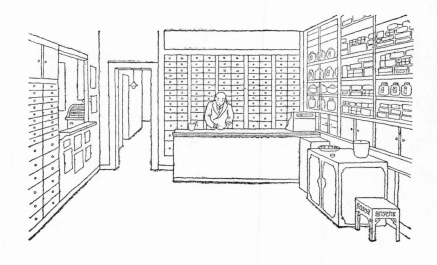

25

THE SANCTUM OF HARMONIOUS SPRING

THERE WAS ANOTHER DISCOVERY FOR JADE SNOW IN CHINATOWN. One day, quite by accident, she passed by a Chinatown store window which carried a display of about twenty large Chinese brushes a half-inch in diameter, a rare item for which there was no domestic substitute. A black-lacquered wooden plaque with gilded Chinese characters, a traditional means of posting a store's name, told her that this was "The Sanctum of Harmonious Spring." Jade Snow saw with surprise that the dark interior was an herb shop, for there had been no samples of herbs in the window.

The store was characterized in the usual way, by one wall solidly lined with long drawers. Each drawer was divided into three or four compartments of different sizes for various herbs. Neither the compartments nor the drawers were labeled. Yet, as Jade Snow knew from experience, the herbalist could unerringly pull out the proper drawer, reach into the correct unseen compartment, and pick up the required herb.

Opposite the wall of drawers were some chairs: some were enormous, handsomely carved Chinese teakwood, others were battered rockers such as those usually found in American second-hand furniture stores. Back farther, there was a wooden cabinet with a tea cozy and porcelain cups in a pan of rinse water. To the left in back, a semiprivate office was divided from the store by a counter. This kind of office was typical.

There were other cabinets with glass doors revealing an endless variety of herbs and medicines in miscellaneous tin and cardboard containers, former tea cans, underwear boxes, and such, arranged without organization but clearly labeled with beautiful Chinese brush characters. "Genuine Gall Bladder of Bear," "Spiritually Effective Powder for Sprains," "Old Mountain Sweet-Oil Cinnamon Bark," "Pills to Stop Ten Thousand Pains," "Genuine Snake Oil," "Pimple Powder." These were a few.

Everything in the dim interior, which was twice as large as most Chinese herb stores, seemed dusty, worn smooth, and age-darkened, giving Jade Snow the feeling that the place was timeless, and that some of the articles placed in their original positions half a century ago had not been moved. The merest hint of a medicinal smell permeated the atmosphere.

The solitary figure in the place, as mellow-looking as his surroundings, came forward to greet her. He was dressed immaculately in a dark American business suit, a once-tall figure now bent to five feet. He was bald, with a pale, calm, and cleanly shining face. Black, bushy eyebrows swept straight up, and then their long hairs just hung at the end, framing gleaming eyes which roved constantly, now looking directly at his customer, now staring out into the street. His expression was kind, his manner courteous and leisurely.

"Good afternoon, Sien Sung [the equivalent of "Sir"], I would like to purchase some of your large brushes displayed in the window," Jade Snow said.

"Look them over and select the ones most suitable for you. There are some fine small brushes too, although you may not know what they are." He slid open the glass case and reached for them. He removed the hollow bamboo casing protecting the tip and showed her one.

"The small ones are genuine black water-bird bristles," he explained. "They have high spring quality and will respond sensitively to the gentlest manipulations, while the large ones made of white bristles are useful only for coarser work."

Jade Snow really needed the large ones for occasional decorations in pottery work. "Five dimes is a very reasonable price, in view of their scarcity. It has been years since new imports," she remarked as she chose some.

"It would be easy to charge more, but I have ethics—and for a few cents it is foolish to take advantage of people. Actually, these are a cousin's brushes, and he was hoarding them. But I persuaded him to let me convert them into cash." He smiled.

Her eyes swept around, and she nodded at his herbs, "Haven't your herbs gone up considerably in price?"

"Of course, I do not need to tell you that there is a normal increase in the prices of many herbs anyway because of age," he said gently. "For instance, you must drink tea. Take my clear herbal tea, which is a remarkable remedy for indigestion."

He thumbed through some memos hanging without apparent organization on a nail, and located a price listing for clear herbal tea. Pushing before her the yellowed paper with its vertical rows of neat characters, he said, "Read this."

Aware of his scrutiny, she read silently, "The Year of the Chinese Republic Seven: $25 a pound; the Year of the Chinese Republic Eight: $24 a pound; the Year of the Chinese Republic Nine: $23 a pound. . . ."

She concluded aloud, "The older the tea, the more expensive it is; a dollar for each year it ages."

"That is only natural," was his reply. "Herb tea improves with age. It is also true of fruit peel. I have forty-year-old fruit peel, which is almost priceless. Do you know how to use it?"

Yes, she knew. Mama soaked it in hot water and scraped off its white membrane before using it as a delicate flavoring for steamed fish or certain soups.

The proprietor disagreed. "I do not recommend that method of preparation. Just grind or pound up the whole dry skin, and use it, lining membrane included, for most dishes. However, one dish which does call for your mother's method is fruit-peel duck. You take about a small rice-bowlful of dry fruit peel and soak it thoroughly; then scrape its inner surface. Cook the peeling in a saucepan with a couple of large spoonfuls of honey until all the honey is taken up. Then put this mixture in the bottom of a large bowl. Place the duck on top and steam until tender. Now pour off the juices and flip the contents of the bowl over on a platter so that the glazed fruit peel, which has absorbed the duck juice, is on top. Make a cornstarch gravy with the liquid and pour it over the fowl. Garnish the platter with shredded green onions or Chinese parsley. I tell you, you will eat the fruit peel and leave the duck!"

Seeing that she was extremely interested, he continued, "Fruit peel comes from a special rare species of the citrus family, the kum (similar to a tangerine). There are many kinds of kum; some are not large enough to be worth drying; some are not suitable for drying. There is the story of an old man in China who raised a special kind of kum tree, admirably suitable for fruit peel, and on Chinese New Year's gave two of these fruits to each of his employees, but only on the condition that after the fruit was eaten they would return the peel to him for drying.

"For the most effective preservation of kum peel," he went on, "dry it in the sun, then store it with dried orange peel; otherwise the kum peel will gradually disintegrate."

She asked how he could distinguish between kum and orange peel when both were mixed in the same drawer. He laughed, amused by the suggestion that there could be any such difficulty for one who knew.

By this time the brushes had been wrapped, paid for, and the change made, but Jade Snow lingered, fascinated. The shop was quiet. No other customer had come in and the proprietor seemingly had nothing to do but talk.

"You are a native daughter, aren't you? You have never been in China, but some day you may be able to study these things at first hand for yourself."

Jade Snow asked how long it had been since his last visit to China.

"Forty-five years—and fifty-five years since I came to America the first time. It's difficult to leave your business after you get it started because it is hard to get a trusted employee. Once I sent for one of my relatives from China to learn my business, but did he want a gentleman's job? No, instead of staying at my store after he arrived, he took a job as a dishwasher to make more money. So now he drifts from job to job. No self-respect, no security. I guess he was too old when he began here. You can't teach a man a new trade or business after he's thirty."

"Daddy told me that in China a father sends his son away at an early age to a good friend for business training," she volunteered, "the theory being that if his son became angered at the friend, he would run away and return to his father, but if the father undertook this training himself, the son might run away from the father. Thus, friends can be mutually free in disciplining each other's sons. I understand that three years is the minimum apprenticeship period."

The proprietor-philosopher agreed. "Business training in China is rigorous indeed. It begins with the most humble duties—what would be merely janitorial work here. The trainee becomes what we call a tea-spittoon-chair boy. It means that his training begins with the maintenance of the shop and the welcoming of the customers by keeping the teapot filled with fresh tea and the spittoon emptied. He pulls up a chair for the customer, and serves him tea. He has to wait until his master retires before he may rest himself. All this may sound strange to you, but, as I say, some day you will see all these things for yourself.

Jade Snow said good-by then, but a few days later she returned for more brushes. Smilingly the proprietor asked if she had cooked fruit-peel duck yet. She said that the current poultry shortage had cut off the duck supply in Chinatown. He looked as astonished as his habitually quiet face permitted. "But there must be ducks!"

"There aren't even any eggs to be had!"

At this remark, he waved triumphantly to the back corner of the store. She could hardly believe her eyes, but there were several galvanized buckets filled with eggs. It developed that his nephew, who delivered poultry from the country to the shops, dropped in every week end after his deliveries with a crate or two of fresh eggs for his uncle to use and retail, along with his herbs, brushes, and notebooks. So Jade Snow happily bought two dozen to surprise her family.

While the eggs were being wrapped up, a listless-looking, middle-aged Caucasian woman appeared from one of the back rooms. She followed a Chinese of slight stature, probably the proprietor's helper. She carried a package of herbs, stopped to pay some money at the counter, then left without having uttered a word. Jade Snow asked what was wrong with her. The proprietor replied in typical Chinese medical terminology, "Her inner unbalance causes a lack of spirit."

"But do you really help her?" Jade Snow asked, remembering that the Chinese case diagnosis was based solely on the study of the appearance and actions of the patient, and diagnosis of his pulse beats. In Chinese medicine "to have one's pulse felt" was the extent of a complete medical examination. As a matter of fact, in China retiring Chinese ladies extended their hand outside the canopy of their bed for such an examination while they remained hidden.

He answered, "She claims that she is better from our prescriptions. She is but one of the unsolicited patients who come in."

Jade Snow's curiosity about the herbs was not yet satisfied. There was, for instance, a glass jar with unpeeled garlic clusters soaking in brown liquid, marked, "The Year of the Republic Thirty." (Nineteen-fifty would be the Year of the Republic Thirty-nine, since the Year of the Chinese Republic One was 1911.) The garlic was thus seven years old. She learned that it was preserved in brine and the longer it was kept, the better it became. Its purpose? A sure cure for indigestion.

Then the proprietor picked up a piece of what looked like a very thinly sliced bias cross-section of the bough of a tree. It was called "dog-elbow root," and its core was good for bone pains. But the fuzz on the root was first scraped off after drying and stored for use on cuts to assist coagulation and blood clotting. The root core itself was then steamed until softened and pliable, and sliced thinly on the bias before redrying.

Pleased with her information, and clutching her precious eggs, Jade Snow returned home. Her family was amazed to hear that eggs were to be found in an herb store where she had bought brushes in the first place, but dismissed the whole account with the remark, "It's just like you to be able to get eggs at such queer places."

On another errand to the Sanctum of Harmonious Spring, Jade Snow found another customer in the store, a nice-looking woman in a fur wrap, Caucasian again, waiting in a teakwood chair. The proprietor hustled around, apparently preparing to attend her. He took the teapot from its cozy on the corner cabinet and disappeared into the back corridor. A few moments later, he returned and escorted the lady into the consultation room.

Jade Snow realized now that the man was more than store owner and philosopher, that his knowledge of herbs was more than that of a dealer—he was also an herb doctor.

When she visited the store again, it was to seek his professional advice. She had had a deep cough for a long time, and she had found in the past that Chinese herbs cured her coughs quickly. She had heretofore gone to any herb store, described her symptoms, told her age, specified a quarter's or fifty cents' worth of herbs, and then watched the herbalist open drawers, take out ten or twelve species of dried grasses, roots, bark, leaves, or insects, in quantities whose weights he guessed with his hand, then wrap them in a package with instructions for brewing: "Use two bowls of water and boil until there is one bowl left; drink before you go to bed." With the purchase of herbs, one was given a choice of imported dried Chinese "loong-ngan" fruit or white raisins to take away the bitterness after drinking the tea.

This method was an informal way of getting well. For serious cases, however, one must consult an herb doctor, have one's pulse felt, and obtain an exact written prescription of herbs in specified quantities. As Jade Snow had never suffered an ailment which required formal herb prescription, the experience of having her pulse felt was a new one. But the proprietor of the Sanctum of Harmonious Spring insisted. He led her to one of his consultation rooms, a small office about nine feet square dimly lit by a hanging central fixture. Its furniture consisted of a table with a straight chair on either side. The table was covered with a faded plush cloth, and on it was a conspicuously red, velvet-covered cushion, about eight by twelve inches.

Jade Snow was asked to be seated and to take off her wrist watch. The doctor, seated across from her, took her left wrist, rested it on the cushion, and laid his curved fingers very delicately on her pulse. Then he closed his eyes and dropped his head low, in a gesture of concentration. In that instant, Jade Snow knew the reason for his stoop. It was from years and years of professional practice. A complete silence was maintained until he had registered in his mind the pulse beats of both wrists. Then he picked up his brush, moistened it on the inkpad, and with a quick stroke of his slender fingers, began scribbling graceful black characters on a piece of buff mulberry paper. In total, he prescribed eighteen herbs in exact weights. While he was writing, Jade Snow asked what he had found wrong with her.

"I wonder that you are not in a greater illness," he said. "You have fire all through your body."

In Chinese terms "fire" and "wind" are two opposite extremes in body state, and roughly correspond to acidity and alkalinity. They are opposite terms, departure points for the Chinese diagnosis of body ills. Fire is allied to an acid condition usually caused by fried foods, rich meats, heavy spices, or excess alcohol. This state can be neutralized by alkaline foods such as fruits, vegetables, or herbs. Wind is caused by sudden or continuous exposure to cold, or by too many cold fruits and raw vegetables which cause a gaseous or "windy" stomach. This can be neutralized by a substance like ginger root. Fire and wind are very complex in meaning as there are several forms of each, and a patient can have a combination of both, in varying degrees, such as "wind wrapped around fire," and "fire collided against wind."

The usual medicinal strategy in attacking a coexistent fire and wind situation is to neutralize the fire, which frees the wind with temporary violence; but it would be almost fatal, on the other hand, to attack the wind without this preliminary neutralization treatment, as the fire would then be imprisoned within the body to cause great fever. For instance, ginger tea would effectively treat wind cases. But if one had fire arising from an acid diet before one caught cold, it would not do at all to take the ginger tea first, which would only abet the fire. Instead, one would first take an herb tea to correct the acid condition, which would quench the fire and release the cold, or wind. Then one would quell the wind with ginger tea.

According to the herb doctor, Jade Snow had fire all through her body, accumulated over a long period of unwise diet, and then she had caught cold, or met the wind, thus trapping the fire. In the face of such a grave situation, Jade Snow decided against telling him about the 50,000 units of Vitamin A and the aspirin she had been consuming, following her research on colds. But she could not help wondering whether they were helping the wind, making the fire worse, or were no help at all in Chinese terms.

Now they returned to the front of the store. The formula was placed on the counter, weighted down, and then the doctor and his assistant worked silently to weigh the ingredients. When Jade Snow asked how fast the cure would work, she was told that she should simply try out the prescription. Normally, only one or two refills would be required for a complete cure.

But she found it unnecessary to obtain even one refill because in a few days the herb tea had completed its work, both in quenching the fire and quelling the wind.

26

ALAS, SHE WAS BORN TOO TALL

IT WAS NOW SEVERAL YEARS AFTER THE MARRIAGE OF FOURTH OLDER Sister, and Jade Snow was obviously the next person in the Wong family in line for marriage. Mama had from time to time hinted, and then openly declared, that in China this daughter would have been married and a mother of several children at her age. In a softer moment, she had pointed out to Jade Snow that affectionate parents couldn't take care of her all her life, and that she should have a husband to nurse her in case of illness and pain. Marriage was a normal thing, and an old maid was therefore abnormal. In China, an old maid was an oddity who must have defeated or refused co-operation in all attempts to arrange a marriage, an oddity to be talked about in whispers. Jade Snow at twenty-two —or twenty-three by the Chinese count from conception, which made a baby one year old at birth—was by that reasoning quite definitely an old maid.

In China, the worst curse upon an unwed maiden was to hurl these words at her: "May your soul be forever homeless." The character for "home" and "family" are one and the same. That is, there is no home without family, or when a Chinese says, "I am going home," he is also literally saying, "I am returning to my family." A woman belongs to the family into which she marries. and only finds a home with her husband; therefore, if she died unwed, she would have established no family and would belong to no home.

When subtle hints on the subject were dropped, Jade Snow would answer impersonally that freedom was also desirable, and housework was tiresome. In irritation, her parents had retorted, "You cannot so independently continue to refute the core of our culture. The time has come for you to give up some of your foreign ideas to insure your own personal future happiness, even though what we say does not attract you now. You know the saying, 'A knife cannot be sharp on both ends, nor can a needle be pointed at both ends.'"

To save their peculiarly headstrong daughter, who had now indulged herself in the luxury of a college education, from the misery into which she was obliviously plunging, Daddy and Mama employed their resourcefulness to arrange for a proper husband for her.

How much they discussed her in privacy she didn't know. But it must have been their common enterprise which led to an enlivening climax one otherwise dull Sunday evening, when Jade Snow had settled herself in the kitchen for her weekly feminine chores.

She had put on her work uniform, which consisted of leftover saddle oxfords from college days when it was not fashionable ever to clean them, odd-colored cotton socks, the oldest navy-blue skirt she owned, and a shapeless, faded sweatshirt. Then she gathered up all her laundry which had to be handwashed, and piled it on the kitchen table. Next she pulled down her straight, long hair, preparing to shampoo it. She planned to do her laundry while her hair was drying.

Daddy came into the kitchen, and noted anxiously, "You are washing your hair!"

"Why, yes." Jade Snow couldn't understand his sudden interest in such a commonplace activity.

Not two minutes later, the doorbell rang, an unusual occurrence, as they rarely had callers. With alacrity, Daddy himself started the long trek from the kitchen to open the front door. This also was unusual.

Jade Snow rinsed her hair after the first soaping and had begun on the second soaping when she heard men's voices coming near. Instead of taking the visitors to the front room, Daddy was escorting them into the kitchen, which was difficult to understand. He and the guests sat down at the kitchen table. Jade Snow was uncomfortably aware that her laundry was scattered in plain sight! What should she do? She didn't know.

The men were talking. Innocently, Daddy opened the conversation. "Fellow Villager, to what do I owe the honor of this unusual visit?"

Jade Snow, her back to the room, peered under her arm, and could see an elderly, portly, slightly bald Chinese gentleman with heavy, dark-rimmed glasses, dressed in a gray business suit.

"Ah," he answered, "my dear Brother Wong, I thought my duty to my son was done when I had raised and educated him, but now I find that it is not done after all."

Again, innocently, Daddy asked, "Why is that, and is this your fine son with you?"

"Yes, this is the son. I find that now I must find a wife for him."

By a little maneuvering, Jade Snow bent and turned so that she could see the young man under her other arm. He was already well on his way to being portly like his father. He had said nothing, but had settled himself back in his chair as if well satisfied with himself.

Daddy commented significantly, "Marriage is a very proper thing. In America, people seem quite confident of finding their own mates without assistance."

Fellow Villager Foo was as jovial as if he were talking about nice weather. "But my boy has been bashful, and I have come to you for assistance."

The facts of the situation were plainly laid down. Daddy wasted no further time with Fellow Villager Foo. Instead, he turned to young Foo. "So you are looking for a wife. I need some information from you."

Young Foo nodded shyly.

Jade Snow now finished her second rinsing. She didn't know whether or not to dry her hair, pick up her laundry from their sight and disappear, or to stay. No one had indicated that he was aware of her presence in the room. Suspecting, however, that the next few minutes would hold interesting disclosures, she decided that she would be hygienically clean—she started on a third soaping.

Mama came into the room with Prosperity clinging in her arms, and remained standing in a corner. It would not have been becoming for her to join in the conversation with two strange men. But of course she was not missing a thing.

Daddy sought his information. "What is your occupation?" When he found that the prospective suitor was an engineer, he asked, "How much money have you saved? Do you have an automobile? What make and year? Is that all paid for? How old are you?"

The poor young man had no defense but to tell all. Then Daddy asked, "When you are married, will your wife have to live with your mother or will you build a house for her?"

Fellow Villager Foo interrupted, "Now, Brother Wong, we would like very much to have a daughter-in-law live with us and help around the house."

Daddy, who had been highly optimistic until now, shook his head. "Very difficult. That will make a problem with these American-born girls." Then he continued, "Is your family home in the country?" He shook his head more vigorously, "Yes, very, very difficult."

Fellow Villager Foo explained, "You know when a young man is first starting in his profession, he cannot afford to house a wife immediately. Yet, my son is advancing in age and must have a wife."

Jade Snow decided that if she washed her hair four times, it would be too dry to manage, so she slowly rinsed it again and again, as she listened to the conversation, like a fly on the wall. She was dying to have Daddy ask the young man or Fellow Villager Foo what kind of a wife he would like. But her curiosity was not to be satisfied. Mama's voice cut sharply across her thoughts.

"Jade Snow, will you stop washing your hair immediately and show your manners. Pour the gentlemen some tea!"

All sounds stopped. Feeling like "Exhibit A" in a court case,

Jade Snow reached for a towel. Peering between the hanging hair, she could glimpse the Foos interestedly waiting to see what would show now in addition to the uninspiring portion of her back view. With her hair covering her face, she reached for the teacups in the cabinet. Mama interfered again, "Go to my room and get some oranges to serve with the tea."

It was a signal that she should comb her hair and make herself presentable. But in sudden stubbornness, she decided to be stupid. She went to Mama's room, and came back again. "Mama, I can't find the oranges."

Mama looked disgustedly at her dripping, shapeless fifth daughter. "They are right in a bowl arranged on my table."

Jade Snow was meekness itself. "Yes, Mama."

She came back with two oranges, but without any improvement in her appearance. "Forgive me," she interrupted the men's conversation. She was provoked at Mama's cutting her off from hearing some of it. As they paused politely, she explained unnecessarily, "I want to get my laundry." She leisurely gathered it up while Mama and Daddy waited, helpless and vexed. Then she returned to serve the tea and wedges of orange.

According to correct manners, she first passed the oranges and tea to Fellow Villager Foo, the oldest male guest. "Thank you," he said.

Then the high light of the evening came. Boy was meeting girl. Jade Snow advanced to young Foo. "Won't you have some orange and tea?" she asked politely. It was apparent that nobody intended to introduce them formally. She could plainly see the young man between the strands of her hair which still hung over her eyes and gave him a thorough once-over, but he had to strain to get a better view of her face.

Jade Snow proceeded to serve her father and, last, her mother. She didn't know what further etiquette the situation called for, so decided to follow Mama's example and stand respectfully next to her. She played with little Prosperity in a half-interested way. But Mama had lost all patience.

"You might as well go and iron clothes now," she dismissed her unhappily.

Eventually the murmur in the kitchen stopped, and the visitors left. The evening was not mentioned for some weeks. Mama and Daddy acted as if nothing had happened. Then one day, out of a clear sky, Mama asked Jade Snow, "Do you remember that father and son Foo who visited us one Sunday some weeks ago?"

Jade Snow giggled, "Remember? How can I ever forget? I hope that the unhappy boy is getting some assistance in his search for married happiness."

Mama replied exasperatedly, "There is nothing wrong with getting some assistance in marriage. Parents, of course, want the best possible in life for their children." Then she came to the heart of the matter. "Do you realize that since you have finished college, it is obligatory for us to find you a suitable person who has comparable education and tastes? In many ways, this young man was quite fine, and your father and I discussed the possibilities very carefully. But I am afraid that we cannot work out any arrangement after all."

"Why is that?" asked Jade Snow in surprise.

"Because a couple must match physically as well as mentally. You never saw the young man stand up, but I must tell you that no shortcoming of yours is responsible for the failure of our plans, because, compared to him, alas, you were born too tall!"

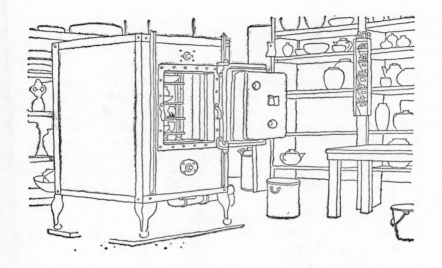

27

A LIFE PLAN IS CAST

JADE SNOW MIGHT HAVE WORKED AT THE SHIPYARD FOR ALL THE war years, except that her boss continued to be promoted until he was in the main administrative offices, to which he could no longer transfer her. "If you go with me to the front office, you'll just become a glorified file clerk under the thumb of the head secretary," he regretfully told her, "and you won't be happy, I'm sure."

Instead, she was assigned to another superintendent in charge of installing fixtures, furnishings, and machinery in the ships after launching. He was a strange man who fluctuated between morose silence and tyrannical teasing. His only concern, day and night, was to get ships out swiftly. If he had to sit up nights with them, he did. When he was in the office for brief moments during the day, it was only to telephone and study blueprints. He did no conventional office work, dictated no letters, and held no meetings.

Suddenly, Jade Snow had next to nothing to do except to answer the phone and maintain blueprint files. She was no longer contributing anything special. She now saw that as a secretary she could not always do the work she wanted. Neither could she hope for advancement except as secretary to a more and more important person. For some time she had been thinking seriously of abandoning her plan for a social service career, for she doubted if within the existing organizations she could really reach the people whom she wanted to help in Chinatown. And she had another reason. After the first shock of adjustment, she was so fascinated by people and experiences of life in the tumbling work world that she was unwilling to bury herself for another two years in the academic world.

After considerable thought, she asked her new boss for his ideas. He gave it to her straight. "Don't you know by now that as long as you are a woman, you can't compete for an equal salary in a man's world? If I were running a business, of course I would favor a man over a woman for most jobs. You're always taking a chance that a woman might marry or have a baby. That's just a biological fact of life. But you know that all things being equal, a man will stay with you, and you won't lose your investment in his training. Moreover, he's the one who has to support a wife and family, and you have to make allowance for that in the larger salary you give him. It's not a question of whether he's smarter than a woman or whether a woman is smarter than he. It's just plain economics!"

It was a practical lesson in economics which the econ major had not digested thoroughly until now. "I'm just tipping you off. If you want to make a decent salary or to be recognized for your own work, and not as somebody's secretary, get a job where you will not be discriminated against because you are a woman, a field in which your sex will not be considered before your ability."

Granted that the advice was good, to carry it out was another thing. After weeks spent in restless attempts at decision, Jade Snow decided to get away from the turmoil of work and the city to do some thinking. Since she had not had a vacation for two years, she went alone to a resort in the Santa Cruz mountains for a long week end.

It was the tail end of the tourist season and there were few people around. She went on long walks alone, or stayed in her cabin in front of her fireplace. In a notebook she wrote down her thoughts as they came to her. She reviewed her philosophy of living and made a few resolutions. Then one morning she rose at dawn and climbed a mountain trail, crunchy with dried autumn leaves. There she sat down on a fallen log under a huge bay tree, and watched the sun warm up the earth with its early rays. Then, in peace and silence, a whole plan came to her in a split second— from where she didn't know. It seemed like an inspiration from above.

Behind her purpose had been a deep desire to contribute in bringing better understanding of the Chinese people, so that in the Western world they would be recognized for their achievements. She wanted to silence the narrow thinking of all the "Richards" and the "placement officers." But she no longer thought that social service work was her answer.

The answer which came to her that morning was that she should try to write. She remembered the advice of her English teachers to send some of her college articles to magazines. At Mills, she had been a member of the English club, which was concerned with helping its members with their creative writing, with occasional assistance from a professor. Most of the other girls had written poetry, while Jade Snow wrote prose. "Helping" meant criticism by their own most candid or ruthless standards as well as encouragement. Their concrete achievement was the annual publication of an attractive, artistic edition of "Mills Manuscripts," which was distributed to the student body. Jade Snow's pieces on Chinatown and her father were included in the issues printed when she was at Mills.

In writing, a woman would not be competing against men. Of course, she had no assurance of success in writing about the life and heart of the Chinese people, but that did not convince her that she shouldn't try. Time enough to look for another answer when this one didn't work. For the immediate present, it seemed like the right lead to follow.

But she didn't have the remotest idea whether one could make a living at writing. She didn't know whether an article was worth ten or a hundred dollars. She just had a vague idea that writers struggled for a living. What could she do to provide a living while she struggled?

The inspiration did not desert her. She would make pottery and sell it! There were friends who admired her work and some had suggested that she try to sell it. Her instructor had encouraged her by saying that she already had a first-rate grasp of the fundamentals.

Jade Snow was deliriously happy. What a wonderful way to live! Write when she wanted to, and make pottery when she wanted to. She could call her soul her own, strike her own tempo as she carved her own niche. How far she would get would depend on how hard she wanted to work, not on anyone else's whims or prejudices.

She sobered down long enough to write "The Plan" in her little notebook, concluding: "Must ask a few people their opinion on this, chiefly my pottery teacher."

The teacher's customary conservatism prevented his giving her enthusiastic assurance, but he did say that the American public was becoming more and more conscious of domestic handcrafts; among them, good handmade pottery. He firmly believed that there was room for pottery of improved quality and that since the war had cut off imported European crafts, there was better opportunity for an American potter to sell his wares than ever before.

He showed Jade Snow a large room which had been added to house new pottery equipment, and also an enormous new kiln. "Since you took the summer session course," he explained, "we have organized a Ceramic Guild at the college. With membership dues, we have been able to purchase this new kiln, and the president of the guild, who owns a contracting business, has built this new room. The guild is limited in membership, but if you want to work in pottery I can recommend you for membership, because one of the basic reasons for organizing was to provide a way for our alumnae to return for further study. Our former college president helped in its founding because of her belief that adult education in the crafts does not go far enough and hasn't a high enough art standard. She wanted alumnae to be able to return for lifelong study. It was her idea that someday there may be a weaving guild, a jewelry and metal-working guild, and so on. Now, our new president is enthusiastic in his encouragement and support."

Jade Snow learned that all the guild members were doing individual research. "I think that's the way for you to learn more about pottery. Come over and have dinner next Sunday, when all the members are here. We take turns cooking."

The cost of equipment, materials and supplies, according to him, was not prohibitive, so Jade Snow decided right then that the money saved for a master's degree in social service would go instead toward paying for a pottery studio.

When she joined the Ceramic Guild for supper the following Sunday, she found them a delightfully informal and co-operative group with a never-absent sense of humor. The president was a woman contractor who was a wizard at figures and as practical as anyone Jade Snow had ever met. After working all day at her business, where she was sole manager, building houses despite the scarcity of materials, she spent hours at the pottery every night to satisfy her need for recreation.

After admission to the group, Jade Snow began making pottery on Sundays. But this was impossible following six days in the ship-yard. One could hardly leave uncompleted pieces of clay work for a week at a time without losing them from overdryness.

In the meantime, her doctor was displeased with her slow recovery. "You had better stop those long hours or soon you won't be able to work at all," he warned her.

"But we are frozen to our jobs," she protested.

"I'll write you a letter to release you. You can still be patriotic and find another half-day job," he insisted.

That night when she met Jade Harp for dinner, Jade Snow told her that she was job-hunting again. Jade Harp had a brilliant idea, "One of the departments under the admiral for whom I am secretary hires the civilian personnel for our naval district. Why don't I send you to see the commander in charge of that office?"

In a few days, the red tape had been unraveled and Jade Snow went to work for the United States Navy. Her job included odd but necessary things—from making up graphs and charts on the manpower forces, to keeping an inventory on office equipment. Later, she was promoted to be the commander's secretary.

When V-J day came at last in 1945, Jade Snow no longer felt obligated to continue her Navy work. The position of commander's secretary didn't seem productively essential. So after a year with the navy she resigned, to spend all her days at the college pottery wheel. Not long before this, the first magazine to which she sent two articles on her Chinese family had accepted and published them. So far, "The Plan" was working.

Not only was she learning about pottery by making it, she was learning about operating a business from constant association with the guild president. Sometimes, when they worked together until two or three in the morning, she would miss the last bus, and her friend would invite her to stay overnight at her home. Sometimes, when she did catch the last bus, she would sleep on it until she got to the city.

Her first shipyard boss, who had kept in touch with her, made a suggestion. "Wouldn't it help you if you made pottery at home instead of going across the bay every day? When it's dry enough to fire, you can pack it up and I will take it over to the college kilns for you, and bring it back to San Francisco when completed. I commute every day anyway, so it won't be any trouble."

It was a blessing to have that help. The guild president had a wheel made for Jade Snow. It was delivered to her home, and she began making pottery there. So she saved two hours of commutation time daily. Younger Brother helped her to nail up a work enclosure in the factory area, which was still unused. Since the housing project had been delayed for the duration of the war, it was not yet necessary for Daddy to move his equipment from their former factory-home.

Daddy and Prosperity were the only other members of the Wong family interested in her pottery activities. Mama ignored her completely. She would walk by the wheel dozens of times and never look at the potter once. Jade Snow gathered that Mama didn't think it was a very ladylike occupation. Mama agreed with the watch-repair man in believing that pottery with the handmade look was too crude to be of value. But Prosperity loved to help his sister prepare clay and "stir mud," as the Chinese called throwing on the wheel. Daddy pronounced no judgment, but quietly made her a present of a beautiful new one-third horsepower motor, which was then almost impossible to buy, and installed it. He also arranged to have some cabinets moved home from his factory in order to give Jade Snow storage space for her work.

By the end of 1945, her labor had given her great pleasure and taught her much, and the cabinets which Daddy had set up for her were filled with a neat stock of pottery from her own hands, ranging from tall vases and large bowls to small ashtrays and sets of mugs. Their emphasis was on good, simple lines and usefulness. Some carried her favorite method of decoration—patterns of natural leaves and blooms, incised into the clay body when it was damp. Bright and subtle colored glazes were applied in harmony with the shape and designs. She counted over three hundred pieces, and decided that at twenty-three she was ready to begin her pottery business.

28

"THE WORK OF ONE DAY IS GAZED UPON FOR ONE THOUSAND DAYS"

CHINESE PROVERB

J ADE SNOW TRUDGED THE FAMILIAR PATHS OF CHINATOWN, LOOKING for a store location where she could make and sell her pottery. She didn't know any of the owners, but instead of following the traditional, established custom of the Chinese, who handle such transactions through a middleman who knows the people and can bargain over a cup of tea, she explored every store along Grant Avenue herself.

As there was no unleased vacant store in those days, she was forced to abandon her first wish to have her own store. Instead, she considered subrenting a portion of an art-goods store. She started with the best corner locations. Some wanted too much rent; some just shook their heads; others seemed interested and asked her to return, only to report that co-owners or stockholders disapproved. All were amazed but interested in what she wanted to do; some almost wouldn't believe her.

It was a discouraging round, in which hope alternated with disappointment. Jade Snow became less particular about the choice of location, and began to work on the smaller establishments. Still without luck, she came to almost the only store she hadn't approached. The China Bazaar near Clay Street was a neat little place, and she had looked into it a number of times. But the proprietor, who sat at his cash register at the back and only waited on customers if he felt like it, always with an air of dignity and stoicism, had been altogether too formidable a figure for her to face. Now, driven by desperation, she made herself enter and tell the proprietor what she had in mind.

He said, "I notice everything and everyone who passes by my store, and I have seen you look in several times before now. You don't look like an American-Chinese to me, with two braids on your head instead of a permanent wave."

"I was born here," Jade Snow replied. "Our family head is named Wong Hong. Do you know him?"

"Yes, I have heard of him, and I know that he is an honest Christian."

Jade Snow waited, with hope beginning to rise again.

"Now, I am not a Christian," he added. "I wouldn't move out of my way to do a good deed. But if a good deed comes to my front door and asks to be done, I have very little choice. A man can go through life minding his own business only until someone comes along who desperately needs his help. A middleman I could have said 'No' to, but you make it difficult to refuse you personally."

Jade Snow assured him, "Everyone has refused me but you. This is my life purpose. All I am asking is to get a start until I can find a permanent location."

"But you can see that I have very little room and a very narrow store. I like to keep it exactly my way. I wouldn't mind displaying your finished things, but there would be no room for you to work in."

"Oh, I must work too, for as my stock is sold I shall have to be ready with more things. I can't have a hired staff yet, and I must both make and sell the pottery."

They both thought hard. Jade Snow got an idea. "Would you let me use one of your two store windows to install my wheel? Then the clay splatter will be confined to a small area, and perhaps my working there would attract people to your store to buy your own wares."

The proprietor was doubtful. "I have only the two windows."

Jade Snow implored him. "Please, try it. If it isn't good for your business, we'll make other arrangements."

They discussed terms. The proprietor said, "Now to be frank with you, I'll never be able to make much money off you. Suppose we just decide on a percentage commission on the total amount you sell. If I am going to try to help you, we might as well be fair about it. My commission will cover what you use in space and utilities. You don't know yet how much you will sell. The plan is new for both of us."

Jade Snow mulled over that proposition. "You don't quite believe what I say, do you?" the man questioned. "Go home and ask your father; he is a fair business man."

So Jade Snow told her family, all of whom were surprised that she had at last found something. Until now, they had thought she was taking the wrong means to a silly objective which she would have to give up eventually. In true Wong family fashion, they weren't preventing her from having her own way, nor helping.

"Daddy, I have today found a store which offers the greatest possibilities to date." And she described her experience in detail.

Daddy agreed that the proprietor's proposal was fair. "Now, it is right for me to go and thank this gentleman for his courtesy and generosity, and to make his acquaintance."

The next few weeks were busy ones. With the help of Jade Precious Stone and a former Navy co-worker, Jade Snow bustled around, ordering supplies, price-marking the pottery, getting announcements printed and sent out, and caring for all the details of starting a business, no matter how small. Her former architect-boss went over the store-window foundation for her, to determine what additional bracing was required in order to support the weight of the potter's wheel. He designed and drew up plans for a set of redwood shelves and cases with concealed lights, so that in the little six-by-five-foot floor space there was room to work, store drying pottery, and display a few finished items. The window floor was paved with bricks laid in a basket pattern. Altogether, the use of natural materials in keeping with the look of pottery made an attractive whole which was certainly unlike any other store window in Chinatown.

With materials scarce, it took Jade Snow days of hunting to find even the bricks for the floor. A Chinese carpenter, a fellow Wong and Daddy's old friend, was the only person who would consent to build the shelves and bracing for her, and he could hardly understand the architectural notations on the detailed drawings. Jade Snow's shipyard training in getting things done stood her in good stead.

At last everything was completed and she was ready to set up the window. Prosperity, who had been most interested in all the bustle, went with her to the store and helped lay bricks. The shelves fitted in exactly. The wheel was set in place, and a stack of plaster bats, molded in pie tins and used to support pottery while being made, was placed near by. A beautiful large philodendron plant curled up gracefully along one corner of the window, gift of Mama and Daddy in honor of the new enterprise.

Even while the brick flooring was being laid, curious passers-by stopped. Jade Snow discovered that one had only to get into a window to attract spectators. As they worked, Jade Snow saw a few insects crawling around; they looked like white ants, and she called the proprietor.

"That is indeed a good omen," he declared excitedly. "White ants do not appear except on very rare occasions. When they appear for a new business, it means that the business is blessed and will prosper."

"Oh, come now; haven't you seen white ants here before when you dressed the windows?"

The proprietor shook his head solemnly, "No, never!"

Soon the curious spectators began to murmur aloud, conjecturing as to the nature of the equipment in the elevated display.

"She must be planning to make bricks for the housing project in Chinatown."

"No, look at those white pies; she is setting up a model kitchen."

"You are both wrong; this is a rice-threshing machine. See the stick across it? I have seen them in China!"

"Oh, look, and it is a China girl too. Look, she has no permanent wave. Her braids are the way they wear them in Shanghai. Here is a Shanghai girl!"

Prosperity listened in curiosity and mounting indignation. At last he ran out to the street and announced: "You are all wrong. This is my Honey's pottery machine, and she is going to stir mud on it."

The onlookers laughed. "Listen to the child; he doesn't know what he's talking about!"

There was little chance for other spectators not to know what Jade Snow was doing in the days which followed. From the time she first threw down a ball of clay on the wheel, the street was packed. There were even people on the balconies across the street, and clinging to the telephone pole. Passing automobiles on narrow Grant Avenue stopped and held up traffic while the drivers watched. The first day, policemen came because they thought there might be a riot. Jade Snow could have an audience any time of the day or night on that busy street.

The morning paper carried a picture and two-column story of the new enterprise. Jade Snow had become a wonder in the eyes of the Western world. They declared that she had invented a new mousetrap.

Chinatown was agog. A woman in the window, her legs astride a potter's wheel, her hair in braids, her hands perpetually messy with sticky California clay, her finished products such things as coolies used in China, the daughter of a conservative family, running a business alone—such a combination was sure to fail!

When Jade Snow went around Chinatown, many storekeepers laughed at her. "Look, here comes the mud-stirring maiden. Sold a pot today? Ha! Ha!" Strangers turned to stare long and curiously.

Caucasians came from far and near to see her work, and Jade Snow sold all the pottery she could make. Even before it had been fired, the first piece was eagerly spoken for by the man who had kindly found her bricks for the window. But the Chinese did not come to buy one piece from her.

Then those who had laughed hardest stopped. After two months, the mud-stirring maiden was still in business! After three months, she was driving the first postwar automobile in Chinatown. The skeptics knitted their brows. It must be those crazy foreigners, who didn't know any better. Some Chinese approached the proprietor for information. Was it because her clay came from China? Was it because she had invented a new chemical process to make pottery?

The proprietor would smile politely. "Ask her," he would say.

But no one ever asked her. Chinese and Americans alike acted as if they thought she were deaf or dumb or couldn't understand their language. She learned a very curious thing about human beings: they would wonder, guess, speculate, but never question the person who could give them the direct answers.

One day two high-ranking Caucasian Army officers wandered into the store. They stood and watched her patiently putting a handle on a pitcher while she sat at the wheel. Since the wheel was being used for a table it was motionless.

"I wonder how that wheel operates?" one officer asked another.

"Oh, she sits there and kicks it with her feet," the other replied. Jade Snow, not two feet from them, heard them plainly, and was amused that apparently they did not observe the one-third horsepower motor which Daddy had installed on the wheel, hung almost at their eye level.

"That seems to me unnecessarily primitive," returned the first man. "But that's just the trouble, you can't teach the Chinese anything new!"

And they went off without further investigation, nodding their heads in self-satisfaction.

The reaction of her friends and family was different. Friends and fellow guild members sent flowers. Later they sometimes dropped in for tea, which she brewed in the back kitchen. And they told their friends about the new enterprise. Dr. Reinhardt never failed to call whenever she was near the neighborhood.

But it was Mama who epitomized the family's change of heart. Where there was formerly only tolerance toward their peculiar fifth daughter whom no one could understand, the tolerance was now tinged by an attitude of respect. Mama, who would not look at the potter's wheel at home, now came to the store to see what everyone was talking about.

Daddy, typically, touched her heart in another way. First, he was critical of her daring in assuming a position in the window above her spectators' heads. But when he saw that she was getting the prices and the market she wished, he ventured a suggestion. "Perhaps you should drape printed percale around your wheel, so that people will not see how crude a piece of equipment you use to make fine things."

Then one afternoon driving home, he sat beside her, lost in reverie. When they were parked in front of their house, he told her a story: "I told you once that your grandfather would have been glad to see that you had learned a handicraft. I can add now that he would have been happier to see that you have established your own business alone, even though you must begin modestly for lack of capital. Grandfather used to brush characters on a small red poster, whenever he wished to impress us with words of great importance or wisdom. This poster would be mounted inside the glass door of a big American grandfather's clock, so that whenever we observed the time, we would also be reminded of the words. I remember that after failure in his first business venture, he posted these bitterly learned words, 'Remember carefully! Remember carefully! With one penny of capital, buy eight bags of peanuts to resell, but do not seek a partner to begin a business.' "

The narrative, unusual in nature and length, was continued, "When I first came to America, my cousin wrote me from China and asked me to return. That was before I can even tell you where you were. But I still have the carbon copy of the letter I wrote him in reply. I said, 'You do not realize the shameful and degraded position into which the Chinese culture has pushed its women. Here in America, the Christian concept allows women their freedom and individuality. I wish my daughters to have this Christian opportunity. I am hoping that some day I may be able to claim that by my stand I have washed away the former disgraces suffered by the women of our family.' "

Then Daddy turned and looked at her kindly, "And who would have thought that you, my Fifth Daughter Jade Snow, would prove today that my words of many years ago were words of true prophecy?"

As for Jade Snow, she knew that she still had before her a hard upward climb, but for the first time in her life, she felt contentment. She could stop searching for that niche that would be hers alone. She had found herself and struck her speed. And when she came home now, it was to see Mama and Daddy look up from their work, and smile at her, and say, "It is good to have you home again!"